Ten Months a Captive Among Filipinos

A Narrative of Adventure and Observation During Imprisonment on the Island of Luzon During the Philippine-American War

By Albert Sonnichsen

Published by Pantianos Classics

ISBN-13: 978-1-78987-180-7

First published in 1901

Contents

Introduction vii
Chapter One - The Trip to Malolos 11
Chapter Two - First Days of Captivity 17
Chapter Three - Close Confinement 23
Chapter Four - Desperate Chances 31
Chapter Five - Jail Life 34
Chapter Six - Relaxation 43
Chapter Seven - Misfortunes of O'Brien 56
Chapter Eight - Santa Isabela 61
Chapter Nine - Sounds of War 66
Chapter Ten - With the Retreat 78
Chapter Eleven - San Isidro 85
Chapter Twelve - News from Outside 93
Chapter Thirteen - Off for The North 97
Chapter Fourteen - On the March 101
Chapter Fifteen - The People of Ilocos 106
Chapter Sixteen - Vigan 114
Chapter Seventeen - An Insurgent Hospital 117
Chapter Eighteen - Lieutenant Castro 125

Chapter Nineteen - Up the River Abra 137

Chapter Twenty - Filipino Friends 141

Chapter Twenty-One - A Wedding in Bangued 150

Chapter Twenty-Two - The Meetings in the Hospital 155

Chapter Twenty-Three - Fugitives 162

Chapter Twenty-Four - Marines from the Oregon 176

Chapter Twenty-Five - In Manila Again 186

Chapter Twenty-Six - Conclusion 196

Introduction

IT was as quartermaster of the Zealandia, one of the four transports of the second expedition from San Francisco to Manila in 1898, that the writer left his native land for the distant Philippines, unconscious that it was to be his fate to experience what fell to the lot of very few Americans during the war.

We reached Manila Bay on July 23d, finding that the first expedition had safely arrived, but as yet had commenced no operations against the Spaniards besieged in the city by the native Insurgents. Disembarking, the troops we had brought joined those of the first expedition, and together they formed an army of 5,000 or more men. Then they took up their position outside the suburbs of Manila, beside the troops of Aguinaldo, who already had thrown up trenches opposite to those of the Spaniards.

Often I was able to visit the camp, or the two camps, rather, for the Filipinos and Americans were encamped side by side; over the white tents of our soldiers fluttered the stars and stripes, over the bamboo huts of the Filipinos the unpretentious tricolor of the new-born republic. Then, for the first time, I saw those people, with whom I was yet to be so closely associated.

On the night of July 31st our boys fought their first battle together with their brown allies— together, for the first and last time. The Spaniards made a fierce attack, and side by side American and Filipino repelled them, seventeen of the former and twenty-five of the latter falling before the storm of Mauser bullets.

On August 13th Manila capitulated, and, attaching himself to the Utah Battery, with various members of which he had made friends on the voyage, the writer entered within the walls of the fallen city; but forbidden to do likewise, the Filipinos remained outside.

Meanwhile, Aguinaldo had conquered all the territory outside of Manila and Cavite, taking some 6,000 Spaniards prisoners. About this time the American commander-in-chief, General Merritt, was relieved by Major-General Elwell S. Otis.

At first the former allies remained on friendly terms, but as the Filipino lines were almost daily forced farther back from the suburbs of the city, the Insurgent leaders became, at each backward step, more sullen, more suspicious, and less friendly.

Such was the situation in January. A letter which I wrote at this time to a friend may further enlighten the reader:

Manila, January 18, 1899.

Mr. Paul Owens,
    Editor of *Weekly Californian.*

My Dear Paul: In accordance with your request, made on my leaving for the Philippines, to supply you with any interesting information that might come within the range of my observations, and thus act as your unofficial correspondent, so to say, I now take the first opportunity since the New Year to send you something that seems worthy of your or my time.

As I wrote you before, Americans are now strictly forbidden to leave the limits of the city, for any person entering the Insurgent lines in an American uniform is at once swooped down upon by them and held as a prisoner until a formal demand is made for his release by our army officials.

Aguinaldo has now established his headquarters and capital at Malolos, a small town some twenty miles up the Dagupan Railroad. An outbreak seems imminent, but still it is hard to believe that men as enlightened as Aguinaldo and his principal advisers are supposed to be should dare to measure strength with our forces, considering their crude and poorly equipped army.

However, I must not forget to give you an account of a visit I was enabled to make into or rather beyond the Filipino lines. In civilian clothes I was permitted to pass their outposts, one day about a week ago, as an English newspaper correspondent, but as I only remained a short time, my visit, on this occasion, was an uneventful one.

Day before yesterday, in company with an old school-mate, Harry Huber, whom I chanced to meet some weeks ago, I passed the Filipino outposts again and succeeded in taking a dozen views with a four by five film kodak.

Early that morning I called on Huber, who is a member of the Hospital Corps, and, donning a civilian suit each, we walked down to the Escolta, hired a four-wheeler vehicle resembling a carriage, and drove out to Fort Malate, a suburb to the south of Manila, where our last outposts are stationed.

Our forces are now holding the same position against the Insurgents that the Spaniards held against the Americans before the fall of Manila. A small creek running by this blockhouse forms the boundary to our territory and that of the Insurgents. In one place it is spanned by a small stone bridge, at one end of which an American sentry paces up and down; at the other end, within speaking distance, an Insurgent outpost sits on the parapet, a Remington rifle across his knees. As I have been frequently told, the two often meet in the middle of the bridge to borrow cigarettes from each other and discuss politics.

We experienced no difficulty in passing both sentries, assuring the questioning Insurgent that we were "Ingles."

Several hundred yards beyond we came into a small village, where a large number of the little brown soldiers seemed to be quartered in temporarily built bamboo barracks.

Seeing no officer about I descended from our carriage and persuaded a number of them, who seemed just to have come in from the outposts, to pose before my camera. Evidently they understood something of the nature of the operation, for they made every effort to appear to best advantage, throwing out their chests, adjusting their belts and ammunition bags, holding their guns prominently before them, as if that was the most imposing feature. Then when I snapped the shutter they crowded around, imagining the result could immediately be seen.

I noticed that with few exceptions they were all barefooted. Their uniform is made of thin cotton stuff thinly striped by white and blue. This is also the uniform of the Spanish Colonial army, and undoubtedly much of it is captured material, although some is woven in the country. Their broad-brimmed straw hats, native made, with the insignia of the wearer's battalion and company on the black band in yellow letters, are also a feature of the Spanish uniform. All those we saw here were armed with old-fashioned Remingtons.

We took three views about the barracks and then drove farther up the road toward the interior, passing through thick bamboo jungles and taking snap shots at anything interesting.

At length, after a long drive, we returned to the village from where we had started, preparatory to crossing over into our lines again. I had just one film left on the roll, so looked about for something to complete my dozen views. Then a most dazzling sight met our eyes.

In front of the barracks stood an officer attired in a white cap, blue coat, crimson trousers with four-inchwide black stripes down the sides, shining black riding boots, and an unlimited quantity of gold and silver braid and tinsel about his person. At one side hung a handsome, polished leather revolver holster; from the other hip dangled a long sword. Truly, neither Solomon in all his glory nor the lilies of the field were arrayed like this brown little gentleman. He was simply gorgeous.

Forgetting for the moment that these dazzling hues would be lost on the film, I lifted up the camera from under the seat and snapped the shutter at this mass of concentrated splendor. The result was surprising.

With a yell he drew his sword and rushed wildly down upon us. At first I thought he meant to do us bodily injury — he did not, though. But the way he whipped that sword about in the air was appalling. Probably he did this to give force to the torrent of words that fell from his mouth, but, beyond the fact that we did not mistake them for compliments, they failed entirely to enlighten us on the cause of all this trouble. Our driver tried some sort of an explanation in our defence, I believe, but was slapped across the face before he could finish. Under ordinary circumstances I should have resented this, but the presence of a number of soldiers with disagreeable looking bolos and Remingtons in their hands, restrained me from making an exhibition of ill-temper. The chances are they might have followed a bad example and done likewise.

Eventually we were allowed to proceed on our way across the bridge, and, had that little peacock officer followed us with his person as he did with his voice, we should probably have sent for an interpreter just to tell him how indignant we were; but he remained on his own side of the bridge, twirling that sword about, while the American sentinel on our side stood convulsed with laughter.

You have now received more than I thought to be able to give you, so allow me to come to a conclusion before you are entirely exhausted. If the Zealandia should remain here much longer, I might be enabled to give you some information concerning the habits and customs of these people, but just now I consider them most interesting at a distance. Should I, however, at some future date, allow my curiosity to lead me once more into their lines, you shall certainly know the result, although I can assure you that my gilded little acquaintance out in Malate will receive a wide berth from my side. At a second meeting he might insist upon my remaining his guest until I could prove my identity, and that might be somewhat awkward for

Your sincere friend,
A. S.

I had promised in the foregoing letter to give my friend, the editor, an account of a second visit into the Insurgent lines, should I make one. A second visit was made, but for reasons entirely beyond my control my friend has been obliged to wait until now, almost two years later, for the promised report. These reasons it is my object now to explain, and not only Mr. Owens, but whoever chooses to peruse these lines, will see how entirely excusable is my delay.

Chapter One - The Trip to Malolos

WE set out on our excursion on a Friday, which, according to an old superstition, was a direct invitation for a disastrous result. At all events it proved true on this occasion, and I still believe that our misfortunes were the result of choosing a wrong day.

Early on Friday morning, January 27, 1899, Harry Huber, of the Hospital Corps, and the writer drove down to the station of the Dagupan Railroad in a *quilez*, [1] both of us apparently civilians, each being attired in a serge suit of unmistakably English cut. With us we carried the same four by five roll-film camera which we had taken with us ten days previous on the trip out beyond Malate toward Paranaque. Arriving at the station we bought two return tickets to Malolos, it being our intention to visit the Insurgent capital as representatives of the British press. The train was scheduled to leave at 9 a.m., but as we had arrived half an hour early we entered a coach and sat down to wait. The cars on this railroad are built on the European plan, in compartments, each being large enough to hold about a dozen passengers. At first we found ourselves alone, but shortly before nine o'clock another passenger entered and seated himself opposite. He was an elderly, well-dressed native, a well-to-do merchant, apparently. By the general expression of his wrinkled countenance, this world had not been made entirely to his satisfaction. Our presence especially seemed to give him great displeasure, but this was mutual.

At precisely nine o'clock the bell rang, a whistle blew, doors banged, and we found ourselves gliding out of Manila at a rapidly increasing speed, until we were flying at a tremendous rate over marshes and rice-fields and through thick, picturesque jungles. On we sped, so deeply interested in the surrounding scenery that we entirely forgot the dark presentiments which the arrival of our sour-visaged fellow-passenger had aroused.

At length the train slackened up and we drew into Caloocan, the first station. We were now some distance inside the Insurgent territory. It was in this place that we expected to meet some trouble, as all strangers were here questioned, and detained if thought suspicious.

Our explanations seemed satisfactory — we were not molested, and when the train once more pulled out, I thought that, for the present at least, all danger was passed.

At Polo, the second station, we were not even questioned; there now remained but four stations more, and Malolos would be reached.

The strange behavior of our travelling companion now attracted our attention. His eyes were fixed upon us with a burning intensity, and, although we returned the stare, he was not in the least embarrassed by that; on the contrary, his behavior became almost insulting. No sooner had the train come to a standstill at Meycauayan, the third station, when he arose hurriedly and left the car. We were pleased to be relieved of his presence. For a long time we waited and wondered what was detaining the train, when suddenly the door of our compartment was reopened, and a young Insurgent officer appeared, motioning us with his hand to descend. Outside on the platform stood three soldiers and our late travelling companion from Manila, grinning maliciously an "Adios" to us as he re-entered the car and the train pulled out once more.

Turning to us, the young officer said: "The Señor says that you are American spies — it is my duty to arrest you." Neither my friend nor I was at that time very proficient in Spanish, and these may not have been the exact words the lieutenant made use of, but what he said gave us the impression that they would have done. He was quiet and polite, but his manner was far more awing than that of the blustering little individual we encountered on our former trip to Malate.

Before proceeding farther I may as well mention that some time afterward we again saw the "Señor" who had caused our arrest, in the full-dress uniform of Aguinaldo's staff, but at that time he was so frustrated by the manner in which some thousands of our compatriots were coming up the same road that we had taken, that he did not notice us. Only on this occasion they could not well be arrested.

Placing us in charge of a sergeant and three men, they made us walk a distance of about two miles before we reached the town of Meycauayan, where the head-quarters of this especial district was stationed. The Filipinos divided the country up into military districts called "comandancias," each in charge of a head officer, or "comandante" (equal to our major), who was held responsible for the observance of the military laws within the limits of his domain. This, however, was quite apart from the civil government.

In the road we attracted almost as much attention as a Fourth of July parade in an American country town — hundreds of men, women, and children flocking around to see us. The sergeant and his soldiers were perfectly willing to answer all questions asked, but I am inclined to believe that they exaggerated the difficulty of our capture somewhat.

Meycauayan could hardly be called a modern town. Some of the buildings would have delighted the heart of an antiquarian. At one time there had been quite a number of medium-sized stone buildings, but now very few of them could boast a roof. In the interior of some, trees were growing, throwing their limbs up through the broken tiles and second-story windows.

The only building that seemed in any state of preservation at all was the church and convent, standing at one end of the plaza; this seems to be a special feature of every Filipino town. Even if there be but a dozen bamboo huts, a large stone building, the church, with a long two-story wing attached, the convent, invariably overlooks the plaza, very similar in architecture to those formerly built by the friars in California.

The Filipinos, however, had converted the convent of Meycauayan into barracks and military head-quarters, the tricolor flag of the Insurgent republic fluttering over the entrance.

To this building our guards conducted us. Quite a throng of soldiers and Spaniards congregated about us as we stood waiting for some time at the door. These latter, ragged and miserable-looking, were part of the 6,000 prisoners that were held by the Insurgent Government that had refused to deliver them at the demand of General Otis.

At length we were taken up to the floor above, and kept anxiously waiting for over an hour in a large ante-room before an audience was granted. Finally a door opened at the farther end of the room, and we were ushered into the office of the local Military Governor, or Comandante.

Now all the Filipino officers that I had ever spoken to (and I had come in contact with a good many in Cavite, before the fall of Manila) had been, with the exception of our eccentric acquaintance in Malate, very polite and courteous in their behavior, tolerating my vile Spanish with patience and affability, so that upon entering the comandante's office I expected to be received with polite bows — "Buenos dias, Señores," etc. Imagine, then, what a shock I experienced when upon entering, on crossing the threshold, we were greeted with a torrent of Spanish profanity, emanating from an excited fat little Filipino behind a large desk, frantically waving a Malay kris over his head with one hand, while in the other he held a Colt's revolver, the hammer of which he was snapping with wonderful rapidity, producing a sound similar to a typewriter in full operation, and on each side of us stood a file of soldiers with Remingtons with fixed bayonets, pointed at us as if about to charge.

The carefully prepared little speech on which I had exhausted my entire Spanish vocabulary was entirely shattered; we stood dazed and stupefied at the vehemence of that hostile reception. But my composure gradually returned as I realized that every dog barks loudest from his own kennel, and we were no longer inside American lines.

Any attempt at an explanation was useless. Every time I ventured a word I found myself looking down the muzzle of the Colt. No explanations were wanted, we were not only Americans, but spies, scoundrels, hogs, dogs, and a variety of other bad things. During the half hour we spent in the presence of this rabid little officer, I learned more Spanish profanity than a two-months' stay in Manila had taught me. His appearance was by no means prepossessing: his complexion was but a shade lighter than ebony, his teeth protruded between thick and prominent lips, and so conspicuous was the upward slant of his eyes that in his anger he bore a strong resemblance to a Chinese Joss. His wearing apparel was far from what I thought an officer in any army should appear in, being limited to a pair of soiled white trousers and an unwashed shirt, the tail of which fluttered in the fresh breeze that came in through the open doors and windows. His feet were bare and the heelless slippers in which he rested them had certainly been worn for years.

Having exhausted his breath, the officer pompously waved his hand to the guards and we were conducted out of the room and down into the street. A short walk down an adjoining road brought us before a small house built of timber but roofed with nipa, [2] into which our guards made us enter. This was the private dwelling of the comandante, the commanding officer, and as we entered I half expected another scene, but the well-dressed, elderly officer who received us at the door was very gentlemanly and courteous, offering each of us a chair. With the exception of a number of chromos and wax figures of the Holy Virgin, Jesus, and various saints, the room was rather barely furnished, a table and a few chairs being the most conspicuous objects. There were a number of insipid-looking women in the room, apparently of the same social standing, yet one was the comandante's wife, and the rest but servants.

Our host, if I may so call him, gave some orders to these women, and soon a small table in the room was set with rice, bread, sardines, bananas, and imported wine, to which we were invited to seat ourselves.

After dinner, the officer who had received us at the convent in such a hostile manner, appeared, now in full-dress uniform, two silver stars on a red shoulder strap on each shoulder announcing his rank as that of a first lieutenant. Apparently he was the comandante's adjutant. The two conversed together for some time, in a low tone, throwing an occasional glance in our direction. At length the two approached us with my camera, and giving it to me asked an explanation of its manipulation. The camera was now in my hands for the first time since our arrest, and unperceived by them I exposed to light the only view we had taken that day, thus destroying any evidence against us. Their knowledge of photography seemed to be limited, and when I showed them the inner mechanism of the "machina," as they called it, they were as surprised and pleased as children. Then I photographed the comandante in his own doorway in different positions, and his delight was childlike in its effusiveness. He asked us to send him the pictures from Manila!

Huber and I glanced at one another, as he said this — evidently we were to be allowed to return.

At about 3 P.M. a soldier came from the convent and delivered a message to the comandante. Glancing at it a moment, he spoke a few words to the lieutenant, and the latter hurriedly left the room.

Half an hour passed, when a second messenger appeared and spoke to the comandante in Tagalog, the native dialect. Our three guards, who had been in an adjoining out-house, were called in, and we were told to return to the head-quarters in the convent with them. Upon reaching the plaza we found a large mob assembled, through which our guards had some difficulty in forcing our way, but at length we entered the building and ascended the stairs to the floor above and entered the office. The lieutenant was seated calmly behind his desk this time, and lined up on the opposite side of the room stood

In spite of the lateness of the hour we attracted quite a crowd, and for half an hour stood there in the open plaza, the objects of insults and abuse. At length an officer appeared and conducted us down a side street to a small stone building, uninviting and cheerless in appearance. By the light of a street lamp we saw above the entrance, in large letters, "Gobierno Militar." This was, as we learned afterward, the head-quarters of the military governor of the entire province, but only the upper floor; the ground-floor was used for an entirely different purpose, as we were soon to learn.

We were at once taken upstairs into an office in which were seated a number of officers about a table. One, a pessimistic-looking middle-aged man, we took to be the governor, nor were we mistaken in this, for we learned to know Don Francisco Donato only too well afterward. Here we underwent some sort of an examination, or maybe a court-martial, but the decision of the court remained a secret.

Having concluded, an officer conducted us downstairs again; a heavy wooden door swung open, creaking dismally, and we were rudely shoved into a room. The bright moonlight came in through a small window, but this only served to distinctly outline the massive iron bars deeply embedded in the solid masonry. The room was not large, about half the size of a railway-car at home, but the floor was covered by sleeping forms so closely that we with great difficulty found a space sufficiently large to stretch our weary limbs. We were soon dead to the outside world, unconscious that this was the first night of an imprisonment and experience through which it is happily but the lot of few to pass in these modern times.

[1] A two-wheeled vehicle resembling a cab, entered from the rear and carrying four persons.
[2] A species of palm, resembling a large fern, and growing in abundance in swamps. Its leaves are used to thatch the huts of the poor, and even the larger houses of the better classes, being much cooler than tiles or galvanized iron.
From the stems a juice is obtained, which, in itself a delicious beverage, is also distilled into what is commonly called in the Philippines "vino de nipa," an alcoholic drink even stronger than whiskey. Every evening the gatherer makes a slight incision in the stems close to the ground, and places underneath a joint of bamboo to receive the drops of juice that ooze out during the night. This is called "tuba," and in the morning is refreshingly cool and sweet, but by the afternoon is sour as vinegar, for which purpose the natives use it extensively.
[3] A light two-wheeled cart with a seating capacity for two persons, drawn by one horse, a sort of buggy.

Chapter Two - First Days of Captivity

U̲PON awakening in the morning, a faint diffused light the dawning day was sending in through the heavily barred window was just commencing to make my surroundings visible, and, anxious to inspect this hole in which we now found ourselves confined, I arose into a sitting posture and glanced about me. What met my eyes was far from encouraging; truly no attempt had been made to disguise the nature of this establishment — it looked every inch a dungeon.

Besides my companion and myself, there were at least fourteen more occupants of this cell, three of whom were Spaniards, and the rest natives. Some had already awakened and sat up rubbing their eyes, yawning; others lay still slumbering on the rough floor, their misery and troubles forgotten for the time being at least. And such companions as these! With the exception of the three Spaniards the rest were apparently of the dregs of Filipino society, of brutish and criminal aspect. A form that had been lying in a dark corner, now moved, arose, and stepped into the light. Lord help her — it was a woman!

At one end of the cell stood a rudely constructed bamboo bed, which, with an old cane reclining-chair, the bottom of which was broken through, seemed to be all the furniture of which the whole room could boast. As the light increased, the form of a young man gradually revealed itself on the cot, whose appearance formed so marked a contrast to the others that my attention was at once attracted to him. So light was his complexion that a casual observer might have taken him for a pure Spaniard, but a slight prominence of the cheek-bones, an almost imperceptible upward turn of eyes and eyebrows, and the sparseness of his mustache betrayed the native blood in his veins. The white pajamas enveloping his limbs were spotlessly clean, and a Spanish uniform that hung by his side on the wall led me to believe that he had been an officer in the Spanish army, but whatever he was, his general appearance gave an impression of education and refinement.

Gradually all the prisoners awoke, one by one, and, rolling up their mats, squatted down on their heels, for want of better occupation. This manner of passing away surplus time is universal throughout the Orient, but the Filipinos have a peculiar way of their own of doing this, which, if imitated by a foreigner, generally causes him to roll gently backward until his heels have reached a greater elevation than his head. At length some lazily commenced to scrape and clean dirty cooking-utensils, while the woman, having collected a copper coin from each individual, placed a large empty basket on her head and began to administer a succession of kicks to the closed door. After a great deal of confusion among the guards outside, and the noise occasioned by drawing of bolts and removal of bars, it swung slowly open and the female passed outside. Evidently she was going marketing.

The door, once open, was allowed to remain so, and, disgusted with my gloomy surroundings, I arose and went out to explore the limits of the prison, while Huber, equally disgusted, tried once more to seek oblivion in sleep.

The main entrance from the street, immediately outside, was crowded with lounging soldiers in all stages of sleepiness. Turning in an opposite direction I found myself in a yard, enclosed by a stone wall of such height that the sun's rays, as yet, were altogether excluded.

Here it was that soldiers and prisoners cooked their meals on primitive stoves of bricks and tiles, the latter having dropped from the roof of the building. From the constant use of water for culinary purposes the ground had become a mass of slimy mud, through which the barefooted natives tramped, evidently with as much relish as the pig that had buried himself so deep in the yielding mixture in one corner of the enclosure that nothing but his snout remained visible, emitting an occasional grunt of contentment. For some moments I stood gazing at this scene, then turned on my heel and re-entered the cell, which, I had mentally decided, was a trifle more endurable.

By this time the young mestizo was up and dressed. He seemed pleased when I seated myself on the edge of his bed, and at once entered into conversation with me, speaking a broken mixture of Spanish and English, the former predominating. Nevertheless, we seemed to comprehend one another fairly well, and in a short time he had given me his history.

Formerly the Spanish Government recruited a number of native regiments, principally composed of Macabebes, they being preferred on account of their stanch adherence to their Caucasian rulers, not due to any particular love for the Spaniard, but to their deadly hatred of the Tagalog. Few in numbers, compared to their hereditary enemies, they found their principal means of defence in faithfully clinging to the Spaniard, knowing well that in case of a successful establishment of a native government their doom as an independent faction would soon be sealed by the hated Tagalogs, especially as the small territory inhabited by them in the province of Pampanga is entirely surrounded by Tagalog country.

Now this young Captain Mariano, as he called himself, was a Macabebe, and, holding a commission under the Spanish Government, had commanded a company of native soldiers. Remaining faithful to their colors, Captain Mariano and his company of Macabebes intrenched themselves in a convent, and held out against the besieging Tagalogs until lack of ammunition, water, and food compelled them to surrender. Since then the young officer had been closely confined, being told that the only means by which he ever could gain his liberty would be by enrolling himself in the cause of the new republic. Six months he had now held out, but the long imprisonment was beginning to tell on him.

The other three Spaniards were but common soldiers, one being confined for attempting to escape into our lines; another was Mariano's servant. (Every Spanish officer is entitled to choose a private soldier as his personal attendant.) The third was a boy of nineteen, whom the others called Antonio. He did not make the best impression at first sight, partly, perhaps, on account of the disagreeable droop to his eyes. He was not in confinement, only making the cell his sleeping-quarters. Evidently he had good reasons for remaining in prison voluntarily, for, as developed later, he was a hanger-on and toady to the officers upstairs, with the object of obtaining that to which Mariano preferred rigorous confinement.

Soon everybody was engaged with the morning meal, but as nobody had as yet offered to supply us with means by which to bring our long fast to an end, we went outside and explained to the sergeant of the guard that we were accustomed to eat sometimes, that it was a habit of twenty years' standing, and that it would be decidedly inconvenient and even disastrous to us to break it off so suddenly. He replied that we had his full sympathy, and that we must not despair; within the next few days we should receive the prison ration of seven cents and a pound of rice a day. We were, however, too unreasonable to be willing to wait a few days, and so at length persuaded Miguela, as our female cell-mate was called, to go out to the market and buy us a few bananas, she being allowed to leave the prison at all times, her husband, also a prisoner, being considered a sure hostage for her return.

That day dragged slowly by. In spite of the almost frantic efforts we made to obtain an interview with some officer, none approached us. That first day was probably one of the worst we ever passed. Forced to remain in close companionship with those repulsive creatures, imprisoned for crimes as hideous as their forms, and then to be treated by them with a disgusting familiarity, was next to maddening.

Mariano seemed to feel a good deal of sympathy for us, and, through his influence, we received an old sleeping-mat large enough for the two of us, and a small space on the floor, whereon to spread it. When night came we retired, but there being sixteen of us, our quarters were cramped, to put it mildly. At one side I found a filthy Tagalog so close to me that his breath, suggestive of decayed fish, fanned my cheek. I tried to escape this horror by crowding Huber, but he was likewise flanked on the other side. A socialist in our situation would have had his ideas considerably modified. That night I became a Darwinist. Later on, rats, lizards, and a species of large beetle appeared and promenaded about the floor and walls. Had they only confined themselves to that I should not have complained, but they became entangled in my hair, crawled down my back inside of my clothes, tickled the soles of my feet, and, in fact, made themselves obnoxious in general.

It must have been past eight o'clock when the door, having been closed at sunset, noisily opened, and two men entered, but so faint was the single light in the cell, consisting of a string in a cup of cocoanut oil, that I could distinguish no more than the bare outlines of their figures, advancing slowly, picking their way, into the middle of the floor. I was suddenly startled by hearing in pure English, "Where are the two Englishmen?" I jumped to my feet and found myself face to face with a white man, evidently Anglo-Saxon. We shook hands.

The new-comer introduced himself as David Arnold, [1] native of Montreal, Canada, prisoner like us; his companion was an Insurgent officer. That afternoon he had ventured on a trip by train to Malolos, but, on arriving, had been arrested. His visit had been intended merely as a pleasure trip, but the Insurgent officials had refused to listen to his explanations, consequently he was now a prisoner.

For some time we stood conversing, the officer standing by listening, as if he comprehended every word, but at length he took Arnold by the arm again and bid us good-night. The door was closed and I lay down to resume the fight with the lizards, the rats, and the beetles, which in the meantime had been reinforced by mosquitoes.

The three or four succeeding days appeared to us like ages, our suspense and anxiety being intense. Whenever we caught sight of an officer we tried to obtain some information, but were invariably met with, "No se sabe!" accompanied by a shrug of the shoulders — if they answered at all.

Arnold had been confined in another cell on the opposite side of the building, and several times we saw him in the yard, but in a few terse words he told us once that he had been strictly forbidden to speak to us.

One day, the Tuesday following our arrival, I believe, we heard a commotion outside in the entrance, which, upon investigation, proved to be occasioned by the arrival of six more American prisoners. We saw them from our doorway, but were not allowed to converse with each other. Evidently they were soldiers, their uniforms told us that, and the brass towers on their campaign hats explained that they were engineers, undoubtedly found following their occupation too far beyond the American outposts. They were confined with Arnold on the other side of the entrance. We could not understand why we two should be isolated; it was somewhat depressing.

A day or two later still another prisoner was brought in, a young man, a civilian, apparently. He stole over to our cell unperceived by the guards, one evening, and held a conversation with us for at least ten minutes before he was discovered. This new arrival proved to be George Peters, war correspondent for an eastern magazine, who, while taking some photographic views close to the Insurgent lines, had been captured by their outposts, but who was too well acquainted with Aguinaldo and his chief officers, he told us, to fear a long imprisonment. We gave him our names, requesting him," in case he should be liberated before us, to report to the proper authorities our presence here. This he promised to do, but just then the sergeant of the guard appeared, calling the interview off. The following day Mr. Peters disappeared, so we supposed that his influence had secured him his liberty.

One evening I had an opportunity to speak a few words to one of the engineers who was cooking a pot of rice in the yard, and, having a vague presentiment that they would be released before us, gave him our names, asking him to report us to the British Consul. As we had entered the Insurgent lines as Englishmen, we were bound to continue the deception, and our only hope was that the British Consul would demand our release without too close investigation.

The following day the engineers disappeared, having been released at demand of General Otis.

As I learned long afterward, the engineer, of whose name I unfortunately took no note, kept his word, and did all he could at the British Consular office, and had the crisis come twenty-four hours later, we would have been saved; but I have often wondered at the probable outcome, supposing the Consul had come to Malolos and discovered the fraud — would he have left us to our fate? Only he can answer that question.

One evening we were interviewed by the Secretary of War, Baldomero Aguinaldo, cousin of the President. He was a short, heavy-set but well-built man, rather Japanese in features, with a small thin mustache, and of dark complexion, even for a Filipino. He wore the usual uniform of the President's staff, a coat of narrow blue and white vertical stripes, crimson pants, and black polished riding-boots. As he spoke excellent English, we had no difficulty in understanding one another, but the interview was short.

"Why did you venture into our lines," he began, "when you knew how strained the situation is? The cord may snap at any moment!" But to our inquiries as to when we might expect to be released, his only answer was a supercilious sneer and a shrug of the shoulders.

This same Baldomero Aguinaldo, seeing afterward how hopeless was the cause of Aguinaldo's Republic, disguised himself as a common laborer, and, coming boldly into our lines, passed through Manila, taking passage on the Hong-Kong steamer, and safely reaching that neutral port, where he is now living on his savings (?).

Our number was once more reduced to three, Arnold, Huber, and myself, but on Friday morning two more were added to the Filipinos' stock of American prisoners. Two white men appeared, evidently soldiers, as both wore uniforms, but we were not allowed to communicate with them either, and they were at once placed together with Arnold. So now we numbered five.

Saturday dragged slowly by, and was an uneventful day to us. At night we lay down on the floor of our cell to battle with reptiles, rats, and insects, as we had done on seven occasions previously, but at about nine o'clock a truce was declared and I dropped off into a quiet slumber. Some time during the night, exactly when neither of us knew, I was awakened by Huber shaking me excitedly by the shoulder. "They've commenced fighting!" he exclaimed. "Listen!"

We listened. With the exception of the heavy breathing of the sleepers, all was silent.

Suddenly we both started, for from the southward we plainly heard a low, deep sound like the buzz of angry bees flying by one's ear. Brrr-um-brrr-um!

[1] For reasons that will develop later, the true name of this man has been repressed, and the assumed one of Arnold substituted.

Chapter Three - Close Confinement

THE tranquillity and quiet which prevailed in Malolos on Sunday morning, February 5th, aroused in us a hope that we might after all have been deceived by those sounds that had disturbed the stillness of the preceding night: they might possibly have been but the rumbling of distant thunder.

Slowly the day wore on. We felt sad and depressed, for Mariano had gone, leaving us alone among those disgusting convicts, whose companionship was even more trying than the confinement. Only the day before he had bid us "Adios," but his prospective liberation had only seemed to sadden him. Long afterward we saw him again, but the shoulder-straps he wore were no longer those of Spain. It had taken six months to break his fidelity to a country not even his own, but at length he had succumbed. Having tried a week already of what he had endured for half a year, I could not blame him. Six months among such companions would have broken the firmest will.

Antonio likewise had disappeared, but when we again saw him, a week later, a second lieutenant's uniform had so transformed his appearance that we hardly recognized him. At length his ambition had been gratified. Spanish-born he was, too!

The unusual quietness seemed almost unnatural until I noticed the absence of the soldiers whose quarters were upstairs. This inspired me with a vague feeling of uneasiness — the soldiers had never been absent before. By late afternoon they had still not returned.

It must have been about five o'clock when I was sitting on a bench outside the cell-door, watching the prisoners cooking their rice for their evening meal, that the sound of an excited voice attracted my attention from the yard to the entrance. A soldier stood haranguing the guards in the native dialect. I could, consequently, not understand a word of what he said, but what caused me to take particular notice of him was the fact that his clothes were spattered with blood and one of his arms had been bandaged and hung in a sling. The guards stood listening to his words with intense interest. Presently the wounded man left them and rushed upstairs, A moment later another appeared in the entrance, his clothes likewise blood-stained, and, saying a few hurried words to the now excited guards, followed the first one to the floor above. I tried to make myself believe that the two had quarrelled and had then settled their dispute with bolos, but when a third man passed by me up the stairs, a bloody bandage about his head, my heart sank. I called to Huber, and he joined me.

By this time a crowd of excited natives had gathered outside in the street, but suddenly a deep silence fell over all, as four men came in bearing a canvas litter upon which a man lay gasping for breath. The canvas upon which he lay had once been white, but was now of a slimy grayish red, while from underneath a steady streamlet of blood was trickling to the ground. His clothing, although torn and blood-stained, was the uniform of an officer of high rank in the Insurgent army, but failed to hide some ghastly wounds on which cotton batting had been pressed. Carefully they bore him upstairs, but it needed no experienced eye to see that the shadow of death was on the wounded man's features.

A loud and hoarse cry now arose outside, the cry of an enraged mob. Miguela grasped us by the arms and tried to push us inside. "Malo!" "Malo!" she repeated when we resisted, and at length we concluded to heed her warning, for even the guards were throwing sinister glances at us.

We asked no questions of our cell-mates, nor was any information volunteered. The subject was a delicate one. Some glared at us savagely, others appeared indifferent, while a very few, Miguela and her husband among them, seemed friendly and even sympathetic. There now remained no doubt but what the blow had fallen.

The cries of the mob outside waxed louder and acquired more volume. Frequently we heard shouts of "Viva Filipinas!" and "Muerte a los Americanos!" but whether the latter words applied only to us five in the prison, or to the whole nation, we couldn't tell, and in either case our situation was not pleasant.

The uproar outside had become almost deafening, when an officer and the sergeant of the guard appeared and beckoned to us to follow them. We were conducted across the passage-way to the door of the other cell in which Arnold and the two soldiers were confined. We stood there but a moment while the fastenings were being undone, but in that short time the mob outside saw us, and became almost frenzied with rage. The guards stood in the portal, barring the way, and beyond them, outside, a seething mass of black heads and half-naked limbs. But the cell door was at length thrown open, we were thrust in and left in total darkness, the door being closed and barred.

Arnold and his two companions were not asleep. One of them lit a match, by the light of which Huber and myself were enabled to crawl upon a bamboo structure, supposed to serve as a bed. We had but little to say to one another, yet I doubt if any of my companions fell asleep before midnight. The sergeant of the guard seemed to be in a state of apprehension on our account; every half hour he opened the door to satisfy himself that we had not evaporated or crawled between the thick iron bars of the window. When at length I did fall asleep, it was only to dream of the crew of the Virginius in Cuba.

The scene that revealed itself to my eyes upon awakening in the morning was not a cheering one. My companions seemed likewise impressed, for they all sat on the bamboo platform on which we had been sleeping, with their backs against the wall, their hands clasped about their knees which were elevated to their chins, staring vacantly at the wall in front of them, nobody saying a word for a long time.

I had likened the other cell to a dungeon, but this one was far worse. Of but half the size, it was more gloomy and had no flooring but the damp earth.

Two bamboo cots, a sort of platform, filled almost the entire space, leaving but a narrow passage between them and one of the walls, in which to walk. Two windows shed a feeble light; one facing the street, being partially boarded up to avoid public curiosity. The other overlooked a massive stone wall, over the top of which could be seen a few palms and banana trees. But, thank God! we were separated from those hideous criminals — we were all of a kind, at least.

The morning passed dismally away. Our conversation was not interesting to ourselves, much less would it have been to any outsider, but we became acquainted with each other.

Arnold, as I have said before, was a Canadian, and proved to be a person of considerable education, having been a clergyman in one of our large Western cities. Being obliged to leave the ministry for reasons best known to himself, he came to Honolulu, where he taught school for some time, until an opportunity presented itself to work his passage across to Manila on the transport Arizona. From having preached the gospel Arnold now tried his abilities in other channels, and just before his capture had been manager of a Manila restaurant. He freely admitted that an overindulgence in strong drink was the cause of his last misfortune, namely, his capture, having boarded the Malolos train while under the influence of too much Scotch rye.

The two soldiers were William Bruce and Elmer Honeyman, both young men, privates of the First Nevada Cavalry, then stationed at Cavite. On the morning of January 31st they had ventured to pay the Insurgents a visit at San Roque, within a short distance of Cavite, They were at once arrested and sent on to Malolos, walking the entire distance from San Roque to Caloocan, several times passing close around the outskirts of Manila, within sight of the American outposts. From Caloocan to Malolos they had travelled by train.

The excitement of the evening before was now somewhat subdued, although several times during the day noisy groups of shouting natives passed by. Numbers of officers and well-dressed civilians came to visit us, and, although no personal violence was offered, on several occasions their patriotic feelings could hardly be restrained. Several told us that as spies we had been condemned to be shot, the execution being set for the following day. Especially Huber and me, who had been taken with a camera in our possession, they had every right to punish as spies, they said. I have since come to the conclusion that this was nothing more than an attempt at humor on their part, but at that time the joke did not reveal its point, as far as we were concerned, at least.

A plate of cooked rice was brought to us twice during the day by the woman Miguela, who had volunteered to act as our cook, but the gray mass of doughy stuff suggested even to us, hungry as we were, the taste of newspaper pap; it had about that color, too.

Only under the greatest necessity were we allowed out in the yard, and then for but a few minutes at a time. Excepting when visitors entered, the door was constantly kept barred.

That evening we received a visit from a young sergeant, who, unlike the majority, seemed inclined to be friendly. He had been to the front and volunteered some information. The lighting, he said, had been precipitated by a blunder, but a conference was that day being held to rectify the same. It was quite possible that all would yet be adjusted to the satisfaction of both parties. This story we could not bring ourselves to believe, although I am convinced that the attack on the night of the 4th was not premeditated; had it been, the troops would not have been in Malolos so late on Saturday night as they were. In other towns, too, as I have learned since, garrisons were called out at midnight and hurried down to Caloocan by special trains after the fighting had commenced.

As we had no means by which to illuminate our cell after dark, it was, of course, necessary to retire with the sun. This, however, was a simple ceremony. Not being able to walk about we were obliged to sit on the bed during daytime, our backs resting against the wall, so that on going to bed we had but to remove our shoes and then slide forward until our heads touched that part of the cot where we a moment before had been sitting. The shoes would then do service as pillows. So quickly and easily was all this done that it did not interfere the least with the conversation. I have read somewhere of a man who considered it a great hardship when once obliged to dispense with a night-cap for one night, but we found other inconveniences of more consequence than that.

But in spite of all our miseries and hardships we appreciated the absence of native companions, we were at least by ourselves, and again I repeat it, we considered that an advantage that more than offset all our other troubles. How great our subsequent disappointment, however!

Let me now pass over the next two or three days, uneventful ones, but fraught with suspense and anxiety to us.

If my memory does not deceive me, it was Wednesday evening, and we had just retired in the manner described, and lay there conversing in the Egyptian darkness, when suddenly we became aware of a low murmur, which seemed to come from some distance down the street. Gradually the sound increased, until it swelled into the loud uproar of an angry mob outside in front of the prison. Once more we heard the cry of "Muerte! Muerte!" and its equivalent in Tagalog: "Pati-e, Pati-e!" At last the mob seemed to have gained entrance, and with a resounding crash our door was flung open. Instinctively we all sprang to our feet, believing that a lynching bee was about to take place, in which we were to play a much too prominent part. The mob burst into the cell, but in a few moments we discovered that this time they had found another object for their wrath — we were not even noticed.

At the head of the crowd, which seemed to be composed principally of soldiers, an officer appeared, dragging after him a trembling wretch, a native, whose arms were tightly pinioned behind him. Pulling him in with a violent jerk, the officer turned and threw the poor fellow against the wall, and as many as could crowd in stood in a semicircle around him. Several of the soldiers bore flaming torches in their hands, and by their light we were enabled to see all. So tightly were the prisoner's arms bound that blood oozed from the cuts above his elbows where the cords sank deeply into the flesh. The officer now drew from its sheath, depending from his waist, a small dagger, and with one cut severed the bonds, thus freeing the prisoner's arms. The light of the torches now fell full upon him, revealing a ghastly sight. Blood was oozing out of two gashes on his head, and some of it had dried in his long hair and matted it together. His clothes were torn into shreds, and his body covered from head to foot with mud and clotted blood. The fleshy part of his leg had been pierced by a bullet, showing an ugly, ragged wound, now black and swollen.

The prisoner was evidently not a Tagalog, as the officer spoke to him in Spanish, and by our combined knowledge of that language we were able to catch the meaning of his words, and those the poor wretch made in reply.

It seems that he was accused of being a "secreto," which means either traitor or spy, or both together, and now for the first time they demanded an explanation, whereupon he began in a low-monotonous tone to give an account of the events leading up to his decidedly unpleasant situation.

The man had been a servant to an American officer in Manila, but had neglected either to obtain the permission of the Insurgent authorities or else to pay his license fee. For this his name was on the Black List. At the outbreak of hostilities, however, he left his employer and thought of nothing more than to join his wife and three children in Meycauayan. Endeavoring to pass through the American lines he succeeded, but was wounded in the leg by a Springfield bullet, and almost captured by the Americans. He at length safely reached the Insurgent lines before they could further disable him. But it was from the frying-pan into the fire! Having no pass, he was arrested as a "secreto." His march to Malolos had been a cruel one, to judge by his appearance.

As he stood relating his doleful story, he would at times falter from fear or weakness, and then the sergeant of the guard would poke him with the muzzle of his Remington, while ogling at his superior for a glance of approval. As the prisoner concluded his narrative, to the truth of which he swore by God, Holy Mary, and the blessed saints, the officer quietly replaced the dagger in its sheath, and no sooner had the last words left those bruised and swollen lips when he drew back and planted his clinched fist between the eyes of the unfortunate. Once, twice, and three times did he repeat it, until the victim lay senseless on the floor, and then, with a last kick, he turned to leave the cell, apparently convinced that the blows just struck were for "la independencia" of his glorious land. As each soldier left the room, he had first to give that mass of almost unrecognizable humanity on the floor a kick, as had done the noble captain. Fortunately they were all barefooted, otherwise the results might have been more serious.

Being once more left in darkness, Arnold struck a match, and by its light we lifted the poor wretch upon the other cot, where he lay groaning throughout the night.

Once, believing that he was dying, we called the guards, but the only answer they gave was a few blows with the butt of a gun against the door, and a command to be silent.

By morning our new fellow-sufferer had fully recovered his senses, but so repulsive was he to look at that none of us really cared to approach him. That day he received no rations, so we gave him some of ours, and the manner in which he expressed his gratitude was touching. Later on during the day we managed to get him some water, and with the remnant of an old shirt persuaded him first to clean and then to bandage his wounded leg, which he did under Ruber's supervision.

We seemed, somehow, no longer to be a novelty compared to the poor "secreto." Numbers of visitors came to see him during the day, nor would they leave without maltreating him in some way, either striking or kicking him.

One fellow, who the week before had been confined in the other cell with Huber and me for murdering a woman, seemed now to have regained his liberty by joining the army. He came in, appearing especially indignant, giving expression to his patriotism by seizing the prisoner's head between his hands and biting it!

This addition to our number was far from agreeable to us, and we did not like it, but the Military Governor upstairs, Señor Francisco Donato, did not consult our wishes, doing exactly as he saw fit.

That same afternoon there was a sudden flap of our door, and two more unfortunates appeared bound together arm to arm. They also had received rough usage, and were likewise accused of wishing to sell their country to the invading Americans. One of these two, whom we at once nicknamed Squint-Eye on account of a defect in one of his visual organs, admitted having been in the employ of General Otis as coachman, but had omitted procuring a license. It seems that the Government at Malolos had once issued a proclamation, declaring it treasonable for any Filipino to enter the service of an American unless provided with a special permit, for which a percentage of his wages was charged. Many neglected to do this, and were at once reported by Insurgent spies and placed on the Black List as "Americanistas!" Had the addition to our numbers ceased with these three, we might have become reconciled to their presence, as they were quiet and well-behaved, but our brotherhood of misery continued to increase. At all hours of the day or night more suspected "secretos" were thrown in, some violently like a shovelful of coal into a furnace, others dragged in by the Governor himself. All were more or less bruised upon arrival, but the worst generally came afterward. Every day we were forced to witness sights that would have horrified the most callous, for violence and brutality prevailed. Never had I seen brute-nature in man more prominently displayed!

One case that occurred then still remains vividly in my recollection of those ghastly scenes; that of a boy of less than fourteen years of age. He also had been a servant with some "Americano," and crossed over into the Insurgent lines to join his family. Arrested as a "secreto" the boy denied the charge, but, in order to force a confession from him, the soldiers bound him to a tree and then burnt his face, neck, and chest with the glowing ends of their cigarettes. When thrown in with us, the poor lad, although by nature of a pleasing appearance, was fairly hideous with his disfigured face and neck, having all the appearance of a small-pox patient. When he told us his story we could hardly believe it, but the pride with which the sergeant of the guard boasted of his complicity in the outrage removed our last doubts. We named the lad Cigarettes, on account of his experience, and by this appellation he soon became known throughout the prison by soldiers and prisoners alike, it being considered very appropriate.

This brings to my memory another similar case, which, did I not have witnesses to prove the facts, I should hesitate to mention. It was that of another boy even younger than Cigarettes, a mere child of twelve, who one day was added to our number. In spite of his extreme youth he received no more consideration than the others; in fact, some of the soldiers seemed to take especial delight in twisting the puny limbs until the victim shrieked from agony.

As we were told, an uncle or cousin of this young boy had committed some offence against the Government and then disappeared. The child was supposed to know of his whereabouts, but, being unable to force a confession from him, the Governor had him added to our number. Every day a diminutive specimen of humanity was permitted to enter the cell, bearing a bamboo basket on its head of such large dimensions that, unless viewed at some distance, the basket itself appeared endowed with power of locomotion. This was a younger brother to the youthful prisoner, who came twice a day with a meal of rice, fish, bananas, etc., in the aforementioned basket, and in leaving took his brother's rations in exchange, the pound of black rice and five out of the seven cents. The remaining two cents were spent on fruit, cigarettes, or betel-nuts. Occasionally the mother, a sad-faced woman of the working class, came also, and, while her son sat eating the scanty meal, crouched beside him, talking to him and weeping by turns, until forced to leave by the guards.

One day our little friend disappeared, and, naturally, we thought he had been liberated. To fully understand what follows, it is necessary that I explain a small circumstance connected with our daily prison life.

The floor above us was composed of three large rooms. The first, facing the street, was the Military Governor's office, wherein Donato and his staff sat daily plotting mischief. Next came an ante-room, and in the rear a third apartment where half a company of soldiers had been quartered before the outbreak of hostilities, but where now the guards and recruits slept at night. Here, out in the rear, a guard would conduct any one of us when obliged to leave the cell, passing up through the ante-room, and past the door to the Governor's office. At times, when the guard chanced to be not too zealous in his duties, we paused a moment at the door to glance in at the officers. The ante-room being very dark prevented them from seeing us. The office was but scantily furnished with a table and a few chairs, but most conspicuous of all was a massive wooden plank which generally stood on end on one side of the room, through which had been cut a row of holes about three inches in diameter. This piece of timber was split through the middle, the split cutting straight through the centre of each hole. At each end an iron rod pierced the two half-planks crosswise, sliding through the upper half loosely so that it could be lifted.

Now this piece of furniture was an instrument of torture similar to the stocks of colonial days, in which the feet of the victim were placed by lifting the upper half and then lowering it over his ankles, the man then being in such a position that he could hardly touch the plank, much less lift it. This instrument is as familiar throughout the Philippines as a stove in our country, each convent being furnished with two or three, although what particular use the fathers had for them might puzzle some people. Probably they were utilized to "convert the heathens."

Such an instrument stood in Donato's office, and many times was it brought into use. But to resume the story of our boy prisoner.

Some days after his disappearance it happened that one of our number, about to make the trip up to the soldiers' quarters, was surprised by seeing the little brother preceding him upstairs, the large basket carefully balanced on his head. Wondering what brought the child here now, he followed, seeing him enter the Governor's office. The guard was not paying the strictest attention, and, looking in through the doorway, he saw the little one placing the basket beside his elder brother, the boy of a dozen years, who sat on the floor, one of his feet in the stocks. So small were his limbs that they had wrapped cloth around the one in the hole, so that it might not slip through. Up to the third day we saw him there, but how long he remained after that, probably only Señor Donato can tell.

To review every one of the fiendish acts of cruelty inflicted on their kind by the patriotic Donate and his crew would require a volume, but the reading would hardly be pleasant.

In less than a week after the arrival of Betel-Nuts, as we called No. i on account of his red teeth, we numbered twenty-five in that miserable hole, which at first we had considered too small for five.

From all classes of society they came: laborers, mechanics, clerks, merchants, doctors, and even ex-military officers; but here all were equals, the lawyer ate from the same dish with the former servant, and the doctor slept beside the fisherman. All were accused of the one crime, being in sympathy if not in actual employ of our Government — all political offenders. At one time a woman was with us for two days, but as she was about to give birth to a child, they had at least consideration enough for the situation to remove her.

I often wondered in what way the poor thing could have offended those fiends; she appeared too insipid even to have a political opinion, much less to express one, but perhaps her grandfather or some distant relative had committed some offence, and, escaping, had left the poor woman as heir to his punishment.

Chapter Four - Desperate Chances

IT does not require a vivid imagination to fancy how twenty-five men existed in a room ten by twenty feet in dimensions. Although we never suffered for want of drinking-water, for washing purposes it was never thought of. In a short time we became covered with vermin and disgusting sores. After eight o'clock in the evening, when the night watch relieved those who had been on duty all day, nobody was allowed to leave the cell under any circumstances, so our floor was soon reeking with filth and dampness. Refuse was thrown out of the window, where it fell in a large putrid heap between the building and a stone wall, breeding maggots and filling the cell with a sickening stench, so strong that it awoke us at nights. From the want of fresh air and exercise the least physical exertion caused such dizziness that, upon rising and standing upon the floor, we staggered about like drunken men.

Then it was that we first began to discuss plans of escape. However desperate the chances, we felt we ought to take them, for, as we then thought, it was either that or death.

Thus we argued among ourselves. Should the Americans begin to advance, the Insurgent army, defeated and demoralized, would retreat upon and through Malolos, a mob of disorganized and ungovernable rabble. Houses would be looted and burned, anarchy would reign, and in their frenzy, what mercy could we expect from such a horde? This seemed to us most logical.

Then, again, supposing the Americans should not advance, but attempt to argue the Filipinos into submission, which might take some time — how long could we expect to live under existing circumstances? In whichever way we looked at our situation, there seemed but one ray of hope, but one manner in which to avoid certain death, and that lay in our escape. This, however, seemed a desperate undertaking, for not alone was the prison well-guarded, but twenty miles lay between us and the American lines. I sincerely believe that the fearful state of suspense which continually assailed us, awake or asleep, would eventually have affected our reason, had we not one day made a discovery which sent a faint glimmer of hope into the prevailing gloom.

One day one of us (I believe it was Bruce) crawled up into the window overlooking the stone wall, endeavoring to obtain a glimpse of the world outside and beyond the aforementioned wall, when he noticed something peculiar about one of the bars. At this window, these bars were made of a native mahogany called narra, almost as tough as iron. In the middle of the window was a horizontal crossbar, through which the vertical bars passed, their both ends buried in the masonry above and below. At first the window had been of double size, but in the numerous fights between Spaniards and Insurgents a garrison of the former had at some time turned the building into a small fortress and built a breastwork of stone and mortar inside the bars, thus filling in the lower half of the original window. The top of this breastwork was on a level with the crossbar. One of the perpendicular bars had been broken off, its stump barely extending below and outside the top of the breastwork. This we had all seen but paid no particular attention to, as the space made by the missing half bar was blocked by the stones and mortar. But Bruce's attention on the above-mentioned occasion was attracted by a wedge, slipped in between the upright and the hole in the crossbar, through which it passed.

On touching this he found it loose, so that by removing the wedge, the broken bar could be slid down to the sill outside of the later built up masonry, transferring the open space thus from below the crossbar to above it, this opening being large enough for the passage of a man's body.

One by one we all examined this defect in the window, and our joy became almost uncontrollable as we now saw the manner in which it could serve us. From the window to the top of the adjacent wall was but a jump, and then — liberty! After this we did nothing but plot and plan; we had at least found something upon which to concentrate our thoughts, aside from the morbid fear of a terrible death, and this, I firmly believe, saved us from madness. Once outside the limits of the town, we reasoned, our chances of reaching the American lines might be considered fairly bright. Bruce and Honeyman, on coming from the railroad station, had observed the surroundings, while Huber and I were well acquainted with the nature of the country where the two armies now lay facing each other. Our combined knowledge served as a foundation upon which we built a plan of action that seemed to us promising of success.

On the other side of the wall, the top of which was on a level with and not six feet distant from the window, was a large space of ground used by the Insurgent officers as a gymnasium, as we surmised by the bars, rings, swings, and trapeze that had been erected there. This was bounded on the other side by a dense banana orchard, and beyond and above that we could plainly see the tops of a bamboo jungle, so we judged that the prison was situated in the outskirts of the town.

From the window over the wall and into the banana grove would be but two leaps, thence into the jungle. At about ten or eleven o'clock on the first stormy night we would quietly extract the wedge, slip down the bar, and steal out while our native companions slept, and if they by chance should awaken and see the hole they also might take advantage of it, if so inclined. Once into the jungle we would circle about the town until we struck the railroad track, and, guided by it, travel along at a brisk pace until we reached the large river that flowed by Bocave. This distance was about seventeen kilometers, or thirteen miles, and, if nothing unforeseen should happen, we would make it by three in the morning. Then we would either have to steal a boat and paddle downstream, or follow the banks until we reached the line of outposts, through which we must pass by swimming, either into our own lines or out in the bay, where the Monadnock lay always anchored, close to the mouth of the river. As we all claimed to be good swimmers this plan was not deemed a desperate one, and was unanimously adopted. Apparently nothing now remained but to wait for a favorable night, and this we expected by the approaching dark of the moon, generally accompanied by stormy weather in the tropics.

Monday, February 13th, dawned gloomily; it being rainy and stormy with every indication of a tempestuous night, and as this continued until the afternoon, we quietly made preparations to take due advantage of the opportunity. Daily we were becoming physically weaker, and felt that by too long delay we might find ourselves unequal to the hardships that such an undertaking would naturally incur. Our impatience was great!

Arnold, who had had charge of our mess funds, receiving our daily rations from the sergeant who distributed them, turned over every cent, and through Miguela it was invested in jerked beef and in bread, which it was our intention to take with us in case we should find it impossible to accomplish all in one night and find it necessary to conceal ourselves in the jungle for a day until the following night made it possible to continue the flight.

As evening approached and nothing remained to be done but to await the hour of eleven o'clock, we all became decidedly silent. Almost without speaking we each of us had taken four slips of paper, written the names and addresses of our different families on them, and distributed them to one another. Some might be more fortunate than others. Then we lay back on the cot, not to converse or sleep, but to speculate on the possible outcome of this game of chance we were about to play, the stakes of which were liberty, and, as we then thought, life itself.

For over an hour we lay there, mentally preparing ourselves for what we knew would be a severe test of our courage and endurance, but for my part, although I will admit that my fears of the consequences of a possible miscarriage of our plans gave me considerable uneasiness, I awaited the hour of action with feverish eagerness, anxious to have it over with, either for good or bad.

It was almost eight o'clock when Arnold arose from the cot, and, remarking that he felt a trifle unwell, knocked at the door and called to the sergeant of the guard, begging to be permitted to leave the cell for a few moments. This was nothing unusual; we all had done this daily, especially at this hour, just before the door was bolted for the night. But on this occasion, by some oversight of the guard, the door was not entirely closed again after Arnold's exit, but stood ajar. A moment later, seeing this, and either being or imagining myself thirsty, I arose, slipped out unseen by the guard, into the yard. Having satisfied my thirst at a large jar which always stood there filled with water, I started to return. In passing the staircase I cast a casual glance up in that direction, when to my surprise I saw Arnold on the upper landing in deep conversation with Donato. The governor was certainly no friend of his, and, naturally, the meeting seemed strange. The expression of the Canadian's face and his gestures filled me with a vague suspicion. Returning to the cell I immediately told my companions what I had seen. We were not long to remain in doubt.

A quarter of an hour passed and still no return of Arnold. Twenty minutes, still absent. Never before had any of us been able to leave the cell for such a length of time.

Suddenly the door was thrown wide open, and preceded by the sergeant of the guard, who bore a torch, Donato entered. Without even glancing at us he strode over to the window, and by the light of the torch examined it, shaking and feeling bars and masonry. Apparently he discovered nothing, so, turning, he left the cell, casting a piercing glance at us as he passed, that seemed fraught with meaning. It was a warning, and we understood. Some minutes later Arnold came in, with a sickly smile and a lame attempt at gayety, accompanied by an armed guard, who held a light while the former gathered up his few belongings. He had just seen the Secretary of War, Baldomero Aguinaldo, he said, and on account of his nationality, or innocence, as he called it, was to be sent through the lines into Manila the next day. Then he commenced to tell us how strenuous would be the efforts he would make in our behalf with the American military authorities, but our silence put a damper on his discourse. Hastily picking up his few rags, he bid us good-by, but again silence greeted his words, so he left the cell, and the door closed behind him. Before long we heard the measured tramp of a new sentinel outside the window.

Chapter Five - Jail Life

HAVING exposed our plans for escape, we naturally expected to see Arnold rewarded, as well as ourselves punished, but neither of these results occurred. Arnold was only separated from us, as he afterward confessed, at his own request, fearing bodily harm from the rest of us, and confined among the convicts where Huber and I had spent the first week of our imprisonment.

The window was again examined the next morning, but as they did not climb up on the sill as we had done, but satisfied themselves with standing on the floor and simply shaking the bars, the secret wedge remained undiscovered, and this probably led Donato to believe that Arnold's denouement had been but a self-conceived trick to gain sympathy and better treatment, and really as such he seemed to treat the whole affair, but, nevertheless, a sentry was so stationed that the gymnasium could constantly be kept under surveillance. At any rate, Arnold gained nothing by his treachery; on the contrary, his situation became worse, alone and among those hideous convicts. Much as we disliked the presence of our native cell-mates, it was from no racial or personal dislike, for the majority seemed honest, and were probably even innocent of the political offences of which they were accused; in fact, the relations between us and our present Filipino companions were ever of the most friendly and even brotherly sort. Some few that had families and received donations of food far beyond the means of the rest of us, were ever willing to divide not only with their own countrymen, but also with the "Americanos." I remember, one day, before Arnold left us, a little incident that took place which illustrates his cowardice and a native's generous behavior.

Arnold had been knocking at the door for some time, on this particular occasion, for permission to leave the cell, but as no attention was paid to him by the guards, he became impatient and commenced to kick at the door. This angered the sergeant of the guard, who at once opened the door so violently that Arnold, thoroughly frightened, drew back. Seeing a native prisoner before him, the sergeant of the guard, supposing him to have been the cause of the disturbance, at once commenced to beat him with his bayonet. The native received every blow in silence, looking reproachfully at the Canadian, who stood trembling in one corner, but who would not say a word to take the blame upon himself, nor did the native ever say a word either. This incident had lowered Arnold in our estimation considerably, so when he afterward betrayed us, the shock was not so unexpected as many might surmise. The sudden change he now experienced must, however, have caused him some mental suffering, for, unprincipled as he was, Arnold had a sensitive nature. From a crack in our door we frequently saw him in the yard, where he now had full liberty to walk about. He grew haggard, and when at times we saw him pacing up and down in the prison inclosure, speaking aloud to himself, gesticulating with his hands and even with his arms, glaring wildly about him, we thought his reason had given way under the mental suffering he endured. But if any of us felt any pity for him, he kept it to himself.

However, Arnold at length found some relief. One day he came laughing and staggering into the yard, an object of amusement to the native prisoners. They had given him vino, a strong alcoholic drink made from the nipa plant, three small glasses of which are enough to deprive any person not used to it of his senses.

But, as the old proverb says, "the blackest cloud rolls by," and soon a great change came to our relief. The reign of Donato the Terrible one day came to an end; he was relieved by a new Governor, and departed to tyrannize and spread terror over some other district. Even the staff and soldiers went with him, and glad we were when they all went. The new Governor soon made his presence felt in a beneficent way. He came personally around on a tour of inspection and seemed highly indignant at the manner in which we lived. We were allowed to clean the cell thoroughly out, and the native prisoners were made to do the same on the entire premises. The putrefying heap outside the window was removed and lime spread there, and the door of our cell was allowed to stand open during daytime, permitting the air to circulate more freely, while by knocking at any hour of the night any one of us could leave the cell. Drains were made in the yard, and soon all the mire had been transformed into solid ground, upon which we were allowed to walk several hours daily. The floor of our cell, which until then had been a pool of water and filth, was also dried up, and disinfectants strewn into every corner. At the end of a few days Donato would scarcely have recognized his former domain had he returned.

About this time Miguela and her husband were liberated, and we were allowed to do our own cooking. I volunteered to act as chef the first week, and at once took charge of the daily rations. My duties, however, were not of an arduous sort, for our meals were simple and easily prepared. At first we found some difficulty in procuring anything in the market not positively distasteful to us, but one day Miguela had bought us some comottes, and, as the patent-medicine advertisements say, "since then we had tried no other." Comottes are a species of sweet potatoes so similar to our American kind that they need no special description. We liked them so well not only on account of their home-like taste, but because they also recommended themselves to us by their cheapness. For one cent we could buy four, and three cents purchased enough to last us all for a day. Rice, boiled in Chinese fashion, comottes and sugar, with an occasional cent's-worth of bananas, at length came to be our principal diet, and if we only had had enough it would not have been so bad.

The native prisoners also lived chiefly on rice, but always had some side-dish, which, no matter of what composed, was always called "vianda," or "ulam," in Tagalog. Sometimes it was shrimps or small crabs, at times a species of catfish boiled with tamarind beans, but their favorite relish was "bogone." I boldly swallowed a spoonful of this mess one day, and survived, which is proof of an excellent constitution. "Bogone" is made in this manner: a quantity of small shrimps, hardly bigger than the ordinary spawn, are placed in an earthen jar, where they are mixed with salt, vinegar, and areca-nut, and allowed to stand a week. The mixture is then ready for use. Sometimes small fish are substituted for shrimps, but the result is the same. With a small dish of this on one side of him, a pot of rice on the other, and two bananas within easy reach, Mr. Filipino is as happy as the proverbial pig in clover. Squatting on his heels in true Oriental style, he reaches into the rice pot, takes a handful, squeezes it into a ball and, dipping it into the "bogone," conveys the whole to his under lip, which in an astonishing manner projects itself to receive it.

This description relates, of course, only to the laboring man, or "taui" as the Tagalogs call him, the Filipino "man with the hoe," he who tills the soil, pays his taxes, and asks no questions. The higher class of Filipino is as much accustomed to knives and forks as we are, but never have I met one so refined but what, if occasion demanded it, he could use his hands with a dexterity that sufficiently proved he was no stranger to the performance, I refer to people prominent in Manila society. The women are, on the whole, more reluctant to drop this custom than the men, and, excepting the most refined and best educated families, do not appear at table if guests are present, unless the latter are on the most familiar footing with the members of the family; intimate acquaintances, whom they know, are so used to this peculiar manner of eating as not to take offence at it.

The lowest class of natives, "tauis," as the Filipinos themselves call them, live in the most primitive bamboo huts, and eat their meals in the manner already described, squatting on the floor. Rice, ulam, and bogone, with a few bananas and an occasional chicken, form their daily diet. Three pesos a month, equal to one dollar and a half American money, suffices as the cost of living. Passing this class we come to the most representative and the most numerous in all countries — the great middle class. In this may be counted small merchants, planters, clerks, tradesmen, mechanics, and minor government officials. The men now begin to afifect European clothing, as far as the climate permits at least, and speak sufficient Spanish for everyday use, the women rarely understanding or speaking more than their provincial dialect. Some live in bamboo huts of larger dimensions and more complete than those of the "tauis," and others in more favorable circumstances have houses of wood with nipa roofs. A tile roof is already a sign of a certain financial standing.

A couple of cases of illustrations personally had by the writer, long after his imprisonment, may prove of some interest to the reader.

I was on one occasion visiting a native friend of the middle class, a prosperous tobacco planter in a small way. Their dwelling was of bamboo, but with a plank flooring, Spanish beds, and modern furniture, that is, considered modern there. His wife, a quiet, meek, insipid woman, could only speak the local dialect, but the children could all read and write Spanish. He himself. spoke it fairly well, had heard of Germany, France, and England, etc., -and even had a fair idea of their population, products, manufactures, inventions, and so forth. He and his family were fair specimens of the great middle class of the Philippines.

Being asked to remain for dinner, I accepted the invitation. The woman set a table in the room, with tablecloth, napkin, knife, fork, spoon, cup, and plate, all in European style. My host requested me to seat myself, which I did, but, seeing only plate, knife, and fork for one, I thought I had done so a little too soon, and waited for my host and family to join me. At length he approached and said, "Señor, why do you not begin?"

"I am waiting for you!" I answered.

"No," he replied, "I will eat with my wife and the children."

I soon became used to this custom, however, for, as I subsequently learned, the knife and fork in my hands were all the house possessed, bought especially for such a contingency. As we became more intimate, and I often partook of his hospitality, this formality wore off; he no longer called me "Señor," but Alberto; he, his wife, and I eating at the same table, they with their hands, although in a much cleaner manner than the "tauis," having fingerbowls on the table, while I plied their only knife and fork.

On another occasion I was invited to dine in Manila by a friend belonging to the upper class, one whose name appeared prominently as a member of

Aguinaldo's former cabinet. Circumstances had made us intimate friends, so long after my release we met again in Manila. There was no ceremony between us, he called me Alberto then as he had done when he knew me in different circumstances, with all my clothes on my back and considerably ragged at that. His wife appeared at the head of the table, handled knife and fork with as much grace as any European, and never spoke to husband or children but in Spanish. They were in all respects equal to a better class Spanish family. Not a drop of Caucasian blood flowed through their veins; they were pure-blooded Filipinos from their remote ancestors. Yet, this same gentleman and I, while travelling at one time, had found ourselves obliged to spend the night in the bamboo hut of a "taui," where knives and forks were unknown, and the dexterousness with which he made use of his fingers had not come to him spontaneously.

But, really, I am digressing from my narrative, and that, too, on such commonplace objects as knives and forks!

As I said before, "comottes" formed our principal article of diet besides rice, consequently our meals were easily prepared, our bill of fare easily remembered, but as cook and caterer another difficulty now presented itself to me, which at first sight seemed likely to cause our financial ruin. Never before had we appreciated how honest poor little Miguela had been in the administration of our funds. We were now obliged to intrust the purchasing of our comottes and bananas to the guards. Generally I gave the price of the desired articles to the sergeant of the guard, who at once sent one of his men to the market to buy them, but the manner in which those men would "desert" was really wonderful. If intrusted with more than two cents they could surely be counted on to desert their cause and disappear. At least, so the sergeant of the guard said. The idea once occurred to us to save up twenty cents by a week of self-denial, and then give each guard three cents, there being six or seven of them, and then send them off to the' market. As they would naturally desert, we could have walked out of the prison unhindered. But this plan had one great drawback. All these deserters had twin brothers who took their place next day. Sometimes we made an awkward mistake and accused them of stealing our two cents, but they at once swore by all the saints that they were innocent, and could not be held responsible for the crimes of their "hermanos!" In this way we even discovered cases of triplets, but our curiosity was not sufficiently aroused to investigate this phenomenal plurality of Filipino family members to any further extent. There may even have been cases of quadruplets, for all we knew, but we could no longer afford to encourage such desertions, it was really too expensive for us, so at length we found a poor inoffensive murderer, who was allowed to go to the market every morning to make the purchases for the native prisoners, and as he proved himself honest, and moreover never deserted, he became our regular caterer.

About this time the gymnasium outside our window was formally opened to the public as a pleasure resort, and we also derived some amusement from it.

Besides the appliances for physical exercise which I have already mentioned as having been established on the ground, two small bamboo pavilions had been added, one so close to our window that, by standing on the sill, we could see anybody inside and have spoken to them so as to be heard in a natural tone of voice. Each one of these pavilions, and, in fact, the grounds in general, were illuminated by electric lights, and every evening the scene was one of life and gayety. We took turns crouching up in our window to watch this scene, where people could laugh, sing, and dance, apparently unaware that brothers, fathers, sons, and friends were falling in a hopeless struggle by hundreds, yes even thousands, less than twenty miles away.

In one of these bamboo retreats stood a number of small tables, and here the higher Government officials would gather of evenings, to forget their cares in beer, checkers, or chess, smoking and listening to the orchestra that played exquisite music in the other pavilion. Our native fellow-prisoners often pointed out to us prominent leaders of the insurrection, such as Luna, Buencamino, the two Pilars (Pio and Gregorio), and the Chinese renegade General Paua. It seems that at this time, when actual hostilities were not going on, these generals often came up to Malolos to consult with Aguinaldo. Antonio Luna, who one evening was pointed out to us, a dark, handsome man in the prime of life, evidently a full-blooded Filipino, was at that time commander-in-chief of the army. This man, had" he been a Tagalog instead of an Ilocano, would probably have been President in place of Aguinaldo, but even as it was, his followers were many. Before the outbreak of hostilities he had been editor of the Filipino Government's official organ, *La Independencia*, but had now been made commander-in-chief to retain the sympathy of his people, the Ilocanos, for the Insurgent cause, who were otherwise not inclined to favor the native government, believing as many of them did that the Tagalogs would hold the reins of government in their hands and rule the country with the same tyranny Spain had done.

Antonio Luna was a man of superior education, having graduated from the Manila School of Pharmacy, as well as from the university. After leaving the college he opened a chemical laboratory in Guiapo, Manila, which he attended during the day, and in the evening he taught fencing in his "Sala de Armas." Being a friend and sympathizer of Rizal, whose connection with and influence on the Insurgent movement are now more or less known, he naturally adhered to his socialistic and even revolutionary ideas. He also was one of the leaders in the famous Katipunan [1] society, that branch of Freemasonry founded by the Filipinos to protect themselves from the constant persecutions of the friars.

There are (or were) of the Lunas four brothers, Antonio, José, Joaquin, and Juan. Jose and Joaquin, besides being educated and refined men, and occupying prominent stations in Filipino society, are comparatively unknown to the foreign reader, but Juan Luna is a prominent artist in Europe, many of his paintings being of world-wide repute. It was he that shot and killed his wife, and was acquitted by the Madrid courts. This incident has frequently been attributed to Antonio, the General, and I have even seen accounts in some of our magazines, in which this was said to be the cause of his deadly hatred for the white race, whereas he was ever a friend of Western civilization and education. Had his policy of meeting the Americans in one decisive pitched battle been adhered to, the war might now have been over with, but from the beginning Aguinaldo's idea was to worry and not to fight the United States forces. We had time and again longed to catch a glimpse of the Honorable President himself, "Capitan Emilio," as the natives affectionately call him. He was at one time the municipal president of a town in Cavite under the Spanish Government, and thus gained the title of "Capitan," according to Spanish custom, and this still clung to him.

One evening Cigarettes, who was sitting in the window, called out to us, "Capitan Emilio! Capitan Emilio!" In a moment as many of us as could, crowded up there and peered through the bars into the bamboo pavilion. There he sat at one of the tables — we knew him by his pictures — small in stature and very dark. His dress was black, all except a colored jockey cap. In one hand he held an empty glass, in the other a bottle. Gradually he poured the sparkling beer into the glass, then drained it. Again he repeated the operation. It was interesting. We could almost hear the sizz of the foam. We forgot the President, our interest centred in the frothing liquid which we had not seen for so long a time. Anyway, I think it showed poor tact on the great man's part in holding that sparkling beverage up under the very noses of four miserable, half-starved wretches, who had been obliged to assuage their thirst with half-putrid water the past month. This was the first and last time our eyes ever rested on the dusky features of Don Emilio Aguinaldo y Famy.

It must not be thought that in contemplating the merry crowds in the gymnasium our eyes did not occasionally drop to the wedge in the crossbar and dreams of escape enter our minds; indeed, we often discussed the advisability of another attempt, but the new guard overlooking that window, our better treatment, and a startling piece of news that arrived about this time deterred us for a while. The news of which I speak, and which for a time demoralized us, reached us on February 23d.

On the evening of that date, shortly after sunset, we were as usual stretched on our cot, giving each other the benefit of reminiscences of our past lives, when suddenly the church bells commenced to ring violently. Bugles sounded all over town, and people in the street ran to and fro, cheering and screaming. In the gymnasium they seemed almost crazy, the orchestra there playing "Aguinaldo's March" amid loud cries of "Viva Aguinaldo! Viva Filipinas! Viva! Viva!" Meanwhile we lay wondering. Presently we heard a great uproar upstairs in the officers' quarters. Chairs were overturned amid trampling of many feet, and a rush downstairs followed. A second later our door was thrown violently open, a group of young officers burst into the cell, one carrying a lamp, which he in his excitement came near dropping among us. All were shouting together, but out of the jumble we caught such phrases as, "Victoria! Americanos muerte! Filipinos entre Manila! Americanos no mas! Muchos prisoneros! Perdido los Americanos!" etc. Then, evidently satisfied that their exclamations would mentally paralyze us, they retired as suddenly as they had entered, and once more we heard them ascending the stairs amid cries of joy. The excitement in the streets continued until late into the evening.

That night we had food for reflection and discussion. Had the Filipinos really gained a victory? We could hardly believe it, but what caused all this public enthusiasm? We were able to arrive at no conclusions, having nothing to found them on, but nevertheless we felt dreadfully depressed, lest the war might yet drag on for a long time. Of course, never for a moment had any one of us expected the Americans to send out an expedition for the rescue of five obscure prisoners whose very existence was not even a certainty, but, as we said to each other, surely in a whole month Otis could have had all the necessary reinforcements to commence an advance.

While cooking breakfast next morning in the yard, I picked up an "extra" of *La Independencia*, copies of which lay strewn about. In large and glaring headlines I read, in Spanish:

VIVA LA REPUBLICA FILIPINA!
AMERICANS ARE DEFEATED!
OUR VICTORIOUS ARMY ENTERS MANILA!
LONG LIVE AGUINALDO! LONG LIVE THE ARMY!

The circular then went on to state that the American army had been defeated after a terrific battle and driven into the Walled City, where the Filipinos were now besieging them. Meanwhile, the valorous Pio del Pilar had surrounded 6,000 Americans at Caloocan, and was about to starve them out. The Honorable President had left for the front to superintend operations in person, and decide upon what terms the Americans were to be spared from complete annihilation. Thousands of prisoners had been taken!

This latter statement interested us particularly. Even if but 1,000, we longed to have them brought to Malolos. We could not but believe that with 1,000 healthy American companions, times would no longer continue monotonous to all parties concerned. But those prisoners must certainly have died on the road. We never saw them, not one of them. But another surprise awaited us that afternoon.

We had now fallen into the custom of the country and took our daily siesta between the hours of 1 and 3 P.M. It helped to pass away time. It must have been about four o'clock on this particular afternoon, February 24th, and the natives were just about awakening. My companions were still sleeping. Cigarettes, the boy, was sitting in the window, as usual, facing the street — the popular feeling against us having by this time been sufficiently subdued to permit the opening of it — and was passing the time away between nodding, dropping his head down between his knees, and then starting up again to watch the passers-by in the street.

Of a sudden the lad gave a great shout — "Americanos! Americanos!" Some of us, awakened by this cry, and believing that he meant armed troops, rushed to the window, causing wild confusion. Above the noise we heard the tramp of marching soldiers in the entrance outside, suddenly terminating by a loud "Alto!" When Cigarettes told us that he had seen one American prisoner guarded by a squad of Insurgent regulars, our excitement grew hardly less, for naturally we supposed that through a new arrival the truth of the whole situation at the front would be unfolded to us, and at least give us an idea of how much longer our sufferings were to last. Looking through cracks and knot-holes in our door we saw a man who was surely neither Spaniard nor Filipino, but before we could thoroughly scrutinize him he passed on in the direction of the stairs, giving us a momentary glimpse of a light beard and hair.

Shortly after we gathered our pots and went out in the yard, ostensibly to cook our supper, but in reality to catch another glimpse of, and exchange a few words with, the new arrival. For a time we were disappointed, for he was nowhere to be seen; but presently a loud "Hello, boys!" caused us all to look up at the second-story windows. There he was, leaning out and calmly puffing at a cigar, apparently very much at his ease — a typical Anglo-Saxon, with blue eyes, blond mustache and beard, and a light complexion. At first the guards attempted to draw him back into the room, but as they did not use any physical force he did not heed them the least. In fact, his bearing was more that of a visitor than a prisoner. As I stood gazing at the stranger's face, his features seemed to me vaguely familiar. Where have I seen him before? I asked myself, but could find no answer.

Having in vain attempted to converse with us, the distance being too great for his words to reach, he disappeared from the window, and a moment later walked into the yard. I stood nearest the door, and as we came face to face the recognition was mutual. He was one of the three Englishmen that Huber and I had met in Meycauayan on the day of our capture, the one who had spoken to us.

[1] A Tagalog word signifying brotherhood. The true origin of this society is enveloped in mist, impenetrable to all but a few of the leaders, and they, of course, do not speak. There is, however, no doubt that it is an outgrowth of Freemasonry, a distinct branch, the result of the peculiar circumstances existing in the country at the time of its organization.

To defend themselves from the persecutions of the monasterial fraternities, the Filipinos sought protection in union, and thus was the secret brotherhood of the Katipunan formed. Its object was to check the persecutions of the friars by intimidating them, pursuing methods similar to those of the vigilance committees of former days in the towns of our Western States. Many friars were secretly assassinated by the agents of the brotherhood, and in return the Spanish clergy and Government exerted all their joint power to crush this terrible enemy, but with small success. Hundreds of natives were executed as suspects, but this only served to strengthen this secret organization, until in 1896 this smoldering struggle burst out into open hostility.

Many are the versions as to its origin. Some claim that Jose Rizal was its founder, others Pilar, and still others believe it to have been Antonio Luna, but even the majority of the members themselves in all probability are ignorant of the truth, and we outsiders certainly are. It is said that at one time its roll of membership contained as many as fifty thousand signatures, but this also can be no more than supposition. Terrible oaths of secrecy were demanded of new members, who signed their names on the list with their own blood, drawn from an incision on the arm, and by the scar of which one member might know another.

Chapter Six - Relaxation

THE Englishman came forward, shook hands with us all around, introducing himself as John O'Brien, a native of London, England, but, as he told us afterward, a citizen of the world. As I already suspected, he had no news, having been a prisoner as long as any of us, confined in a neighboring town. The most pressing questions being answered on both sides, we all sat down on a woodpile in a corner of the yard while the rice was boiling, and O'Brien related the story of his capture and subsequent experience. I will here let him tell his own adventures:

"In order to thoroughly explain my presence here you must know that I am a miner, or, to be still more exact, a prospector. Since leaving home as a sailor while still a boy, I have been prospecting in Australia, California, the Klondike, and last year brought up in New Guinea. The climate of that country did not agree with me, however, nor had I any great success, so I left there, and last November came to Manila with the intention of exploring the mountains of Luzon for gold, which, I have every reason to believe, are just as rich in the precious metal as those of New Guinea.

"Upon arriving at Manila I immediately set out to obtain as much information as I could, and I soon found enough to satisfy me that the country was promising. My intention was to go to Malolos, and as an Englishman ask the Insurgent authorities for a passport throughout the country. Having secured this I expected to continue on the train to Dagupan, where I would have hired a number of native servants, bought provisions, pack-horses, etc., and continued my journey on foot to the province of Benguet, about three days' march north of Dagupan. I have been told by old English residents that the mountains of Benguet, Lepanto, Bontoc, and Abra are so rich in gold that the natives of those parts, the Igorrotes, a tribe of naked savages, pick the free gold out of the rocks and sell it to the European traders for half its value; but on account of the aversion of the friars to any foreign immigration, which the opening of new gold fields naturally would attract, such heavy taxes were levied on mining privileges that the riches of the mountains of Luzon were never developed, but left to the Igorrotes who would wash out small quantities in ox-hide or bamboo baskets. One Englishman, who even now lives in Benguet, buys gold from the natives at sixteen pesos per ounce, and sells it at sixteen dollars, just doubling his money. But, considering the quality and quantity of the gold the Igorrotes extract from the rocks and soil in their primitive manner, and I have seen numerous specimens, I believe that any money invested there is a 'sure thing.'

"On the afternoon of January 27th I left Manila on the two o'clock train for Malolos. I found on the train with me two other Englishmen, bound on a pleasure excursion, Captain Scott, of the steamship Pelican, and the chief engineer of the same vessel.

"Arriving at Polo we three were arrested and taken to Meycauayan. I was the only one that possessed a consular certificate, so Captain Scott suggested that we all claim to be of one party, making the certificate do service for the three of us, to which I gave my consent. The lieutenant who examined us in Meycauayan seemed satisfied with that, but told us that we would have to return by next train to Manila. It was then that you two were brought in" (here O'Brien addressed Huber and myself) "and taken out again a few moments later. This was done in order to enable us to judge whether you were Englishmen or not, as you claimed to be. No sooner had you two left the room when the lieutenant asked us, 'Inglese ese?' As I could not truthfully assert that you were, I did not express an opinion and merely said, 'No sabe.' The engineer did likewise, but Scott, who seemed thoroughly frightened, said, 'Those men are Americanos! Spias! Spias! Mucho malo!' and to us: 'The presence of these men increases our danger. We may be taken for accomplices; what can we expect when such people claim to be Englishmen!'

"Scott's words seemed to please the lieutenant, who smiled grimly.

"That same afternoon we were taken to the station, and Scott and his companion returned to Manila. I waited for the next train for Malolos, and, continuing my journey, arrived there after dusk.

"Upon inquiring of an officer where passes were issued, I was shown to the office of the Secretary of War, where Señor Baldomero Aguinaldo himself received me. As he speaks excellent English we had no difficulty in understanding one another, but on explaining to him my wishes, his brow darkened and he answered: 'I cannot guarantee your safety throughout the country. Popular feeling is so strong just now that no matter how many passes I might give you, you would not be safe from a mob. I advise you to abandon your scheme until the country shall be in a more settled state, and the present troubles between us and the American Government satisfactorily adjusted, when we shall be glad to invite foreigners to assist us in developing the country.'

"That, of course, ended the question. Without a pass it was of no use attempting to carry out my idea. I saw I would have to wait some time.

"We remained in conversation together a long time on other topics, the Secretary being well informed on almost any subject, but we drifted back to the political situation and the possibility of war. He tried to convince me that the Filipinos had good prospects of winning in any coming struggle, but I made the mistake of expressing my honest opinion, comparing the Americans to the British in Egypt, giving a brief description of Lord Kitchener's victory over the dervishes. A slight darkening of his brow showed me my mistake, but as he still continued to converse pleasantly, I thought no more of it.

"At about eight o'clock Señor Aguinaldo arose, and, stepping out of the room for a few moments, returned with an officer. Turning to me he said: 'I have instructed this gentleman to see that you are well cared for until morning, when you must return to Manila. Now, good-night!' We shook hands and I followed the lieutenant downstairs. There stood a corporal and two soldiers, and turning to me the lieutenant said, 'These three men will conduct you to a secure place for the night, and at the same time will act as your body-guard and escort.' So, bidding the officer good-night, I went out with the three soldiers, who at once led me down the street.

"As we kept on walking for some time without entering any house, I began to grow uneasy, wondering why they should take me such a distance, but when I noticed that we had left the town and were out on a country road, I became really alarmed and insisted upon returning. At first they paid me no heed, but when I turned to leave them, one raised the butt of his gun and brought it down on my shoulder with such force as almost to stun me. Then, while two presented their bayonets to my chest, the third commenced to relieve me of my hat, coat, and vest, and all my pockets contained. Next he proceeded to unbuckle my belt, but as this contained forty English gold sovereigns I resisted. They then struck me two or three blows on the head, and when I fully recovered from the effects my belt was gone.

"Forced to continue with those I now knew were my guards, we walked on for about an hour, when we entered a small village, the most conspicuous building in which was a large church and convent, the rest of the town being composed of bamboo huts, with the exception of a small house built of boards and thatched with nipa, that stood on the plaza opposite the church and convent. Into this I was taken.

"Apparently the house contained but two rooms, and in one of these sat three men, two officers and a civilian, all writing at a table. To one of them, a captain, the corporal gave a letter, which he opened and read and then glared ferociously at me as if he had just received an order for my execution. The three soldiers then turned to leave, when I commenced to complain of my treatment and the robbery in broken Spanish. The captain told me to keep quiet, but as I still insisted he jumped to his feet in a threatening manner, and, thumping his chest with his hands, exclaimed in a shrill voice: 'Me Capitan Filipino, me officer. You no speakee me — sabe?' That, of course, settled the question, so I said no more.

"Later on, the same night, I was taken across the plaza to the convent, where a company of soldiers was stationed. Conducting me upstairs they shoved me into a room, or rather closet, formed by partitioning a portion of the balcony off. You know how wide these convent balconies generally are, say about six feet. Well, this was cut off by a thin board wall about five feet from the end, forming an enclosed space of five by six. In this hole I was confined for twenty-five days, subjected to daily insults and indignities not only by the soldiers, but also by officers — at least they wore the stars of officers. Three times daily a plate of dry, cooked rice without salt was brought to me, and nothing more. This treatment and the loneliness of this existence almost drove me mad.

"On the night of February 4th, I heard the guns pounding away to the southward, and then my hopes of a speedy release rose high, for I believed that in one week the Americans would sweep up through the country, along the railroad track at least, at ten miles a day, as the English frequently have done in India, with less men and a more numerous enemy. But, although I occasionally heard the guns again, a few hours at a time, nothing disturbed the quiet and peace of Santa Isabela, as the town was called. My guards were now composed mainly of bolo men, the regular troops having been hurried down to the front after the outbreak of hostilities.

"Frequently I received visits from officers and Government officials, to all of whom I showed my consular certificate, which I had been fortunate enough to retain in the pocket of my overalls; but, beyond stating that they were sorry and shrugging their shoulders, I got no satisfaction.

"Two days ago, however, I received a visit from Captain Espina, a Spanish renegade, in the service of the Insurgents as captain of engineers. Upon showing him my paper he at once appeared interested, and, upon leaving, promised to exert himself in my behalf.

"That evening I was removed to one of the large rooms of the convent, which encouraged me somewhat, especially as the guards treated me with more respect.

"This morning I was taken back to Malolos, upstairs here to the Provincial Military Governor, and he has just given me a pass that holds good about the town and vicinity, but I am not to be allowed to go through to Manila. I am to sleep upstairs here, eat with the guards, and can leave the building at any time that I feel inclined to stroll about the town."

O'Brien having concluded his tale of woe, we continued to converse, telling of our own troubles, our attempt at escape, and Arnold's perfidy. He promised to make as careful a survey of the surrounding country as was possible under the circumstances, and give us the result in the form of a rough chart for future reference. During his twenty-seven days of solitary confinement he had picked up a few words of Tagalog from his guards, and this might enable him to overhear little bits of news as spoken between the officers upstairs, and these he also promised to communicate to us.

Shortly before dusk we separated, he sauntering quietly out of the gate with his hands in the pockets of his old blue overalls, a turban on his head instead of a hat, and a cigar between his teeth at an elevation of about forty-five degrees. In the evening we again saw him in the gymnasium, performing some really wonderful feats on the rings and bars before a crowd of admiring Filipinos, some of whom narrowly escaped broken necks and bruised themselves in vain endeavors to imitate him.

We did not see O'Brien again the next day until late in the afternoon, and then, to our great surprise, he was permitted to enter the cell for a friendly chat.

He had that morning been to see the Secretary of War, Don Baldomero, to complain of the robbery of his forty sovereigns, but that gentleman's only reply was, "that such was life, and such the fortunes of war"; of course accompanied by a French shoulder shrug. A small hand-bag that he had taken charge of for O'Brien, containing instruments for a rough assay, compass, etc., he now denied ever having seen. They had, however, given him a slip of paper on which was written in Spanish, "This man, John O'Brien, is allowed the full liberty of the town, and all persons are hereby cautioned to allow him to pass unmolested, as he is an Englishman and 'No Americano.'" The last two words were heavily underscored, and the whole stamped with the official seal of the War Office, a sun in a triangle.

Being now, after a fashion, kept in touch with the outside world as far as Malolos was concerned, at least, we found our time passed more rapidly. Every day O'Brien came to visit us, relating his little experiences about town, until we began to look forward to his coming as a welcome treat. Notwithstanding the fact that the officers looked upon his intimacy with us with disapproving glances, he continued to come, regardless of the annoying looks of these gentlemen. His rations were about the same as ours, those of the guards, dry cooked rice and "vianda," brought to him at each meal in an army mess-plate by one of the soldiers.

I must not omit here to mention an incident that occurred at this time, of which we then thought but little, but which was later the means of making families, relatives, and friends acquainted with our presence in the world of the living.

One afternoon, while we were outside in the yard, several officers came in, and in quite a friendly manner attempted to converse with us. At length they asked us our names, and upon hearing them they laughed heartily at the strangeness of the sounds to their ears, requesting us to spell them; whereupon Huber, who was cook for the day, pulled out a charred brand from under the rice-pot, therewith writing our names on the wall, quite unconscious how they, long afterward, dim and begrimed by smoke, would be copied and even photographed. One of the Manila papers has called them our self-written epitaphs.

Notwithstanding the rather mild tendencies of the new Governor, we still continued to number from twenty to twenty-five persons in our overcrowded cell, but the possibility of cleaning it out once in a while, and the privilege of spending a great part of the day in the yard, helped to offset this great disadvantage. That there was no room for all these men was no excuse, for opposite on the other side of the passage was a cell of the same size as ours, practically empty. This reminds me that I have never told of the solitary occupant of this cell, the mysterious prisoner, a Filipino "Iron Mask!"

We had often noticed that the door to this cell was always kept closed except at meal-times, when a sergeant entered with a basket containing food of exceptional quality and variety. The rice was white, the meat and chicken of excellent aroma, and the fruit the finest in the market; everything being served in white china. Evidently the prisoner confined there was no ordinary person. Although we had for a long time tried hard to catch a glimpse of the inmate, we had never been successful. One day, however, our patience was rewarded. The sergeant, on entering with the food, had evidently forgotten something, and, leaving the door open, ran upstairs. A middle-aged and rather good-looking mestizo came to the threshold and stood there for a moment, but on seeing the sergeant descending the stairs, he disappeared once more in the gloom of his cell. By the fine white pajamas this prisoner wore we knew that he must be a person of some consequence, and this, of course, increased our curiosity.

One day I found the door open again and the mestizo stood there, his intelligent features pale and haggard from the close confinement. Quite unperceived I walked up to him, saying in my best Spanish, "Good-morning, Señor — fine day!" My words caused him to start nervously, and, turning to me, he replied in fairly good English, "I am prohibited to speak;" and closing the door himself, he retired into his cell.

What crime this mysterious prisoner had committed remained a riddle to us, nor did anybody seem to know, or, if they did, they kept it to themselves. When he had first come there, or who he was, was likewise unknown, but that he occupied a whole cell by himself when the prison was so crowded, showed him to be of some importance.

About this time half a company of regulars returned from the front and were quartered upstairs. That they had come in contact with the Americans was evident, for they seemed to regard us with some respect. It has always struck me as an infallible rule, those soldiers who have met and fought the enemy have more respect for their courage and abilities than those who have never fought but with words.

And this does not only apply to Filipinos!

Every evening at twilight the soldiers gathered together in the yard for athletic sports, such as wrestling, jumping, arm twisting, etc., and we also were invited to join them, which we sometimes did.

Often I have heard Americans speak with contempt of the small stature of the Filipinos, and we also had much the same opinion, telling each other what we could do with half a dozen of them if only they were not armed. On these occasions, however, we all had a chance to learn how deceiving appearances sometimes are.

I still remember my first wrestling match in the Malolos prison yard. It was with a Filipino sergeant who hardly reached to my chin, and in ten seconds he laid me on my back. Time and again we were at it, but I generally got the worst of it, until once I managed to throw him by virtue of my superior weight, and after that I would never wrestle with him again, in order that I might say that I had gained the last bout. Of course, from poor and insufficient food and the want of physical exercise, I was at that time in poor condition, yet I have seen tall and husky beef eating Americans fall down under a little black mass of sinews only five feet four inches in height, and too much self-conceit.

But the accomplishment of which they were proudest was the moro-moro play, a kind of fencing in which each of the combatants has a bolo in the right hand and a dagger in the left. This is a relic of the times when the Malay Filipinos all were Mohammedans, ruled by rajahs, before the advent of the Spaniards. As boxing is to the British and Americans, so is moro-moro to the Tagalog. Although he may be lazy and disinclined to exert himself, the Tagalog youth is willing to stand for hours giving and taking blows with sticks in this exercise, until he is bathed in perspiration.

Here in Malolos we saw a good deal of this and even had it taught us, but we did not prove apt pupils. Two men would stand facing each other, each a long stick in the right hand, to represent the bolo, a short one in the left to serve as dagger or "campit," as the Tagalog calls it. Then commences a giving and warding off of blows bewildering to a stranger, but in which there is undoubtedly a crude science. Sometimes they would stop all of a sudden as if petrified in some position, while the bystanders would loudly argue which of the two had the advantage, and, when at length decided, the fight was resumed.

Considering the fact that I had finally been able to throw my little antagonist, the sergeant, he proved himself rather friendly toward me.

For a long time I had felt a great desire to visit the market personally, and one day I confided this to my friend, the sergeant. He promised to assist me, and, if possible, to obtain the necessary permission from the Governor. The following morning he buckled on his bayonet, and, calling to me, said that he had succeeded in obtaining the Governor's consent, and that we could "vamos." I was almost overcome with delight.

The bright glare of the sunlight outside almost blinded me, and the pure air swelled my lungs, giving me the sensation of a thirsty man who is enjoying a cold draught from a spring. Passers-by turned to stare at me, but the sergeant seemed proud of this.

Presently we found ourselves in front of a barbershop. The people inside raised a shout as I came into view, and, rushing out, dragged me bodily in. The shop was evidently a gathering-place for the young aristocracy of the town, all well dressed in spotless white suits, and some with low-crowned derbys that made them look ridiculous, at least in my estimation. Nothing is more unbecoming to a Filipino than a derby, yet it is almost universally worn by both upper and middle classes, and when worn out, what is left of them is appropriated by the "tauis" for their "go-to-mass" suits.

The young men in the barber-shop were not inclined to be hostile, but the bantering questions they addressed to me were anything but flattering to my countrymen, as: Did the Americans shoot from the hip? or, did they saturate themselves with whiskey before going into battle, in order to get courage? etc. It was a popular belief among the Filipinos that the Americans shot from the hip, but we saw the day when they were thoroughly disillusioned of this fallacy.

To keep me from going away the barber offered to shave me, as I attracted trade to his shop. I accepted his offer and was about to sit down when, upon turning, I found myself face to face with a stranger. A white man he probably had been, or was yet, though his appearance at first glance belied it. I did not like his looks; he made a decidedly bad impression. His clothes were ragged, his hair was long, and his face had not felt a razor for some time. He had all the appearance of a bankrupt pirate or brigand. The fellow was impudent, too, and kept staring into my face, so I returned the stare. Still, his features seemed familiar — where had I seen them before? Suddenly a smile of mutual recognition lit up our faces simultaneously — certainly, we were old acquaintances! But it made me mad to think that I had been fooled by a mirror.

I sat down in the chair, but a moment later would gladly have paid the full price of that shave just to escape the torments this barber inflicted. Apparently he had never heard of lather being used for shaving, nor perhaps even seen a shaving-brush. A razor and a wooden strop for honing were his only tools. They were probably enough to remove the black down on the upper lip of a Filipino, but I swore he should never operate on me again.

Leaving the barber's establishment, the sergeant and I continued our walk down the street, lined on both sides by Chinese stores, toward the plaza. We passed through a group of dirty, ragged, sickly, hungry, and dissipated-looking Spaniards, who greeted us with a shout, whether of welcome or derision was hard to say, but the thinness of their faces gave them a sarcastic expression whenever they attempted a laugh. Laughter did not become them; it seemed unnatural.

Presently we found ourselves in the plaza. A crowd gathered about us, but, although the men scowled and significantly touched the hilt of their bolos, none dared to insult me. One, indeed, had drawn a knife from his belt and was advancing through the throng to exhibit his valor, when the sergeant struck him with the back of his hand and then kicked him to boot, causing the bystanders considerable amusement. My would-be intimidator disappeared down a side street, having evidently decided to keep his great courage as a warrior bold a secret for some time longer.

We now passed the large convent which Aguinaldo then occupied as his residence. The entrance was well guarded by his own body-guard, men selected for their fine physical appearance and good training, all having been soldiers under the Spaniards. Their uniforms differed from the rest of the Insurgent army's in that they wore dark red pantaloons, and, also unlike the others, they wore shoes. The black bands on their broadbrimmed straw hats bore no inscription, but one side of the brim was pinned to the crown by a red and blue cockade, in the centre of which was a white triangle, with the two letters G. P. in black, which I suppose meant "Guardia del Presidente." As a whole they would compare favorably with any body of European soldiers that have come within the range of my observation.

Having crossed the plaza, we now passed down another small street, and soon found ourselves in the market. Large roofs of nipa had been erected here, and under them the stalls were systematically laid out in rows, one for dry-goods, another for vegetables, a third for fish, and so on, similar to the markets in any other civilized country, with the exception that all the wares were spread on the ground, and buyers as well as sellers squatted beside them on their heels.

As my companion and I appeared on the scene, all business was, for the time being, at least, suspended. The majority were women, and that a real live "Americano" had dropped down among them caused quite a sensation. The sergeant was as proud of me as if I had been a tamed lion which he was leading about unchained, with nothing to protect himself from my ferocity but his own personal courage.

Both young and old crowded about me to touch my clothes and in other ways examine a specimen of the much dreaded race, the name of which they used to frighten the children into good behavior, a sort of Filipino bogie.

Some were evidently disappointed, saying that I differed in no essential part from the "Castiles." They had been under the impression that the Americans were "mucho grande," something like a palm tree, and wore large plumes in their hair, as the illustrations in the friars' school-books portrayed them.

A spirit of friendliness toward me seemed to prevail among them, however, for one made me a present of an ear of corn, another of a cake of black sugar, and a third a small piece of brown soap. All were thankfully received. One young señorita offered me a flower with a most bewitching smile, and, although at that time I really had no particular use for flowers, I nevertheless expressed my thanks the best I knew how. This caused a young gentlemen with her, half choking in a high white collar, to glare at me savagely, and say to the crowd in general that instead of lionizing the Americans it would be better to kill them all off, or words to that effect; and when I replied that there were over 20,000 within a day's travel to begin on, the bystanders laughed at his confusion. The sergeant and I spent over an hour strolling about among the stalls, and for the time being I was as happy as a school-boy at a country fair.

The first department we stopped to examine was dry-goods, and the variety on hand surprised me. There were piles of imported calicoes, and all sorts of cotton stuffs, but the sergeant called my attention to one stall where a woman sat weaving the native cloth on a primitive sort of loom made of native wood and bamboo. The thread she used was of cotton, grown in the country, not on bushes, but on tall trees. I have myself seen these trees towering over the roads, covered with fluffy white balls, some bursting out of the pods.

The cloth this woman was weaving was a very coarse stuff, finely striped blue and white, the material from which the Insurgent's uniform was made. Almost every household of the lower and middle classes has these looms, as well as old-fashioned, spinning wheels. It is very common to see people walking about the streets spinning by means of tops hanging at the end of the twine or thread, and upon which the fabric is wound as finished. The top, suspended in mid-air, is set spinning by twisting the thread, the operator holding it in his right hand, while in his left he holds the cotton. Thus the Filipino paterfamilias often takes an evening stroll, the baby sitting astraddle of his hip, his arm around it, while with his hands he spins, no time being lost. Meanwhile his wife may be at home spinning at the wheel or weaving.

Another cloth that attracted my attention was what the natives commonly call maguey cloth, made of the coarse fibres of the maguey plant. This plant grows in the northern provinces of Luzon in great abundance, and is a species of cactus. From my own observations I can see no difference between it and the maguey of Mexico and California, also known as the American aloe, the agave or century plant, from the juice of which the Mexicans get their "pulque" by fermentation, and their "mescal" by distillation, and likewise employ the fibres in the manufacture of a sort of cloth. The word "maguey," by which the average Filipino knows the plant, seems to be of Mexican origin, so it is but natural to suppose that the plant itself was introduced by the Spaniards in early times from their American colonies.

The leaves, all shooting up from a common root, having no stem, are thick, and very thorny on their edges, averaging in the full-grown plant from four to six feet in length. These, when considered of sufficient size, are cut off close to the root and thrown into running water, where they are allowed to remain about a week until the pulpy substance between the fibres is half rotten. They are then taken out and beaten on a rock with a heavy flat club until nothing but the coarse fibres remain, which are then hung up to dry. So closely does this maguey fibre resemble that of the hemp or abaca plant that an inexperienced eye could not tell them apart, still the plants themselves are entirely different, the latter resembling a banana-tree. The maguey fibre is, however, much inferior in strength, and, not being fit for the manufacture of rope, is used for the loom.

I have seen the Filipino housewife sit for hours, patiently pulling the long, coarse fibres out, one by one, test their strength, knot them neatly together at their ends, winding them on a large spool made of a joint of thick bamboo, until, by the work of weeks, enough was gathered to make sufficient material for one shirt!

From this cloth is made part of the national costume of the lower- and middle-class Filipino woman, viz.: the upper garment, a loose, low-necked chemisette, the wide, puffy sleeves of which are so short as hardly to reach the elbow. I have heard some of our people call this piña, but that is an error, piña being a valuable fabric made from the pineapple-leaf fibre, and much worn by the gentler sex of the upper classes, in the same manner as maguey is worn by the middle and lower classes.

Having passed through the row of stalls or "tiendas," as the sergeant called them, where cloths were sold, we next came to the pottery department, where clay pots were on sale, from little sugar-bowls the size of a teacup to large "tinajas," or water-jars, in which a ten-year-old child could have hidden himself. There was a large heap of clay, and beside it the potter sat on a small bench turning with his foot a low, flat, and horizontal wheel, upon the centre of which he banged down a lump of the damp clay, set the wheel in motion, and, presto! before I knew it he had a small cooking pot before him, such as we used for our daily rice. His two assistants piled the thus fashioned pots on a board, and, when they were thoroughly dried, put them into a long brick oven, to be baked. Later these now finished products were taken out, of a beautiful terra-cotta color; I bought a small one for a cent. An old woman who stood by took it from my hands, tapped it with her knuckles, pronounced it unsound, and gave the potter a good scolding in Tagalog for trying to take advantage of a poor prisoner by selling him wares which he could not get rid of otherwise, and, disregarding the expostulations of him and his assistants, commenced sounding pot after pot, from a large heap, until assured that she had found one worth the cent it cost. I saw other women imitating her on the spot, and the poor potter seemed the most uncomfortable wretch in the whole market.

Next we came to the fruit and vegetable stalls where the venders, mostly women, sat amid the heaps of their wares. Bananas with red, green, and yellow skins were on sale, all ripe, too. I am told there are over fifty varieties of these in the island, but all poorly cultivated. Never have I tasted any to be compared to the luscious golden banana of Honolulu. There were heaps of green mangoes, ripe ones not having arrived yet. They are about the size of a man's fist, shaped nearly like an almond kernel. The natives seem to like them green as well as ripe.

Oranges, lemons, guavas, shaddocks, and pineapples were plentiful, even watermelons. The latter in their decided want of flavor reminded me of bread soaked in water. Another kind of fruit of which the natives seem to be fond is the paw-paw. It resembles a small muskmelon and is even more tasteless than their watermelon. It grows on small trees without branches, a cluster of leaves at the top resembling those of a fig-tree.

Cocoanuts also were considerably in evidence, some so green as to have no perceptible husk as yet. The juice of these is superior to the older ones that reach us in America, the milk of which is generally oily and tasteless, whereas that of the young and green nut is agreeable and tart, reminding one of lemonade. The cocoanut does not grow inland, however, requiring the sandy, lime-containing soil of the low beaches under the tropical sun.

One tienda was occupied by a girl making up the betel-nut packages, of which the natives are so fond. She would take a leaf resembling in shape and size that of a poplar-tree from a heap in front of her. At her side she had a pot containing a white paste of lime and water, which she smeared on the leaf with a small stick or spatula; then folding it, and taking a slice of the nut, resembling nutmeg, wrapped the folded leaf about it. It was now ready for use. The sergeant took one and gave me another. That was the only time I ever tried chewing betel-nut, or areca-nut, to be more exact, but it did not remain in my mouth long enough to enable me to expectorate a bright blood red, as the sergeant did. The natives call it "buyo," which is the proper name of the leaf in which the areca-nut is wrapped. These nuts grow on small palms in clusters, looking much like small, immature cocoanuts. I have seen American soldiers, when short of tobacco, chew the buyo leaf as a substitute, its taste being hot and very pungent.

There were vegetables in abundance, such as small pumpkins, squashes, peas, beans, and onions, the latter only in a green state; also cucumbers of a warty appearance and exceedingly bitter taste, used for flavoring soups. Tamarinds are likewise used for this purpose, and garlic and Chili peppers galore.. Potatoes grow in some of the northern provinces of Luzon, on the higher table-lands and in the mountains, but are rarely larger than walnuts, and much inferior to those grown in temperate zones. Comottes, of which I have already spoken, take their place.

As it was now growing late in the forenoon, we started to return, stopping in to see the "tiendas de los Chinos" on another street. The Chinese are the true merchants of the Philippines; every town has its percentage of them. A Chinese country-store looks very much like one in our country. The Tagalogs hate the "inchic," as they are called by them, the children insult and stone them as they do in some parts of America, the men frequently taking part in the abuse, yet, if the despised "Chinos" were to leave the islands, the natives themselves would be the greatest sufferers. The Spanish law at one time prohibited the Chinese from following mercantile pursuits in the colonies, restricting them to agriculture, but either the law was repealed or became a dead letter, for now all the Chinese in Luzon are merchants or traders of some description.

At length we returned to the prison, and the dream was over!

After this we were always permitted to do our own marketing, the sergeant of the guard being instructed to send a man each time with the would-be purchaser. We had but to walk up to a soldier, saying: "I wish to buy!" As many of the soldiers did not understand Spanish we learned to say this in Tagalog, it serving as a sort of password. Whether it was all one word or composed of several we never knew, but I remember it still, nor am I likely ever to forget it: Acoobibilimoolám! (to be pronounced "Ah-coo-bee-bee-lee-moo-lám" — the stress on the last syllable). The advantage we gained repaid the effort of learning it, however. We could use it with telling effect on the market-women, who became so tickled at the idea of an American speaking Tagalog that they sometimes knocked off ten per cent, from the price of their goods.

Our greatest difficulty lay in the proper valuation of the different copper coins.

The money system of the Philippines was established on a silver basis, and, a Filipino or Spanish gold coin, unless worn as a watch-charm, I have never seen in the island. Their largest coin was the silver peso, either the official Spanish Colonial "duro," or that of Mexico, of about half the value of the American dollar. Next came the half peso and then the peseta, a Spanish coin, five of them having the value of a peso. These were again divided into half pesetas, or ten cents, a small silver coin about the size of an American dime, but of only half its value.

So far all was simple enough, but the coppers! Ten copper cents were worth half a peseta, a coin the size of an English penny, with a Spanish king's head stamped on its face. But there was also another copper coin, valued at one cent and a quarter, or eight to half a peseta. These were called "motas" and were old Spanish coins so worn that on very few could the stamps be made out. Some still showed dates from the last century, as far back as 1750. They had been condemned in Spain and sent out to the Colonies for circulation among the natives, and are seldom seen in Manila. There were also smaller coppers, or half motas. Ten motas were called "un real fuerte" or "cincapat." Four motas were simply called "un real," and this gave rise to a good deal of confusion at times. One mota was also called "delava qualta." A cent was called "un centavo," or "un centimo," or "una perra." This confusion of names was naturally the cause of much trouble between the market-women and us when we priced their goods, until necessity compelled us to learn their respective values. Seven motas was our daily allowance.

One afternoon we asked and received permission to go down to the river to bathe. Huber and I went first, accompanied by an armed guard, but on reaching the river were not a little embarrassed by at least a score of young ladies seating themselves on the opposite bank. We moved up-stream a hundred yards, but they also moved. Then we besought the guard to help us out of our predicament and either drive the young ladies away or shoot them, but he either wouldn't or couldn't understand us. There remained nothing but to appeal to the señoritas themselves, and this we did, begging them to spare the feelings of two helpless prisoners, but they only giggled and hid their faces behind their hands. There was no help for it, so while Huber bathed I stood before him shielding him with his shirt, and he afterward performed the same service for me. Meanwhile the young damsels on the opposite bank became so shocked that they retreated behind a fence, through the cracks of which we could see their little black eyes sparkling mischievously.

We returned in time to allow Bruce and Honeyman to have their turn, while we two cooked the supper. That evening we experienced a feeling of restraint among us. We seemed strange to one another, as if we had but met an hour before. The bath had indeed transformed our appearance.

Times now became rather monotonous, O'Brien having been unsuccessful in gathering any news from the front as to whether the American army was still in existence or not. We; were all in the second month of our imprisonment, still not once had we heard the guns again from the southward. One day O'Brien conceived the bold idea of going down to the front to find out for himself; and to how this came about and how he did it I will devote the next chapter.

Chapter Seven - Misfortunes of O'Brien

ONE evening O'Brien paid us a visit, bringing with him a copy of *La Independencia* stating that a fleet of American vessels had anchored in the Gulf of Lingayen, and threatened Dagupan. What hopes that article raised as we sat spelling out the words! I remember it ended up with: "Brethren, the times are dark, but let us not be pessimistic!" If even they admitted that times were dark, there was hope for us, for the old saying, "what is one man's meat is another man's poison," could well be applied here. Another article stated that the Americans had lost three generals, one being General MacArthur, a dozen colonels, and minor officers in like proportion. The number of "soldados Yankees" killed was something frightful; they were "as the sands on the seashore and the stars of the heavens," stated this veracious and sanguine paper. "All the churches in Manila were being used as hospitals, and so numerous were the dead that it had been found necessary to have recourse to cremation instead of burial. Meanwhile Otis was ruling Manila with an iron hand."

"Thank God," we said as we read this, "even these people acknowledge that Manila is still in the hands of the Americans."

"A Filipino," continued *La Independencia*, "dares not appear in the streets of the metropolis of his own native land. The Yankee soldiers enter the houses, kill the men, insult the women, and rob them of their valuables. The gutters of Manila stream with the lifeblood of our innocent countrymen, the air is filled with the shrieks of women and the groans of dying men. In fact," continues this graphic journalist, "the situation can well be compared to the Reign of Terror of the French Revolution. The blood of our innocent brethren cries to us for revenge, and let it not appeal to us in vain, O fellow patriots! Let us rise as one, my brethren, and strike while yet strength remains, for the liberty which is our birthright. Let us boldly face and fight this venomous serpent before he has us helpless in his coils, and, if we must die, let us rather fall from the bite of his fangs than be slowly suffocated by the weight of his ponderous body. Rise! fellow countrymen, and drive the accursed Yankee from the land, and if it must be, die for your glorious country, for your homes, and your families! Viva Filipinas!"

This is a fair specimen of some of the articles that appeared in *La Independencia*. Even now, two years later, I have a good-sized bundle of them before me, from which I could choose language more fiery and statements more reckless than the above. But to do the paper justice, all articles were not like this. Never once in its most vehement outbursts have I seen it advocate anything inhuman or criminal in character, beyond fighting the enemy, but, like some other periodicals, its lying was unlimited.

All this rant, which at that time we but imperfectly understood, gave us no news. A few small skirmishes, generally enlarged to important battles, gave an account of the tremendous loss of the enemy compared to that of the Filipinos — Cabo Sanchez receiving a trifling scratch in the shoulder, or Teniente Somebody else falling seriously wounded after first slaying half a dozen of the enemy. We always believed that more than one teniente had fallen where six Americans were slain.

Another faint ray of hope came, to O'Brien at least, when he learned of an Englishman, living in the town, a Mr. Higgins, manager of the railroad, owned by an English syndicate. The natives all spoke with great respect of Señor Higgins, a man of great influence with the Insurgent Government officials, and in him O'Brien saw a possible friend, who, being his countryman, would in all probability not refuse to assist him in his present trouble, even if but to give him some decent clothes, the means of obtaining something substantial to eat, or even a few English books. Unfortunately he was not in Malolos at the present time, being up or down the line somewhere, but in the next town, Calumpit, resided another English employee of the road, Mr. Clark, whom O'Brien intended to visit next morning, for he was now ragged and penniless, and in no better condition than the rest of us, excepting his privilege of walking about town.

Accordingly, the following day he did not make his appearance until shortly before sunset, when he came into the yard looking tired and disappointed. He had tramped the seven kilometres to Calumpit, under a burning sun, only to find that Mr. Clark had just that morning left for a two days' inspection tour. Leaving a note asking where and when a distressed countryman could find him, O'Brien returned to Malolos, obliged several times to show his pass from the War Office to save himself from arrest or even assault.

Next day Higgins returned to Malolos, but, notwithstanding his untiring efforts, O'Brien could never succeed in obtaining an interview — he was always "out!" Several times he met him driving in the street, but neither shouts nor gesticulations would attract his attention. Meanwhile days passed, nothing was heard from Clark, and at length O'Brien determined once more to pay him a visit. Again he was disappointed. Mr. Clark was not at home, his native wife averred, and even if he was, she did not think that a man in such rags as the visitor wore would be welcome. As for him being a countryman of her husband, she did not believe it — he surely was one of the hated Americans, and had better make himself scarce. This was the manner in which the dusky Mrs. Clark received the poor fellow on his second visit, which was rather significant, considering that on his first visit she had been exceedingly pleasant. He was now heartily discouraged and determined to pay no more visits to Calumpit.

One day, while strolling about the railroad station, O'Brien saw a white man coming up the track on a hand-car. Asking a native employee of the road who this gentleman was, he was told, "El Señor Clark." As he passed, O'Brien spoke to him, but "Señor" Clark heeded him no more than if he had been a native beggar. Poor man, no wonder he was "a citizen of the world."

One evening our English fellow-sufferer came to us with an account of an interview he had had with the Rev. Mr. Arnold, while that gentleman lay on the floor in his cell in a maudlin state of intoxication. Being in a rather sentimental mood, he had grasped O'Brien's hand, and with sobs and tears confided to him the whole story of his treachery from beginning to end, admitting that he had betrayed us, his excuse being that "cast in a finer mould" (his own oft-repeated expression) from the rest of us, "his finer nature shrank from such a foolhardy enterprise as we had contemplated, and believing that if he remained behind and allowed us to escape, the guards in their anger might kill him!" Consequently the object of the betrayal had been but to protect himself. He "trusted to an Overruling Power to prove his innocence." After he had related this to us, O'Brien's only comment was: "Well, he's not a true Britisher, anyhow."

We witnessed an incident one evening which suggested to us that even the Filipinos were beginning to think it wise to prepare for the defence of the capital itself. Hearing a loud noise in the street, we rushed to the window and observed at least two hundred natives pulling on a stout rope, dragging a large Krupp gun of at least six inches calibre, dismounted and wrapped in coarse matting, out of which both ends protruded. Several days later we saw it lying in the plaza, and O'Brien had seen two similar ones in other parts of the town. However, one day it was gone, and a certain unevenness of the sod on the surface caused us to surmise that it had been buried there. That we judged correctly was proved afterward when the Americans took the town, finding and unearthing the cannon there, its location being revealed by the Chinese.

O'Brien, usually of a rather optimistic disposition, had now, after repeated disappointments, become much discouraged. It was the evening of March 3d when he came to us and said: "Boys, I can't stand this any longer without making some effort to regain my liberty. To-morrow I'm off for Manila. I'll stake the little privileges I've got to get through, and if I fail, well, then I'll probably be lodged with you."

That evening we all wrote, on the veriest scraps of old and dirty paper, so-called letters home, and when O'Brien came in next morning to bid us good-by, he hid them in his shoes. To meet the expenses of living and railroad fare to the front, for which he did not possess sufficient funds, we managed to squeeze our mess-funds to the extent of thirty cents, which we added to his own scant treasury. We did not dare to shake hands, in sight of the natives, but when he left us he took with him our most fervent wishes for his success.

When evening came and O'Brien did not appear as usual, we knew that he had at last "struck out," to use his own expression, and would never return unless brought back by force. As the next day passed without his reappearance, our hopes for his success increased. Surely if he failed he would be brought back to Malolos, or would they possibly once more confine him alone in the convent of Santa Isabela? As evening again approached we became almost certain that our English friend was now within the American lines.

It was shortly after the church-bells had tolled the "Angelus," when all was still and darkness had almost settled over the town, that a disturbance outside aroused our curiosity. Men were talking excitedly and running about, when, suddenly, above the tumult we heard a familiar voice: "Hello boys, home again!" There was no mistaking that. The doors were thrown wide open, and Jack O'Brien was shoved violently in. "Well, I've come to stay," he quietly remarked, as he seated himself on the edge of the bed.

Although much disappointed, O'Brien was too much of a philosopher to make any display of his feelings. Being almost famished he begged us for something to eat, and, after satisfying his hunger with some rice and camottes, he related his story of how he had attempted to pass through the Insurgent lines into the American camp, and how he failed:

"Going down to the station yesterday morning," he began, "I persuaded a boy to buy me a ticket for as far as the train now goes, which is only to Meycauayan, as I did not consider it wise to present myself at the ticket office, and when the nine o'clock passenger came along, I found no difficulty in boarding her. Nobody molested me until we arrived at Meycauayan, when, on stepping off the train, I was arrested and brought before the commanding officer, to whom I at once showed my consular certificate and the War Office pass. This seemed to thoroughly convince him, for he became polite at once and promised to send me through under a flag of truce. It being Sunday, however, he informed me that I should have to wait until the next day, as the officers were all attending mass, but that I should be looked after the first thing in the morning. You can imagine what an uneasy time I spent that night. True to his word, he instructed a young officer to take charge of me, and the two of us together stepped into a carromata and drove down the road to Manila. The fact that we two were alone and entirely unattended by soldiers encouraged me a good deal — evidently I was not regarded as a prisoner. Soon the increasing number of bamboo barracks convinced me that we were fast approaching the main body of the army. Rapidly we neared Caloocan, and just as he pointed out to me a small hill on the top of which the Insurgent soldiers lay intrenched, facing the Americans, we reached a temporarily built village of soldiers' barracks. These had been built about a large house which seemed to be the head-quarters of the officers. Before this we dismounted and entered a room, where the young lieutenant bade me be seated. A fine breakfast was here served for two of us, for, said the officer, you must not leave us hungry. A telegraphic instrument was ticking in another room, and that spoiled my appetite. At last we got into the carromata again, much to my relief, but before we could drive off an officer appeared in the doorway of the house and called us in. I was left alone while the two officers went into the adjoining room, but as that telegraphic instrument was still tapping away so distinctly that I fancied I heard it pronounce my name, a sickly feeling overcame me. When the lieutenant came out and we stepped into the vehicle once more, he simply said: 'We can't send you through today, they have commenced fighting Mariana!' Then I knew all was lost.

"The drive back to Meycauayan seemed long compared to our coming. I knew that I was once more a prisoner, for two guards accompanied us on horseback. No sooner had we arrived than they hustled me aboard the afternoon train for Malolos. In the same coach with me I found another white man to whom the Filipino officers spoke with great deference. So Anglo-Saxon did he appear that I addressed him in English: 'Are you Mr. Higgins?' 'No,' he replied, 'my name is Murray, and I am inspector of locomotives on this road.' He furthermore informed me that he had had some trouble with the Insurgent officials about the number of special trains they wanted without paying for the accommodation, and he had refused to furnish any more. This had caused some words, and he was now on his way to Malolos to consult with Higgins. When I commenced to ask him whereabouts the Insurgent forces were posted and how many they numbered, he seemed suddenly to become suspicious of me and snapped out: 'I don't know.' When I told him of my twenty-seven days' imprisonment in Santa Isabela, he made no reply, but afterward remarked that I had been foolish in attempting to escape. 'Why don't you wear decent clothes?' he continued, surveying my ragged raiment, and when I explained, 'For the simple reason that I have none,' he said no more. In fact, for the rest of the trip he answered only in monosyllables."

"As the train pulled into Malolos station, and we stepped on the platform, a number of Filipino officers and a white man came forward to meet us. The latter walked up to Murray, with: 'How are things going, Murray?' 'Beastly, Higgins,' answered the inspector of locomotives. 'Never passed a worse time in my life; the beggars are actually disrespectful to me. Haven't had tiffin today.' Murray then told Higgins who I was, and then and there I asked the latter as a countryman to do something for me, at the same time showing consular certificate and Insurgent pass, to prove my nationality. 'All right!' he answered, 'I'll see about it.'

"All of us now walked up to the Secretary of War's office, where Higgins was received with a number of bows from all present, the officers begging the Señor Higgins to sit in a reclining chair close to the window where the air was 'mas fresco,' and would the 'excelentisimo Señor' have a cigar! I was then hustled out again, Higgins promising once more to exert himself in my behalf, but, to tell the truth, his manner did not inspire me with confidence. So then I was brought over here, boys!"

O'Brien having finished his narrative, we fell to discussing the situation, trying to see a favorable sign in the fact that the Insurgent lines extended no farther than Polo, or at least not to Caloocan. This was certainly proof that the Americans had pushed on up the country that far.

Once more we now renewed our plan for an escape. There was now no traitor among us, that much we knew, and on the next favorable night we would slip that bar and be off for the jungle. Finally we fell asleep, little dreaming that it was really to be our last night in Malolos!

The morning of March 6th broke a dull one. We went through our usual routine of cooking, eating, marketing, and lounging in the yard. We could not even get up the excitement of an argument among ourselves. At last Arnold came staggering into the yard, recklessly drunk, and started to fight with a native, who promptly knocked him down. We were just in the midst of this commotion, when the sergeant of the guard appeared and told us to prepare for marching. We were to "vamos!"

This caused the longed-for sensation! But where were we to go? Had the Americans begun the advance? We could only surmise. Could it be possible that they were going to exchange us? It was with suppressed excitement that we lined up outside in the entrance. Arnold caused quite a disturbance; he did not wish to join us, but his expostulations did not avail.

Antonio, the renegade lieutenant, the ex-prisoner, who had sold his country for fifteen pesos monthly salary, now appeared with three guards, and, giving the word to "sigue," we bid our few acquaintances "adios!" the little sergeant especially — he had been good to us.

Down the street we marched into the plaza. Now, would we turn to our left over the stone bridge to the north? No, we passed it! Right on by the Presidencia and down the road leading south. We were going *toward* Manila!

Chapter Eight - Santa Isabela

SOON we left the town far behind and were marching down a country road on both sides of which the bamboos grew so thickly that their leafy tops intermingled overhead, forming in some places natural archways of tropical foliage.

Suddenly O'Brien cried: "Hello, I know this spot! Here the three soldiers held me up— we are on the road to Santa Isabela!"

He was not mistaken. In less than an hour we entered the plaza of a small "pueblo" of bamboo huts, and the inevitable church and convent. All the former piled together could have found ample room under the lofty roof of the latter. It reminded me of a vampire bat, having grown large and fat by the blood sucked from its victims.

Opposite the church, on the other side of the plaza, stood the largest house in the village, a wooden hut built on a stone foundation and thatched with nipa. Taking us up into one of the two rooms of this habitation, Antonio delivered us over to the municipal president of Santa Isabela, and then left to return to Malolos. This shanty was the "presidencia" of the town, or, as we might call it, the "city hall." Shortly after our arrival our new guards conducted us across the plaza into the convent, passing up a broad staircase, and through a succession of large rooms until we finally brought up in one of these spacious apartments, four times the dimensions of our Malolos cell. Two bedsteads of massive mahogany and of a size corresponding to the room were all the furniture to be seen, and these we immediately took possession of, as our guards informed us that this would be our new prison. "In this very room," O'Brien remarked, "I was confined for two days, and tomorrow you will see the cage outside on the balcony where they kept me the other twenty-five days. Look at the walls here!"

Taking up a small cocoanut-oil lamp, made of a common tumbler and a string, we held it to the walls the better to examine them. They had at one time been frescoed, but now appeared faded and dirty. All over had been written poetry, political treatises, reflections on the war and a sort of vocabulary of English, Spanish, and Tagalog, all O'Brien's work, the pastime of a lonely prisoner.

We experienced a novel sensation that night in sleeping in so much surplus of space in which to kick about our limbs without bringing them in violent contact with a neighbor, and we appreciated the luxury.

Early in the morning we awoke, all anxious to inspect our new quarters. As before stated, we had occupied a roomy apartment, but the one adjoining, in which our guards kept watch, was much larger, and also showed traces of former grandeur. Ceiling and walls had been frescoed artistically, but were now faded and covered with cobwebs. The floor was of polished mountain mahogany, and the bedsteads, four in number, were of the same material and elaborately carved. Pieces of ragged hangings and of once rich laces of beautiful design hung from the frames above. In the centre of the room stood a table, wonderfully carved, but much the worse for rough usage. Its round top, at least four feet in diameter, consisted of a single piece of polished "narra" wood, hewn from the log, and in our country would have brought a considerable sum of money. Candles had been allowed to burn down on and into it, and besides, it was covered with dents and deep scratches.

In one corner of the room the guards pointed out a large dark discoloration, or stain, on the floor. The walls close by were speckled with black spots, as if a bucket of paint had been spilled and splashed up on them. Here, we were told by those who claimed to be eye-witnesses, it was where the three padres, who formerly had occupied this convent, had fallen in a screaming heap, their black robes rent and stained with their own blood, begging for mercy from those to whom they themselves never had shown any. The local president himself had struck the head off Padre Tomas with one powerful sweep of his bolo, his arm gaining strength by the recollection of this same holy padre's denunciation of his son, who subsequently fell on the Luneta at Manila under the fire of a squad of Spanish soldiers.

Returning to our room we opened a door and walked out on a balcony or gallery about six feet in width, extending along the side of the building. The main roof, of tiles, projected its eaves down over this also, and by closing the sliding shell windows or blinds, resembling transparent checker-boards, the whole became a long, narrow room incorporated with the rest of the building. One end of this gallery was spaced off by a wooden partition, forming a closet about five by six feet in dimension. Entering this by a small sliding door in the partition, we found it barely roomy enough to hold the five of us. This was O'Brien's "cage," as he called it. Every available square inch was covered with writing, some of the lines not over-elegant in expression or execution but very much to the point, nevertheless, and all inscribed with a rusty nail.

Returning to our sleeping quarters we passed through the guard-room and out on an extensive tile-floored balcony into the open air. It was at least thirty feet square, about fifteen feet from the ground, and protected by a solid stone railing on its three exposed sides. Here, in the old days, the friars were accustomed to sit in the cool of the evening with their friends, the garrison officers, enjoying the glowing sunsets, sipping black coffee and smoking their Cagayan cigars.

From here we had a fine view of the surrounding jungles, rice paddies, and the nipa roofs of the village, while far off in the distance through a break in an intervening jungle a piece of the railroad could be seen. We had indeed reason to be well pleased with our removal from the "Gobierno Militar" of Malolos to the convent of Santa Isabela, not alone on account of our greater personal comfort, but because as we stood on this elevated platform and gazed southward we realized that we were three miles closer to our lines and to Manila. Never in Malolos had we had such favorable surroundings for carrying out the plans which we so long had awaited an opportunity to put into execution.

During the day many curious natives of both sexes came to gaze upon us with a persistence and stupidity of expression truly bovine, but beyond this did not make themselves offensive. It was late in the afternoon before our rations of rice were issued, and by the time we had cooked them out on the balcony on a primitive stove of broken tiles, we had been fasting just thirty-six hours.

It amuses me now to call to mind how we spent that afternoon, before the rice finally came, lying on the beds trying to imagine that we had but lately eaten, cursing the Filipinos in general. At noon we advocated the shooting of all their leaders as a just retribution for starving their prisoners. By one o'clock, as the pangs of hunger became more acute, we all agreed that hanging them would be more appropriate, by this time including every Filipino officer. At three we made no more distinctions — every male Filipino deserved death. Four o'clock found our sentiments still more sanguinary — every native man, woman, and child should be put to slow torture; and by five o'clock we had the whole land drenched in blood! Then the rice appeared, and after cooking and eating it we would have been quite willing to spare the women and children. I may laugh at these recollections now, but *then* they were all too serious.

Our guards, who numbered about nine, were composed partly of the local police, and some were militia or bolomen. These latter lived in their homes, cultivated their fields, etc., but were drilled with wooden guns, and were obliged to be ready at a moment's call. Their only arms were the native sword or bolo, and their uniforms scant and ragged. The police were armed with Remingtons, and wore dark blue homespun uniforms, resembling suits of American dungarees or overalls. Santa Isabela had about six of the latter, three of which guarded us continually — the bolomen being relieved every morning. All were under the command of the local president or mayor. This strikes me as an opportune moment to describe in short the civil government of the Insurgents.

At the head of each province, and quite aside from the military governor, was what was called "el presidente provincial" or "gobernador." His position was practically the same as that of a governor of an American State, he being the executive of civil law. Under him came the "concierjo de justicia," or supreme judge of the province; the "Concierjo de Rentas," or tax collector; and the "presidentes locales," or as the Spaniards called them, "capitanes municipales." These latter were what we would term mayors of towns, one being at the head of each pueblo. On his staff came the "concierjo de policia," a chief of police, and his lieutenants, and, if the size of the town warranted it, the local tax collector and a justice of the peace.

The town was divided into "barrios," or quarters, there being at the head of each a "cabeza," or wardmaster, who represented his particular barrio at the municipal councils in the "presidencia," or city hall. All these offices were filled by the election of the people; none but civilians were appointed. Every male above twenty was an elector. Each province also elected a "representante de la provincia," for its representation in Congress at Malolos or wherever the capital might be. All this was apart from the military government, but the "comandantes" of districts could demand food and quarters for troops from the local presidents if necessary.

Such was the Civil Government of the Insurgents, based almost on the same system as ours, although more crude and imperfect, but answering its purpose nearly equally well. Under normal conditions the Filipino is naturally a peaceful and law-abiding citizen, but, of course, it must be remembered that at this time the excitement of war, never the promoter of law or order, existed throughout the country. It has been admitted by the natives themselves that in the beginning, after the downfall of Spanish rule in the provinces, and while the persecutions by the friars were still vivid in the mind of the populace, many outrages were committed, but, gradually, as the internal government became more firmly established, these became less frequent. In many cases Spanish prisoners obtained redress by appealing to the native courts.

As stated above, we now began to watch for the first opportunity to carry out our plans for escape in earnest, being sorely pressed by the almost constant hunger we suffered here, for the seven motas brought not half as much in Santa Isabela as in Malolos, and comottes were scarce. The only chance for consulting with each other was on the balcony while cooking, for inside Arnold was always present. He cooked by himself, the rest of us together, for we did not desire any closer association with him than what was necessary. On account of him we were obliged to be extremely careful in our conversation, for we knew that if he should hear one suspicious word he would surely again endeavor to sell us out to the Insurgent officials.

The 13th of March was gloomy and stormy. Again the moon was dark. The two or three preceding days had been similar, and had the opportunity presented itself we would have been off before, but the door to the outside gallery had always been closed at sunset. On this particular evening, at seven o'clock, it was still open. A strange fatality had marked out the 13th for us again.

It was already dark, though only seven; I was lying on one of the beds, my canvas shoes slipped off, but within easy reach on the floor. The guards had taken the only light into their room, and were now all absorbed in a game of monte. My four companions were in with them. Arnold lay in a corner on the opposite side of the room, and, as he had not moved for some time, I thought him asleep.

Suddenly a dark figure glided by me and moved toward the door to the gallery. I heard a faint whisper: "Come on, let's hit the trail!" It was Bruce's voice. Jumping up I slipped on one shoe. Meanwhile other figures were moving stealthily by. I was tying the lacing of my second shoe, when I heard a thud on the ground outside — Bruce had made the drop. All at once a loud cry rang out: "Guards, guards, the Americans are escaping! Guards!" And Arnold leaped up from his corner and ran to the door of the guard-room. In a moment the room was full of armed men, and, together with the last one of the figures that had passed me, I found myself hurled bodily back from the door to the bed. The light had been brought in and a torch made of a twisted sheet of paper brightly illuminated the room for a few seconds. I now saw that my companion was Huber. Three hammers clicked, and the muzzles of three Remingtons were pointed at us. I half expected to hear the report, but slowly they were lowered again, as the bolomen bound us together, arm to arm. One, thoroughly bewildered, stood over Arnold, his weapon raised as if to strike, while the latter had dropped to his knees, holding his clasped hands beseechingly up. All this took place in about thirty seconds, but Bruce, Honeyman, and O'Brien were gone.

Chapter Nine - Sounds of War

So furious had I expected the guards to become on discovering the escape, that I feared the worst treatment possible, but in this I was mistaken. Having securely tied Huber and me together, they now stood stupidly staring at each other in confused terror. What punishment might they not expect now after allowing half of the Government's greatest treasures to slip through their fingers? The only trophies of the war, and now half of them gone! It was a national calamity.

Finally the corporal of the police recovered his senses and ran over to the presidencia to raise the alarm, and a few moments later the President and all his councilmen came rushing over. The chief of police, the tax collector, the justice of the peace, and all the ward masters, who had been sitting in grave consultation in the city hall, weighing important questions concerning the public welfare, broke up the meeting to run over in a body to the scene of the great disaster. Half the American prisoners escaped! It was terrible!

Huber and I were bodily dragged downstairs, across the plaza, and thrust into a small cell under the municipal council chamber, where the greatest excitement prevailed, as we could see through the cracks in the floor. Bells were now ringing and drums beaten to spread the alarm abroad, and in an incredibly short time the populace had flocked into the plaza from all directions, running to and fro with flaming torches in their hands, giving vent to their excitement in shrill screams. A stranger ignorant of the cause, would have supposed a sudden night attack of the enemy. Of course, we naturally supposed that it would be their first aim to pursue and capture the fugitives, but instead of doing this they came over to revile us as being the cause of the catastrophe.

The place in which we three now found ourselves (Arnold again having gained but little by his treachery, being shoved in after Huber and me) was an old stable, about large enough for two horses. The walls were stone, with one side almost entirely open, though heavily barred. Besides ourselves there were at least a dozen native prisoners, showing it was the municipal jail. So crowded was this hole that the only available space in which to lie down was a bamboo cot that stood close up against the bars, which was a most undesirable position, as soon became evident.

Soon there appeared on the outside of the bars a solid mass of black faces, their teeth visible in shining white rows like those of snarling curs. Bolos were poked through, stones thrown in, and they even spat in our faces. The cell being small and crowded, we lay there helpless, unable to withdraw out of the mob's reach. Unfortunately for myself I lay closest to the bars; Huber came next, and then Arnold. Thus we were obliged to partly shield him with our bodies.

Toward midnight the majority of the rabble withdrew, but even then there was no sleep to be had, for no sooner had my surroundings grown indistinct, when a stone thrown or the contents of a glass of water brought me back to reality.

By morning the excitement had cooled down considerably, for, although crowds of natives still came to abuse and insult us, no personal violence, as on the night before, was perpetrated. There was one curious exception to this statement, however.

Shortly after daylight the door opened and the corporal of police entered, his Remington slung over his shoulder. Of all our guards he had been the most friendly, and now as he came in on this morning his behavior was the same as ever. Coming up close he slapped Huber and myself on the shoulder, called us his "amigos," and even insisted on shaking hands. Meanwhile he paid no attention to Arnold, who rose to greet him. All at once the smile on his face died out, and, slipping the gun off his shoulder, he took it by the barrel, and, with the stock, dealt Arnold a stunning blow, knocking him over backward on the cot. Three or four times he repeated this, grinding out "bueno" between his clinched teeth each time. Then, once more shaking hands with us two, he left the cell. Here was at least one of our enemies who did not admire a traitor.

We now found ourselves in a bad plight regarding rations, for O'Brien, having been caterer and cook, took with him the two days' ration money received the morning before. Thus we would be obliged to dispense with eating until the money again was issued, another day. Fortunately the rice for the whole party was left behind, and, going over to the convent to recover our cooking utensils, we found this rice and brought it with us. Having, thus, a surplus, we sold some for ten motas, and there was no starving this time.

At first only Arnold was allowed outside the door to do the cooking, his action of alarming the guard now being appreciated for the first time. Later he was called upstairs for an examination by the President, a long, lean, cadaverous-looking old gentleman, while one of us was allowed to continue the culinary operation. Arnold now made good use of his tongue, as we could hear from below, running down the Americans, and the three fugitives in particular, who he said were "mucher maler!"

In the afternoon, shortly after the siesta, we received a visit from three Spaniards. Two of them I had often seen passing before the convent; they were but prisoners quartered on the town, but the third was a stranger to me, wearing the uniform of a Filipino captain. Compared to the natives he was tall, his Roman nose and clear-cut features disclaiming the least drop of Malay blood. At first he entered into a friendly conversation with us without introducing himself, but a brass tower on his coat collar, the insignia of the engineer corps, led me to believe that we now were speaking to O'Brien's benefactor. Captain Espina, and in this I was not mistaken, as we soon learned.

By this time we had all gained sufficient knowledge of Spanish to keep up a lame conversation on commonplace topics, and, seeing that we understood him, the captain seated himself and commenced to have a long talk with us, his distinct manner of enunciation making him easy to understand. Soon I found my surmise verified: he told us of his meeting with O'Brien, and how he had interceded with the Secretary of War to have the Englishman's condition bettered. "On account of his escape," he continued, "I could do but little for you now with Baldomero Aguinaldo, but it may be that Mr. Higgins, a personal friend of mine, can do more for you than I can, as his influence with President Aguinaldo is very great, and I will try to get him interested in you." We told him how apathetic Mr. Higgins had been to O'Brien's misfortune, whom even the Secretary of War admitted was an Englishman; what assistance could be expected from such a man! However, we requested him to beg Mr. Higgins for some English reading-matter, if he had any, something with which to pass away the tedious hours. This he promised to do. "But," he said, before leaving, "I will make an effort myself to have your condition ameliorated, and you must promise me, if I succeed, not to take advantage of it to attempt an escape." This we readily promised. Bidding us "adios" he departed, giving us to understand that we should soon see him again.

The three or four succeeding days were dreary ones to us. Arnold and I never exchanged a word. He was intoxicated, most of the time, into the bargain; vino was given him for the asking. Had the President been as liberal with rice to Huber and me, we should not have been obliged to endure the constant hunger we did. Never before had we suffered so much on this score; we could often have only one meal in the twenty-four hours. And then, as if to tantalize us, the President's son and his friends would often toss pesetas and pesos before our eyes in a game similar to "toss-up."

One little incident that embittered my mind at that time I shall never forget. I was outside cooking one day, when the President's wife came down the steps from the house, and, throwing me a package in an old *La Independencia*, cried: "Here, Americano, is something for you! Poor little things, how hungry you must be!" On opening, I found it contained some entrails and heads of the native cat-fish, such as many people would not feed to their dogs. This caused a general laugh among a group of idlers that stood about — the lady's joke was considered clever! But when I walked up the stairs and laid it in the doorway, saying, that my conscience did not permit me to eat it, knowing how fond the Señora herself, being a Filipina, was of such a dish, her smile faded into a snarl, and she called me a name unfit for publication.

But not to give the Filipino women in general a reputation for heartlessness, I will mention another incident to offset the behavior of the President's wife.

An old woman of the "taui" class came to the bars one day and slipped in an ear of corn and a few cigars to each of us. When she saw how hungry we were, the tears rolled down her withered cheeks. She then asked us questions of the American soldiers — were they so bad as reported? did they kill their prisoners? etc. We assured her that such accounts were but baseless calumnies, and she hoped that they were indeed false, for her only son, together with his whole company, had been taken prisoner. What did we suppose had been done to them? Would the Americans repeat the Spanish cruelties, and shoot their captives on the Luneta? She came often after that, the old gray-haired woman, venerable in spite of her naked feet and stooping shoulders, and seemed to derive comfort from our assurances of her captive son's humane treatment.

True to his word, Captain Espina returned at the end of several days with an order for our reinstatement in the convent during the day. Every evening we were to return to the jail to spend the night there. He had tried his best to have us entirely removed to the more roomy quarters over there, but his efforts had failed. Nevertheless I, for my part, felt deeply grateful to him for what he had succeeded in doing. He had also seen Higgins, but that gentleman would have nothing to do with us.

On the succeeding morning, after breakfast, we returned to the convent with three policemen as guards. We took our cooking utensils with us, that we might prepare our afternoon meal over there, but at sunset we were obliged to return to the cell under the presidency. And this became our daily routine.

Times now became dull and monotonous again. What had become of our three companions we didn't know. Some told us they had been killed, others that they were recaptured, but, as the reports were so vague, I believed that they had made good their escape into the American lines.

A native lawyer of the town, Señor Santiago, loaned us an old Ollendorf's Spanish-English grammar, with which we passed away many a weary hour, copying verbs, nouns, sentences, and phrases on the white walls and then memorizing them. It was here that I laid the foundation to a pretty fair knowledge of the Spanish language, which afterward became of great usefulness to me. Occasionally we received visits from Mausilla and Santa Maria, the only two Spanish prisoners in the town, and they assisted us in pronunciation.

Our daily life had now settled into a routine that at times became almost unbearable. Often we would lean over the balcony railing gazing southward; as far as we knew, the American army had ceased to exist. The feeling that we were considered dead by friends and relatives, and were unable to relieve their anxiety, was highly depressing.

Over the way from the balcony, in a little bamboo hut, lived an old couple, Francisco and Joaquina. Notwithstanding their large family and extreme poverty they would often throw up small offerings, small to be sure, but not fish entrails. An ear of corn, a green mango, or a few cigarettes would from time to time come flying over the balcony railing as a grateful token of their sympathy.

One day Francisco called to us from the window of his abode, asking us if we cared to earn a few extra motas by pounding rice. Huber and I shouted back that we would, most gladly; Arnold shook his head but said nothing. Francisco promised to arrange with the proper parties that night. On the succeeding day Francisco appeared shortly after the siesta with permission to take us with him, our guards to accompany us, of course. He conducted us down a street leading off from the plaza and into an extensive enclosure, where over a dozen women were shelling rice in large wooden mortars, by pounding it with huge mallets of heavy mahogany. The superintendent, or owner, an old toothless Filipino, explained to us that for each mortarful we pounded, a copper mota would be placed to our credit. Arnold at once explained that he was not used to manual labor, but if they had any employment wherein he could use his head, he would gladly work, with his hands — never! No, never!

Huber and I, however, seized one of the heavy mallets each and set to work, causing the rice to fly about in all directions, much to the amusement of the women and the horror of the owner. It took us half an hour to finish our first mortarful. The women could do the same work in half that time, having a dexterous way of slinging the mallet, weighing at least ten pounds, with but small exertion. Then we commenced on our second mortar. Arnold was sitting close by, giving Huber a good deal of advice as to the best manner in which to manipulate the mallet. Soon the handles burned in our hands like red-hot iron rods, our arms ached, the small of our backs became weak, and our bodies covered with perspiration. We each finished a third, but had my life depended upon it I could not have pounded any more. Our earnings were given to us, and the owner's wife brought each of us a plate of cooked bananas, very welcome after that terrible exertion. Arnold received all that we did, and was called "Señor" in the bargain!

When evening came, Huber and I vainly tried to satisfy our ravenous appetite with the bananas the extra three motas could purchase; but as we felt of our blistered hands and watched Arnold quietly munching baked rice cakes, in which he had invested one of his three easily earned motas, we decided then and there never again to pound rice with wooden mallets.

One day the military governor of the local comandancia honored us with a visit. Comandante Antonio de la Peña was his name — he wrote it on the wall. He was a small, very black, heavy-set man of middle age, and, unlike most Filipinos, wore a heavy mustache. What surprised us most was the fluency with which he spoke English. In his younger days, he told us, he had sailed before the mast in British and American merchant vessels. Hearing that I also had sailed on the briny deep, he was delighted and opened his heart toward us to the extent of ten cents' worth of bananas, for which he sent one of the guards. For nearly two hours he sat conversing with me of foreign seaports where both of us had been. Later he ventured a little war news. Fighting was going on continually, but as yet the Americans had not gained one fathom of ground. As he further expressed it: "They were putting kinks in Uncle Sam's tail and were well to windward of him." In his mind, there was not the least reason for doubting that the Filipinos would eventually gain their independence; in fact he already counted upon having command of one of the finest vessels in the future Filipino navy. But in spite of all these bombastic words, there could be detected an air of doubt in the manner they were expressed, that impressed me with the idea that he himself had not the faith in them he professed.

Another visitor that also made his appearance during those tedious days, and caused us some little amusement, may be found worthy of a few lines.

One afternoon after the siesta, always the customary visiting hours in the Philippines, a number of natives of the very lowest class entered and stood gazing at us with open mouths and eyes. This in itself was nothing unusual, but when one of them, a small, withered old man, stepped forward, pulled an imaginary lock of hair on his forehead, a manner of saluting peculiar to seafaring people, and said quite plainly in English, "Good-morning," our attention was attracted. Although surprised, we retained our presence of mind and answered quite calmly with another "good-morning." He was sadly disappointed — the effect was not stunning enough. Suddenly, in a loud, hoarse voice of which a navy boatswain might have been envious, he roared: "Bear a hand there, stand by yer topsel braces!" The effect was all that could be desired — we *were* stunned! Then, as if to follow up his advantage, he added in a still deeper roar, "Splice the main brace!" After which he turned around to his admiring companions as if to say: "You see, for me the language of these people has no mysteries. A man of my learning and experience knows a thing or two." But it soon became evident that he had just about exhausted his whole vocabulary, and was now obliged to resort to a strange gibberish in which an occasional English word could be recognized. At first we thought he was addressing us in Tagalog, until we noticed that the natives likewise could not comprehend him, to judge by their blank and surprised features. What he spoke of we could not even guess, but it probably made but little difference to him whether we understood or not, since he was making the desired impression on his countrymen. Of course, we quite entered into his little game, and answered back in real genuine English to heighten the effect, and that delighted him beyond measure. At length we shook hands and said "Good-by," and the manner in which he stepped out at the head of his admirers showed that he was well aware of the importance he had gained in their estimation.

Bigoted as well as ignorant as were most of the officers by whom we were interviewed, it is but just to mention a notable exception.

A young second lieutenant came in one day and greeted us with some show of friendliness. I remember he made a good impression on me at once by his manner, but his appearance was far from prepossessing. Being unusually black, he was short of stature, thick-lipped, and pock-marked, a typical full-blooded Filipino. In spite of these physical disadvantages, his features appeared to me remarkably intelligent when he spoke. Accompanying him was a sergeant, who carried, slung over the shoulder by the strap, an American Springfield rifle. Seeing that we looked at it with some curiosity, he gave it into our hands to examine. Sure enough, it certainly was a United States rifle. Upon asking him how he had come into possession of it, he related the following story:

"It was captured during a skirmish on the Pasig, wherein a number of Americans fell back, leaving their dead behind. This rifle I found on the field after the fight, and this belt of ammunition I took from one of their dead." Then Arnold, either to curry favor or draw him out, made the remark that the superior courage of the Filipinos would certainly insure their ultimate victory in the war. "No," the lieutenant replied, "that is impossible. Although they have not yet commenced to advance, I believe our cause is already lost, or will be, ultimately. In two or three months they will overwhelm us with numbers. Even now there are two American soldiers to each armed Filipino, the difference being all the greater on account of their superior training and armament. We shall probably be swept out of existence, for surrender we never will."

"Yes," admitted Arnold, "they will gain by mere superiority of numbers, but their courage is of poor quality."

"No, again you are mistaken; the Americans are 'valientes' — I admire them for their courage. Their tactics are bolder than those of the Spaniards. The latter take advantage of every possible shelter, while the Americans boldly advance upright, their bodies exposed. No, the Americans are brave men."

Arnold was crestfallen, and, notwithstanding his glib tongue, could find no suitable reply. With his intelligence this young lieutenant, had he but possessed a little better personal appearance, would probably soon have risen to be a colonel or even general in the Insurgent army, but often these high-ranked positions were bought, directly or indirectly, or obtained by social influence, thus placing intelligence and experience as secondary in importance. A young, ambitious man would promise to help out the cause with so many thousand pesos, and was at once made a colonel or a general, and in some cases general officers were not yet out of their teens. These positions could certainly not have been coveted on account of fat salaries, for an Insurgent general's pay amounted to about the same as an American sergeant's. To begin with the common soldier, he was supposed to receive one and a half peso a month with rations, but later on was seldom paid. A corporal had three pesos and a sergeant six. These non-commissioned officers bore the insignia of their respective ranks on their sleeve, just above the wrist, as do the Spaniards — a corporal two, and a sergeant three, stripes.

The rank of the officers, as in all armies, was designated on their shoulder-straps. These ran lengthwise on the shoulder, not across as in our army. A second lieutenant wore three silver stars on each shoulder, and had a monthly salary of fifteen pesos. A first lieutenant wore two silver stars, and a captain one, their respective salaries being twenty and twenty-five pesos. A major or comandante's shoulder-strap bore three gold stars, a lieutenant-colonel two, and a colonel one, their salaries increasing five pesos each step. I was told that a brigadier-general only received fifty pesos a month, but cannot testify to the truth of this statement. Possibly the salaries varied according to their respective merits or ability. That any of them, including Luna, the Commander-in-Chief, ever drew more than fifty American dollars a month, I do not believe. The civil officials were, as a rule, better paid, as that lay within their own power. These had excellent opportunities for stealing, and did not allow them to slip by, either, for, as several told me afterward, their opportunities might never come again.

According to the general testimony of intelligent natives themselves, a Filipino in office can never be honest, the Spaniards having taught them that a dishonest peso is worth two gained fairly, and it will take a long time before the effect of their examples can entirely be eliminated. It is likewise necessary that those who in time will teach them that "honesty is the best policy" live up to their teachings, but "there's the rub."

But to return to Santa Isabela. Had it not been for the Spanish grammar, our mental sufferings would indeed have been great, for, when idle, fearful visions sometimes arose. I thought of a relation of mine who long ago disappeared in the Australian wilds, and was found twenty years later, his reason gone, nothing but the animated clay left. I did not believe that such a fate could befall one here, but still such thoughts would enter my mind at times.

This demoralizing monotony was one day interrupted by our friend and benefactor, Captain Espina, who came to pay us a visit. I happened to remember it was on March 20th. He remained a considerable while, and, after conversing on various subjects, finally told the story of his entering the Insurgent service.

Formerly, under the Spanish Government, Señor Espina had held the rank of "inspector of mountains," literally translated; and somewhat similar to our timber commissioners. When the war with America broke out, he was made an officer of volunteers, but when the Americans entered Manila on August 13th he surrendered his arms, and became once more a civilian, having a family in the city.

Being the owner of vast estates in the interior, he was given a pass to Malolos in order to arrange with the Insurgent authorities for the protection of his property from the depredations of the mob, but found that all had been confiscated. This was on February 3d. The following night hostilities broke out and Señor Espina found return to Manila and his family cut off and himself penniless. For two weeks he endeavored to exist, but, not being considered a prisoner, was not even allowed rations. Knowing him to have been employed before, both by the railroad company and also by the Spanish Government as a civil engineer, the Insurgent officials approached him several times with the object of persuading him to join their cause, and at length, driven by sheer want, he accepted a commission as captain with the monthly salary of twenty-five pesos, the highest rank to which a renegade could rise. Only one Spaniard ever rose above a captaincy, becoming a comandante (major), and he was related to Aguinaldo by marriage, his wife being a native.

It was Espina that superintended the digging of the trenches at Caloocan, and later at Calumpit, which even our experts admit, show remarkable scientific skill.

But he became most interesting when he volunteered the information that the Americans had notified Aguinaldo that they would commence to advance on Thursday, March 24th. The information was common property, but the embellishments will interest the American reader.

All the European Powers had combined and notified the United States Government that it must take some decisive measures to end the insurrection, otherwise they would intervene for the same reasons that the United States had done in Cuba, finally expelling the Spaniards. The Powers had sent an ultimatum to McKinley, making it incumbent on the American army to advance on Malolos by March 24th, which capital they must take by April ist. This being done, the war might go on, but should the Insurgents successfully defend their capital until after that date, then combined Europe would demand the independence of the Philippine Islands.

Such was the news as Espina had it from official sources, and as he told it to us, and at the time we believed enough of it to feel deeply interested. Espina seemed somewhat gloomy over the prospect, and remarked: "I greatly fear that we cannot resist an American advance for a whole week, but, if the war would then be at an end, it might be for the best. The Americans believe that by taking Malolos they conquer the country, but the war will not be over by the end of this year, nor the next, either. Aguinaldo's policy is to worry the Americans, and not to meet them in pitched battle. The Filipinos can carry on a guerilla warfare in the mountains for ten years to come, and they will surely do so if the United States Government persists in refusing to define the exact degree of autonomy they intend giving us. Having been eighteen years in the country, and being married to a native lady, I suppose I also can consider myself a Filipino. If we were promised the same form of government that Canada has under England, we would, every one of us, lay down our arms and become as loyal to America as the best of her citizens, for our leaders are not extremists; but, above all, to insure permanent peace, the monastic corporations must be banished, for as long as a friar treads Philippine soil, so long will the Filipino Catholics be discontent."

The intervening time between Espina's departure and next Thursday seemed to me an age of suspense. The native prisoners over in the jail also had heard the report, so there seemed no doubt but what it had some foundation. Since the night of the 4th we had never heard the least indication of the struggle going on to the southward. Occasionally we had seen a red glare in the heavens over where we thought Manila to be, but could draw no deductions from that in our favor. Sometimes we could not but believe that foreign complications hampered our Government in some way.

When Thursday morning dawned, our nervous excitement and expectancy was plainly visible to each other in our behavior. Nobody thought of cooking breakfast, we were far too anxious to hear the guns open up. All day, after going over to the convent that morning, we stood out on the balcony anxiously listening for the least sound that might float up on the southwest monsoon breeze. Once a door below banged several times, and we became almost frantic until we learned our mistake. But the day passed slowly away, and not a sound disturbed the faint rustling of the bamboo thickets and the mango-trees. Evening came, and we returned to the cell under the presidency, believing ourselves victims of false rumors.

Friday morning again found us in the convent, but hope had died out, and we resumed our Spanish lessons inside on the white walls. It must have been about ten o'clock in the forenoon. Huber was asleep, and Arnold and I paced the floor with lists of Spanish words in our hands, which we were memorizing. We never spoke to each other, not one word had passed between us since the night of the 13th, but now, suddenly, he stood as if petrified and shouted, "Listen!" The guards had rushed out on the balcony and were talking excitedly among themselves. All three of us went out to join them, Huber being awakened by the excitement. For a moment we stood breathlessly listening, when faintly but distinctly came that same deep intonation that we had heard on the night of the 4th, a low, angry "b-r-r-um," that thrilled my whole being. Faint it was at first, like the hum of insects on a bright summer day in the meadow, but we knew now that the advance had really begun.

What my sensations were is hard to describe. At times I did not know whether hope or fear was most predominant. How it would affect us remained to be seen, but our countrymen were really coming; to rescue us or not, the end of the week would tell, for we could not believe that they would require a week to advance twenty miles. A crisis was approaching, that we knew, either for good or bad, and, naturally, to be preferred to the fearful suspense of the preceding two months.

All that day we remained on the balcony, even forgetting to prepare our scanty meals. Whenever the firing ceased we walked about like caged animals, but it was always resumed again, more distinct than before. By the afternoon we could plainly distinguish each separate report. Shortly after our removal to the jail at sunset the firing ceased, and we heard it no more that night.

Excitement of the wildest sort prevailed in Santa Isabela. Throughout the night companies of regulars and bolomen passed down the road toward the front, singing and laughing as if going to certain victory.

Saturday morning we were again allowed to return to the convent. At about ten the cannonading was resumed, but much more distinct, that is, nearer than on the preceding day. Small groups of Spanish prisoners passed through the town toward Malolos.

At noon we were made to return to jail on account of the decreased number of guards, the bolomen of the district being called together in the plaza and marched off to the front. Before leaving the convent we wrote our names on the wall, knowing we would never return, also adding a few words giving date of capture, condition, etc. Some of the native prisoners were now utilized for guard duty over us.

By evening carretones, drawn by carabaos or water buffalos with tremendous horns, commenced to pass at short intervals, going toward Malolos, loaded with household furniture, rice, women, and children. All night we heard the creaking of passing vehicles. Late in the afternoon cannonading again ceased.

Sunday morning vehicles of all sorts were now passing in great numbers, — carretones, carromatas, and quilez, all heavily laden with the household goods of the fleeing families trudging alongside. By afternoon the exodus became a living stream of humanity. Some carried their goods on poles after the manner of the Chinese, others on their heads. Carromatas crashed into carretones, the drivers swore at each other, and the horns of carabaos became entangled in the wheels. Bundles were dropped and crushed by heavy vehicles. Women with dishevelled hair and crying children in their arms plodded beside the family carreton, some sobbing quietly, others expressing their alarm and grief in loud shrieks. There were blind and crippled and old, who were tossed helplessly about by the panic-stricken mob, too frightened to hear their cries. Everywhere was terror and confusion.

By afternoon soldiers intermingled with this fleeing throng, first in twos and threes, later by dozens and companies. Some still had their guns, others had lost them and were bareheaded and half-naked. But, above all the noise and din of this confusion, the banging of guns and bursting of shells could be heard apparently not five miles away. Although this latter ceased again at dusk, the refugees still continued passing, their numbers not perceptibly diminishing.

At about nine o'clock a mob of bolomen gathered outside the prison, and amused themselves by jabbing their long knives in between the bars at us. We were now alone, the native prisoners had disappeared. It was bright moonlight, and plainly could we see the crowd of half-naked savages outside, the long blades of their bolos flashing in the yellow light as they flourished them overhead. Again those vicious cries of "Muerte! muerte! muerte a los Americanos!" Then they tried to force our doors, but they were strongly bolted. Every moment their fury increased, and it seemed to us that the long-dreaded climax had arrived.

But just then, in the veriest heat of the excitement, we heard the trampling of horses' hoofs outside, and the next moment a mounted officer dashed into the midst of the turbulent mob, laying about him with a heavy riding whip, and thundering out oaths in Spanish and Tagalog. We could hear that whip whizzing through the air, followed by cries of pain. In two minutes the horseman was alone, glaring about him as if seeking more victims. Approaching the bars, he shouted to us: "All right; I told 'em; they not trouble you again!" It was Peña, the comandante or military governor of the district. We admired his style of telling them. "Plenty fight now," he continued, coming up close to the bars and speaking in a loud whisper. "The Americans is advancing, but not possible can come here. I'm going down to the fight with my men! I knock seven bells out of de damn Yankees. I keelhaul 'em all. We not possible can be licked! "Then he turned his horse as if to depart, but once more lowering his head to the bars, he added, doubtfully: "I doan know, mebbe I mistake — good-by!" and, digging his spurs into the horse's flanks, he galloped off toward the south, to fall the next day, as I was informed afterward, before the deadly fire of the American rifles while leading a hopeless charge against the "damn Yankees" that he wanted to "keelhaul." But worse men than he fell that day! It must have been about midnight when I dropped off to sleep, and by that time the creaking of vehicles and shouts of refugees had considerably diminished.

Upon awakening in the morning not a sound broke the unnatural stillness, not even the usual cock's crow, to which we were so accustomed. At eight or thereabouts our doors were opened and we were allowed to go outside for the purpose of cooking breakfast, but what a change! Every hut within our sight appeared to be deserted, except the presidency upstairs. Not a dog nor cat to be seen, everything appeared dead. With the exception of the President and his family, and our few guards, the entire population of Santa Isabela seemed to have fled, and even now two carretones stood before the door, being loaded with the furniture of the rooms above. The road which but yesterday had been the scene of so much commotion, was now again deserted.

But what would now become of us? Should we be permitted to remain to welcome the advancing troops? Should we be forgotten in the excitement? Our hopes rose. Any moment we might now expect to see the last remnants of the Filipino army retreating through the town with the pursuing Americans on their heels. If we could only have hidden, but we were helplessly caged up in that stone jail. We were, however, not to remain in doubt much longer.

While we were eating our scanty breakfast of saltless rice, the President entered and motioned to us to come out. We followed him outside, where we found a squad of regular soldiers, and to these the President gave us in charge. Ten minutes later we were tramping up the Malolos road.

We had barely left Santa Isabela when the firing recommenced, but in such close proximity that the shells seemed actually to burst overhead. Intermingling with the roar of the cannonade we distinctly heard the volley firing and the rattling of the rapid-fire guns. Every house on the road was deserted, not an animal remained. Nobody now to shout "Mucho malo Americanos!" as they did when we came down.

In less than an hour the church towers of the capital appeared above the intervening bamboo thickets, and soon we entered the town — but what a scene presented itself! We had seen panic and confusion the day before, but that couldn't be compared to what we observed now. Men, women, and children thronged the main thoroughfare in one compact, screaming mob, stricken with a terror that seemed to have bereft them of all reason. They all ran into one another. Officers shouted orders and soldiers shouted back, nobody obeyed.

Fighting our way through this terror-stricken mob for us, the guards at length turned down the old familiar street on which fronted the "Gobierno Militar." We had just passed the convent, and the redtrousered guards were frantically exerting themselves in throwing the President's furniture into vehicles, which, as soon as loaded, tore across the crowded plaza and over the bridge out on the northward road, black with people as far as the eye could reach.

A few minutes' walk now found us before the "Gobierno Militar" building, the same old familiar mass of gray stones. Again those old wooden doors swung open. Everything was as we had left it. We were roughly shoved in, the darkness blinding our eyes for the moment, but, suddenly, there arose a loud shout, old familiar voices, and Huber and I were shaking hands with Bruce, Honeyman, and O'Brien.

Chapter Ten - With the Retreat

OF course, the recaptured three were less surprised at this meeting than we were — they had expected us for several days. I had mentally decided that they had effected their escape, since nothing but vague rumors concerning their fate had reached us, but here they were, sure enough. As my eyes became accustomed to the gloom, I was shocked to notice the change for the worse in their appearance; their sunken eyes, sallow complexion, and emaciated condition told a tale of suffering. But a glance at the surroundings explained all. The cell was in the same condition as during Donato's *régime*, and for the last week had contained never less than thirty occupants. It had not been possible to lie down in all that time — there was no room in that hole for such a crowd to stretch themselves on the floor at once. What sleep was had could only be obtained by sitting and leaning up against each other.

In very short time we had exchanged accounts of our respective experiences, but theirs had been more eventful than ours.

After leaping from the balcony on that eventful night of the 13th, they had heard Arnold's outcry of alarm, and, rushing blindly down the road, found themselves on the railroad track. Under ordinary circumstances the plan had been to follow this as a sure guide in the right direction, but having heard the alarm raised, they feared pursuit, the more so as Arnold being familiar with the old idea of following the rails, might divulge this to the President, who then would send a party to cut them off; so, instead of adopting the old line of action, they dashed across the railroad embankment into the jungle and rice-paddies beyond. The night being dark, they, of course, lost their bearings, and, after stumbling about for two hours in ditches and swamps in a vain endeavor to regain the track, they soon realized that what one considered north another felt certain was south, while the third declared it to be east. Allowing Bruce to take the lead, they plodded on as best they could, crossing creeks and carabao wallows, until about midnight, when, exhausted and discouraged, they sank to the ground to confer. For some time all were silent, none having the heart to make a suggestion, when they became almost blinded by a flash of brilliant light across the sky. Springing to their feet, the three fugitives recognized the rays of a searchlight from the American war vessels in Manila Bay, and, following the direction whence it shot up on the horizon, they again trudged hopefully on, knowing that should it remain stationary for a little while, it would eventually guide them to the railroad track. Had the officer in charge of that searchlight, walking comfortably up and down the vessel's bridge, known what use his light was put to by those three despairing fugitives, he might have left it in that position all night, but as he could not possibly surmise such a thing, the light was turned away and once more the trio found themselves in almost total darkness. Fortunately they had not wandered so far from the track as they feared, and, accidentally starting in the right direction, they soon found it, but almost in the same spot where they had crossed it four hours previously. With renewed hope and strength they set off at a smart pace along the guiding rails, pushing desperately on, regardless of the stations through which they passed, unheeding the danger of being challenged by sentries by so doing. The sky was commencing to lighten over the mountains to the eastward, when they reached a large river, and, turning off here, hid in a clump of bushes on the banks, intending to continue the flight the following night. Daylight came, and with it a drizzling rain. Toward noon a small herd of carabao came down to wallow in the mud, but, seeing the three men in the brush, stood about sniffing the air and staring in a manner that seems indigenous to the country, with people and animals alike. In no way could they scare the stupid animals off, and, his curiosity excited by their suspicious manner, a small boy came down to inquire into the cause of it. Discovering the three fugitives in the bushes, the lad ran back to the village close by and raised the alarm. In a few minutes they were surrounded by natives, who, seizing them, bound their arms behind their backs and dragged them up into town, which proved to be Bocave. The unfortunate captives were placed on exhibition in the convent windows while a brass band played martial music, and the church bells tolled the news of their capture throughout the adjacent country. Work was abandoned and the day given over to a "fiesta," for now the Government's great treasure was safe again.

That same afternoon they left Bocave in great state preceded by a brass band, keeping step to the slow time of a dead march. On each side of them marched a file of soldiers with Mausers and fixed bayonets, two black'-robed priests bringing up the rear. There are occasions when music is not cheering, and this was one of them. Imagine the feelings of these three men, finding themselves in the midst of such a suggestive procession, their arms bound behind their backs above the elbows!

This proved to be nothing more, however, than a merry joke on the Bocave President's part, he seeming of a sort of humorous turn of mind. Two kilometres outside of town the band and priests returned, leaving the prisoners to proceed with the guards as far as Bulacan, where they slept that night. Next day they continued their march to Malolos, arriving in the afternoon at the old "Gobierno Militar," where they found Cigarettes, Squint-Eye, and all the rest to welcome them. Betel-Nuts, the badly abused, had joined the army!

We were still conversing when the sergeant of the guard appeared and ordered us to fall into line outside in the passage. This did not take us by surprise, for Bruce had told us what they had known for several days, viz., we were to be taken along on the retreat.

Picking up our few cooking utensils (for they were really too valuable to be left behind), we filed out on the street, where we found a column of about fifty Spaniards waiting for us to join them. We six were placed at the head, completely surrounded by guards, and then the officer in command gave the order, "Sigue!" and we "signed" accordingly. The streets were now almost deserted, and, entering the plaza, we turned to the north, over a stone bridge and out on the road, which for miles ahead was black with the rear of the retreating population.

Once clear of the town we came out on a broad stretch of bare rice-fields, and, far off in the distance, to our right, we saw the smoke of the two firing lines. In several places black columns of dense smoke arose where buildings were burning, set afire by the retreating Filipino soldiers. Fighting seemed to be going on less than two miles away, and, seeing this, our guards became almost frantic in their efforts to drive us along at a double-quick pace. The Spaniards, notwithstanding their sickly condition, flew helter-skelter up the road, urged by sharp pricks of the Remington bayonets, but in spite of blows and threats we would not do more than walk. O'Brien suggested that we lag behind as much as possible, and, though we suffered for it, we gradually found ourselves far to the rear of the rest. Huber and Arnold had gone ahead with the Spaniards, so we numbered but four, but for each one of us there were two well-armed guards, and the hope of being able to take advantage of the proximity of the American troops finally vanished in thin air. Honeyman and O'Brien were the last pair, and blow after blow from the stock of the enraged sergeant's gun rained on their backs, but doggedly they refused to accelerate their steps. Bruce and I also came in for a good share.

At last we entered a heavy thicket of bamboos, the road at the same time taking a more northerly turn, thus hiding the firing line from view. This had a quieting effect on the soldiers, who recovered their composure somewhat, and from then on we had nothing worse than Tagalog curses heaped upon us.

In two hours we reached a small town where we found Arnold, Huber, and the Spaniards resting, the two former in a cell under the convent, where we joined them. In this place, Quingua, as the Spaniards called it, we remained until shortly before sunset, when the march of the prisoners was resumed.

They now bound us together in pairs, arm to arm, with rattan cords, evidently fearing that we might make a break for liberty under cover of darkness.

For about four long weary hours we tramped the dusty road, when we reached the bank of a rather wide river, on the other side of which could be seen by the bright moonlight the stately "convento" of another town. Thirty at a time were ferried across on a large bamboo raft, which with soldiers, Spaniards, and ourselves made three trips. This was the town of Baliuag, and here the rest for the night was to be made. We Americans were taken into the convent, and at once confined in a cell under the main staircase, miserably small, and the presence of two canvas litters daubed with clotted blood did not add to the attractions of this hole. But, being tired out, we were soon fast asleep.

Early in the morning, the day hardly breaking, our slumbers were brought to an abrupt termination by a number of pebbles striking against our bodies. As many black faces as could conveniently crowd into the space of the window, were glaring at us through the iron bars, waiting to see what efifect the stone throwing would have on us. As we did not fly at them and attempt to bite the iron bars in two, their disappointment became evident, and sticks were brought into use in the hope of awakening our dormant ferocity. Later the doors were opened and the populace were allowed to file by to see us, the sergeant of the guard acting as master of ceremonies.

At about eight o'clock we were formed in marching order, but not bound. The Spaniards formed just ahead of us, and then at the word "sigue" (pronounced "seegay," from "siguir," to follow, here meaning "hurry up," "get," etc.) the retreat was resumed. Many of the poor "cazadores," as the Spanish soldiers were generally called, were now in a deplorable condition, but the guards formed in a line across the road behind them, prodding up the stragglers with their bayonets, meanwhile shouting at the top of their voice: "Sigue, sigue, sigue!" That word I shall never forget. The Spanish drover makes use of it in driving his stock to market, and now it was applied to us.

One Spaniard, unable to proceed farther, dropped to the ground. A guard kicked and poked him, but the man lay there, apparently dead. For a moment I thought that the raised bayonet would descend and end his sufferings, but, giving him a last kick, the guard stepped over him and went on. What became of this poor unfortunate I never learned — never did I see him again.

My heart sank within me when I observed that our line of march seemed to lead toward the mountains. We had been dreading this. At noon we entered a town called San Rafael, and, as usual, were confined in the convent. Here Arnold and myself had our coats stolen, although mine was later returned, minus the contents of its pockets, a few much-needed copper motas.

At about four the march was resumed, and glad we were to leave this inhospitable place, where they tore the rags from the backs of helpless prisoners. To our relief the road took a more northerly turn, keeping parallel with the foot-hills. The country now became wilder and more rugged, vehicles being useless in places. The Spaniards had a woman with them, a pure-blooded Castilian, wife to one of the officers, and she was now obliged to tread the rocky road with her delicate feet. Her husband tried to carry her, but she would not consent, and I much doubt if he, or any of the prisoners there, for that matter, could have accomplished it.

Late that night we hobbled into a town whereof the convent had fortunately been burnt down, so there were no cells in which to confine us. We were allowed to sleep with the Spaniards in a bamboo enclosure shared with us by a few pigs, whose domains we thus usurped, and who resented our intrusion with angry grunts.

Since leaving Malolos we had eaten nothing. The Spaniards, not being restricted on reaching towns, could do some foraging, but, as we were closely confined, we were obliged to depend on our captors. At all our appeals for food we had been told to wait until the end of our march. As the general impression seemed to be that this might take a month yet, if the Americans continued to advance, we found no comfort in the assurances that our hunger would be assuaged upon reaching our destination. In this town, San Ildefonso, we each received a dried fish and as much rice as we could grab out of a pot with one hand. How diminutive that fish and how genteelly small our fists on that occasion! Yet, when we afterward complained of hunger, our Insurgent officers would exclaim: "What? Did you not dine sumptuously in San Ildefonso? Would you unfit yourselves for the march by overloading your stomachs?"

We spent the forenoon of the next day in standing in the road under a broiling sun, several Filipino officers sitting on the veranda of the President's house in reclining cane chairs, smoking and maybe speculating how many more of the poor Spaniards would succumb to those pitiless rays, as so many already had done. The prostrate forms were dragged by their comrades into the shade under the house, where they lay until either their senses returned or perhaps were extinguished forever. I missed several familiar faces afterward.

At noon the President gave orders for the continuance of our march, and, after being stoned by a mob until a mile outside of town, we found ourselves on the northward-bound winding road once more, which lay entirely through an open plain, with not a thicket or even a tree to give shelter from that scathing tropical sun. It was hard to believe that those ragged, dirty, limping, and hopeless figures, marching with heavy, halting steps beside me, were only a year before the spruce and orderly soldiers of proud old Spain.

Late in the afternoon we entered the town of San Miguel de Mayumo, and, escorted by what seemed to us a million of natives, entered the plaza, where we stood on exhibition beneath a life-size representation of the "Last Supper," the latter on a wheeled platform, it being some of the church paraphernalia, used in their religious processions. Why they in any manner should connect us with this is hard to say, but as I gazed on the silken robes of Jesus and his disciples I wondered if, had he been alive, he would have approved of what he saw. But the native priests, who gathered around to feast their eyes on our condition, apparently did, since, their glances held nothing but hate!

The Spaniards had dispersed in various directions to beg food from the inhabitants. At sunset we were conducted to the public prison in the plaza, where many of the Spaniards also were quartered for the night. Here our bad fortune seemed to leave us for a while, for an old Spanish resident of the town, whom we afterward knew as Ramon Rey, gave us two chickens, rice, meat, bananas, cigars, and a bottle of real old whiskey, besides cheering words. Another, a former Spanish officer, who declined to give his name, gave us two pesos to be divided among us. Ramon Rey enjoyed some privileges, being married to a native woman and having lived thirty years in the country; yet he, too, had suffered imprisonment in former times. He informed us that Aguinaldo had arrived in town that morning, and a meeting had been held in the convent, the object of which was to decide upon what terms to negotiate a surrender to the Americans. Aguinaldo had been in favor of surrendering on the best possible terms, but Luna was for concentrating the whole Filipino force for the delivery of one decisive battle. All this we were told by Ramon Rey, whose native wife had learned it from one of the servants claiming to have been present at the conference held at the presidency, and naturally imparted her information to her husband. Aguinaldo was still in town, we were told. We had seen his private carriage, drawn by four handsome black horses, pass us on the road, but the President was not inside, only two women with a child, his wife, mother, and son, the Spaniards informed us.

We had the honor of sleeping in the same stable with those four black horses that same night, as we were considered more secure there, but we were now in excellent spirits, as the Spaniards had informed us that several regiments of cavalry had landed at Dagupan, thus cutting off the Insurgents' retreat to the northern provinces. This seemed so reasonable that we implicitly believed it, especially as we had read a month before in *La Independencia* that American war-ships threatened that town.

When morning dawned, almost the first sound to reach our ears was the cannonading to the southward. After a good breakfast we were lined up in the plaza to continue our march for San Isidro, which we now learned was to be our destination for the present, at least, the new capital having been established there. The Spaniards able to walk were now reduced to thirty, the rest having fallen by the wayside and then disappeared. To our surprise we were allowed to depart in peace. No mob accompanied us for miles out of town, stoning us, as had been done in the other places.

As we came out on the broad rice-fields again we observed far to the southward a dense column of smoke rising, too voluminous for one house, which the Spaniards declared to be Quingua in flames, and a few of them, bolder than the rest, cheered a "Viva! viva los Americanos!"

Throughout the entire day it was tramp, tramp, tramp! over roads smothering us with dust. Since leaving Malolos we had evidently followed a semicircular course, for during the whole march we had on our left a solitary sugar-loaf mountain, always about the same distance off, and always "on our port beam," to use a nautical phrase. Since then I have learned its name to be Arryat, but we continued to call it the Lone Mountain.

Toward evening we reached the outskirts of San Isidro, where a delegation of several thousand natives turned out to meet us. Our reception here was the most furious we had ever been subjected to — several of us were even slightly wounded by bolos, and, had the guards not been re-enforced by the local police, I do sincerely believe our travels and adventures in the Philippines would have come to an end then and there. We were at length dragged in through the gates of an extensive brick building, and as they closed behind us, leaving the furious rabble beating on them outside, we experienced a great relief.

Experiences like the foregoing are too apt to generate prejudices even in an otherwise well-balanced and unbiassed mind, and I believe that on this particular evening we would have given our consent to any proposition for the extermination of the whole Filipino people, regardless of age, sex, or tribe!

The guards themselves were not inclined to be gentle, but threw us into a cell with small ceremony. Our new quarters were capacious, we had sufficient food and money to keep us from starvation for a week, and, above all, our troops were advancing up through the country, with the retreat of the Insurgents cut off at Dagupan. No wonder we were in high spirits. A good supper of one of Ramon Rey's chickens, rice, bananas, and tea, cooked outside the cell, added to our satisfactory state of mind. Why should we be saving with our provisions? In two weeks we should be free, for were not the advancing Americans driving back our captors until they would be only too glad to accept an unconditional surrender? So sure were we of all this and our speedy prospective liberation, that in our exuberant state of mind we indulged in a song, the words of which seemed so appropriate to our condition, and were probably never sung with more feeling and true appreciation of their encouraging spirit than on this particular night under the old tile roof of the San Isidro Prison. It was "In the prison cell I sit," with the chorus:

"Tramp, tramp, tramp, the boys are marching!
Cheer up, comrades, they will come.
And beneath the starry flag we shall breathe the air again
Of the freedom in our own beloved home!"

How the chorus of this inspiring war-song was repeated over and over again in this old Spanish prison, where in all probability words of freedom had never before found voice but in low whispers!

Chapter Eleven - San Isidro

FEELING as certain as we did of the Americans blocking any further retreat at Dagupan, we were not surprised at not being obliged to march next morning. We did not hear the guns that day, but this was easily accounted for by the Spaniards who reported that Aguinaldo and his staff had met the Americans at Quingua, arranging for a conference, which was granted. An armistice of fifteen days was declared, at the end of which time the Insurgent leaders were to give a decisive answer. All this the Spaniards told us, and we believed it.

What seemed most significant, however, was the sudden change in the conduct toward us of the prison officials and guards. Although the night before they had treated us with but little ceremony, they were now almost respectful. The "alcaide," or prison governor, paid us an early visit and anxiously inquired if we were comfortable, but we received his attentions somewhat haughtily — we now thought we could afford to.

San Isidro is not a small town, and was always the capital of Nueva Ecija, one of the largest provinces of Luzon; we were no longer in Bulacan, in which province Malolos, Santa Isabela, etc., are situated. From our only window, which overlooked the plaza, we observed that the streets were thronged with Spanish prisoners. Many of them came into the prison to visit us, making us presents of cigars and fruit, and even offering us money. The latter we did not feel justified in accepting, for they evidently were not aware of the gifts of money and food which had been made us by Ramon Rey and the Spanish officer in San Miguel. Most of the poor fellows had earned their few coppers by pounding rice, and were willing to share with us, whom they thought in a worse condition than themselves. The majority of them were quartered on the private houses in the town, some in the hospital, and about fifty in the prison with us, but in other cells. Counting all, they numbered at least seven hundred. After a few days, however, over one-half of them were marched out to neighboring towns, the burden of their support becoming too heavy for the municipality to bear.

As stated above, the prison at San Isidro was a large, rambling structure, built of brick, of but one story, with a capacity for holding about three hundred prisoners. In all, Spaniards, Filipinos, and Americans, we numbered about two hundred. Only the Spaniards were permitted the freedom of the streets; the natives were as closely confined as we. The cells were each capable of holding at least fifty prisoners with some comfort, excepting ours, which was the smallest. In the centre was a broad, sunny courtyard, in which we could walk a certain number of hours daily.

Our old companions from Malolos, Squint-Eye, Cigarettes, and all the rest of them, had arrived before us, having come by a shorter route, but, fortunately, we were not to be confined together again. In addition there were confined in a cell adjoining ours almost one hundred Macabebe prisoners.

These were treated more harshly than we were, and forced to live upon four motas apiece, daily. This tribe inhabits a small district in the province of Pampanga, on the shores of the bay. In spite of their limited numbers as compared with the Tagalogs, the latter had not dared to invade their territory, although open hostilities existed between them, the Macabebes having successfully repelled several attacks made on them. These one hundred prisoners with us had been taken in various fights, being held as prisoners of war. In appearance they differed but little from the Tagalogs, seeming to me to be even physically superior, of somewhat larger stature, and the majority of them not so dark complexioned, but at that time some lurking prejudice may have impaired my judgment. But few of them could speak the Tagalog dialect, their native tongue being so different that often Spanish was resorted to as a means of intercourse with the guards. I spoke to many of them later on, inquiring the cause of this racial feud between the two factions, and was told that it dated far back from the time of the rajahs, and would continue until doomsday, as my informant added with a snap of his teeth.

Our rations had now been decreased to four motas and about one pound of black rice a day each. This, as O'Brien termed it, was coming down to bedrock. But we appreciated the roomy dimensions of our cell, which, although much smaller than the room in the Santa Isabela convent, was, nevertheless, of generous dimensions, about ten feet wide by thirty long, a bamboo platform, upon which the six of us found ample space to sleep, running along one wall from end to end. The door to the courtyard at one end, and the window overlooking the plaza at the other, caused the air to ventilate our cell thoroughly.

It was fortunate for us that we had those two pesos, otherwise we would have suffered severely. When at length they gave out, we fortunately found another means of helping out our meagre rations by a few coppers: We would sing for alms! Starvation humbled our pride, and one day we began to sing "John Brown's Body" until quite a crowd had collected before our door. Then we took one of our mess tins and passed it around, with the result of bringing us in twelve motas. And while it remained a novelty, it kept us from enduring pangs of hunger. Arnold had a fine bass voice. Ruber's was a tenor, and the rest of us anything between. "John Brown's Body" was our favorite, as we all knew it and could roar out the chorus until the old brick walls trembled.

One day we were treated to a genuine surprise. We had just struck up the strains of "John Brown's Body" again, and were about to join in a mighty chorus, "Glory, Glory, Hallelujah!" but were struck dumb with astonishment, when from the adjoining cell, where the Macabebes were, that chorus rose up with a volume that could be likened only to a tremendous roar, one hundred voices strong. Again we joined in, and together with our neighbors, the Macabebes, we sent the notes of that old hymn rolling over all San Isidro, so that Aguinaldo could easily have heard it at his residence, the "convento."

So often had we sung that chorus, that the Macabebes, with their natural aptitude for catching the notes of a melody, had picked it up, and, with the exception of adopting words of their own, which made no practical difference, it might just as well have been one hundred Americans. Often they would sing with us after that — they always fell in with the chorus; and as often as they struck it up alone we would join the chorus.

We were now forced to reconcile ourselves to the presence of Arnold, for the time being at least, although several of us persisted in our determination never to exchange a word with him. He, for his part, tried to make himself as agreeable as possible, to bring about a reconciliation, and in this he partly succeeded with some. Besides having a splendid bass voice, he could entertain us by the hour with stories of his adventures before and after leaving the ministry. He had been through Hamlin College in Minnesota, and his anecdotes from there were highly amusing. Occasionally he would get on his feet and commence a sermon on the most sacred subject, and for, say, half an hour, would speak with such an appearance of genuine feeling and sincerity, that a stranger would have been affected to tears; when suddenly he would finish up with a hoarse laughter and a string of vile oaths! To a man with his education, however, the situation must have been trying; our contempt for his hypocrisy could not always successfully be concealed. O'Brien, his own countryman, remarked one day in his presence: "I don't like the idea of Arnold cooking for us: a man of his character would not hesitate to poison us." But Arnold had trained himself to listen to similar remarks in silence, although many times I saw his eyes flash and his teeth gnash.

On several occasions we had seen Arnold go into the alcaide's quarters, a small dwelling inside the courtyard, and chat on the veranda with that official, but the object of these secret discourses we never learned, we could only guess. One afternoon the alcaide's clerk came to the door and called for the "Ingles." O'Brien, being an Englishman, stepped forward, but the fellow said, "No, not you, hombre, I want Señor David, the learned man that speaks the good English." Arnold rose from the bed and followed the messenger out, nor did he return until late in the evening. Although we asked no questions, he volunteered the information that the "presidente provincial," or Governor of Nueva Ecija, who resided in the convent, had sent for him, wishing him to become his teacher in English. Every morning he was to go there, and only return to the prison before the gates were closed, to spend the night with us. This continued for several days, during which period we only saw Arnold at nights. One evening the gates closed and Mr. Arnold had not arrived, and for almost a week we saw nothing more of him. A young officer, who visited us about this time, told us that Señor David was "mucho bueno," and had become a "Capitan Filipino." This I would not believe. Arnold was not the man to fight for a losing cause, nor for any cause, for that matter, but it showed the way the wind blew.

Once, while several of us were contemplating the gambols and rompings of the very youngest of the inhabitants of the town in the plaza before our window, who should suddenly appear on the scene but Mr. Arnold, attired in a spotless white suit, patent-leather shoes, a new hat, and arm in arm with a gaudily dressed Filipino officer. As they came opposite the window Arnold turned, and, bringing two fingers up to his forehead, made us a sweeping French bow, and then walked on. Some of us took that bow in good earnest as a gentleman's salute, others again as a token of derision, but I wondered how he wished us to interpret it.

The daily routine of our existence became tedious; as yet we had noticed no indication of a peaceful settlement. The soldiers still drilled in the plaza, and once a band passed at the head of a column of recruits marching to the inspiring strains of the "Marseillaise." Our hopes were centred on those regiments at Dagupan, and in case Aguinaldo should decide to hold out after the 15th, the end of the armistice, we had no doubt but what the two forces, the one to the north and the other to the south, would come together on the Insurgents and crush them as a nut-cracker does a nut, freeing the imprisoned kernel inside. Of course, we considered ourselves the kernel. But some nuts are very hard, too round, and roll.

Our principal pastime was the study of Spanish. O'Brien and I amused ourselves by competing with one another, to see who could learn a given number of words by heart in the shortest time. We could also sit in the deep window-sill and watch the passers-by, but for the fact that they likewise wished to watch us and did not hesitate to sit on the sill outside of the bars to do so. We soon learned that we need not tolerate this, and, procuring long sticks from the bed platform, poked them off. As the ground on the outside was over five feet below the window-sill, and only about three on the inside, we had the best of it, and enjoyed their rage at their own impotence. As we, though unofficially, were backed up by the alcaide, their efforts at revenge failed, and every time a hand grasped the bars from the outside it received a rap. On several occasions they tried to overcome us by throwing stones, but here the guards interfered.

Gradually the rabble learned to leave our window alone, something we could never have accomplished in Malolos. The alcaide and several of his officials were far-sighted.

Small groups of Spanish prisoners often came straggling into town from the southward, passing our window on their way to the presidency. One afternoon I sat leaning my forehead against the bars, watching some twenty or thirty of these poor fellows, dusty, ragged, and barefooted, marching into town, when I noticed one of them stare at me and then slowly approach the window. I paid but little attention to this man's singular behavior, until he stood below the window, calling me by name. I was startled: the voice was familiar but the features strange. He called again and reached up his hand. Then I recognized him, more by his voice than by his features.

Two years before, when the name of the Philippine Islands was hardly as familiar to the average American as that of a remote province of China, the writer formed one of the ship's company of a steamer trading in Mediterranean waters. On this trip we spent a week in the Spanish port of Cartagena, and while here two Spaniards were added to the number of the crew, one an old salt who had sailed the briny deep for many a year, the other a boy of about sixteen, not long from home. The latter, whose name was Antonio, was he who now stood below the window. While on board the ship he learned English fairly well, that being his ambition, and on account of his youth and good-nature we all liked him. At the end of three months he left us to join the Spanish navy, and since then I had not seen him until now. I had known him as a sprightly and robust youngster, able to fly up the ratlines in the twinkling of an eye, or to climb up stays hand over fist in a jiffy. There he stood, a sallow-complexioned, hollow-eyed weakling, panting from the exertion of carrying a blanket-roll, his features so thin that the lips were drawn away from the protruding teeth. He still wore an old ragged, blue navy suit, and on the band of his cap the name of his vessel, the Isla de Cuba, in faded yellow letters. I could not repress an exclamation of surprise mingled with pity, whereat he gave expression to a weak and mirthless smile. "One year, almost," he said, "since your countrymen delivered me into the hands of these people. Why did they do that? Could they not have taken us to Manila? I might now have been in Spain once more to greet my old mother, had they not turned us over to these barbarians that neither feed nor clothe us!"

"Never mind, Antonio!" I replied, "in another month we shall all be in Manila." He laughed, and a dry and sarcastic laugh it was,

"What, do you believe these foolish stories? Those same words I heard a year ago, and, like you, believed them. One month more, they told us, only one month more, not more, and never less."

I tried hard to argue poor Antonio out of his pessimistic views, but I lacked conviction myself. Then we spoke of former days, when, as shipmates, we sailed over the blue waters of the Mediterranean together, unconscious in the buoyancy of our youthful spirits that a dark cloud was rising on the horizon of our near futures, to prove cruelly fatal to him, poor fellow. We were still recalling to one another episodes of our past acquaintanceship, experiences that we had had in common, when the sentry at the gate saw him and drove him away, striking his thin, wasted body with the butt of his gun; "Booh — sigue — diablo!" each word accompanied by a blow causing a sickening thud!

I saw him waving his hand at me as long as he remained in sight, but soon he passed beyond the limited range of my vision, and I never saw him again. Long afterward I made inquiries for him in Manila, but no one seemed to know what had become of him, until one day on the Escolta I noticed a Spaniard in navy uniform, on his cap-band, in large yellow letters, the name Isla de Cuba.

Stopping and addressing the stranger, I asked him if he knew Antonio Rodriguez. He knew him well. Since leaving Spain they had been companions until the surrender of the naval garrison in Subig Bay, when the Americans intrusted them to the Insurgents as prisoners of war. They had been companions as prisoners for eighteen months, until hunger and sickness had so reduced them that their companions had carried them both together to one of those charnel-houses called hospitals. There this man saw Antonio close his eyes forever. Three days later the Americans captured the town and he himself was sent to Manila, where proper nourishment, good nursing, and intelligent physicians effected his recovery.

My impression had all along been that the Spanish prisoners consisted entirely of soldiers, marines, and a few sailors, but one afternoon a party of about two dozen "padres" appeared in the courtyard of the prison. This somewhat surprised me, for so revolting were the stories I had heard of these Spanish friars, especially of their cruelty and persecutions, that I had naturally supposed them to have shared the fate of the three in Santa Isabela, but here were some twenty-four or five, and as I subsequently learned, there were at least five hundred in captivity.

Not only do the Tagalogs hate the friars, but all the natives of Luzon, Ilocanos, Macabebes, Mestizos, and even the Spanish soldiers regard them as human birds of prey, and the stories I have heard of their fiendish cruelty and cunning trickery would fill volumes and make a fitting parallel to the Spanish inquisition. From nobody, not even the Spanish officers, have I heard a word in their defence, and the native clergy unite in calling them oily hypocrites and tyrants. There were, of course, exceptions, for once I heard of a good friar who lived in a small provincial town, and as "cura" ruled his flock with sympathy and love, but then he died.

They were mostly of the Franciscan, Recollet, Augustin, and Jesuit orders, and, strange to say, the Filipinos are not so averse to the latter as to the rest. The Jesuits have founded schools and done less harm, but the Recollets seem to be the most hated. I have had men show me crippled limbs caused by the friars by torture inflicted in underground chambers, in order to force their victims to reveal the hiding-place of Insurgent refugees. Another showed me scars on the soles of his feet where they had tortured him by placing burning candles to the bare flesh. I have myself entered secret chambers under their convents and seen hideous instruments of torture. [1] I have spoken to men returning from years of exile in Fernando Po to find parents and relatives dead, from whose embraces they had been torn for engendering the enmity of the village cura. How many hundreds fared even worse than these for daring to complain of the injustice and tyranny of the oppressive "frailes," or for daring to say that taking what is not your own is a crime, in falling on the Luneta in Manila! Read the story of Rizal; his is but the fate of hundreds of others, less gifted, less illustrious, perhaps, but none the less martyrs!

Some of the most prominent of the Filipinos have assured me that the insurrection of 1896 and 1897 was but the upheaval of a slumbering volcano, the bursting out of a smouldering fire, which for years had been fed and fanned by continual oppression and outrages, until at length the flames leaped up to spread revolution, bloodshed, and greater misery throughout the land.

Had Spain been willing to abolish the monasterial corporations as a political institution, and left only the Catholic clergy, the Filipinos would not only have remained faithful to Spain, but would have fought and died side by side with the Spanish soldiers under the red and yellow banner, defending their country against the American invasion. The laws of Spain were, many of them, wise and just, but when an archbishop or even a bishop could interpret them to suit his own purposes, of what use were they?

When Aguinaldo, in 1897, at the Treaty or Agreement of Biacnabato accepted 400,000 pesetas to lay down his sword and declare the insurrection at an end, he did not receive this money, nor was it given to him as a personal bribe, as many of our papers and magazines have declared, but intrusted to his care as a fund with which to educate the Filipino rising generation abroad in foreign universities.

The stipulations of this treaty were, that the religious corporations be abolished, 800,000 pesetas be given as an educational fund, as stated above, and representation be granted in the Cortes with internal self-government.

All this was agreed to by Governor-General Primo de Rivera, in the name of the Spanish Government. Half the sum agreed upon was actually paid, and Aguinaldo and seventeen of the principal leaders given passage to Hong-Kong, but as soon as the Insurgents had disbanded as an armed body, the rest of the agreement was ignored; the other 400,000 pesetas were never paid, the friars remained undisturbed, and new executions took place on the Luneta. When it became known that Aguinaldo and his companions were entering into negotiations with the Americans, the Colonial Government at once made the most profuse promises of reforms to come, but it was then too late. The 400,000 pesetas already received remained in a Hong Kong bank and was afterward used to purchase arms and ammunition, but never have I heard any Filipino accuse Aguinaldo of misappropriating one cent of that money. Although the people do not reverence him as a superior being, nor regard him as a demigod, as many of our newspaper correspondents have asserted, Capitan Emilio is beloved by his people rather for his well-known patriotism and generous character than his mental abilities. Many Filipinos, even Tagalogs, admit that Luna was the abler man, but he, again, lost many friends by his harshness and strict discipline, and, as will afterward appear, this eventually cost him his life.

Had Rizal lived, there is not the least doubt but what he would have been Chief Executive instead of Aguinaldo, as he, according to my numerous informants, combined the gentle and mild disposition of Capitan Emilio with the learning and mental abilities of Antonio Luna. But I have been wandering from my narrative, and, meanwhile, left those poor, ragged, foot-sore friars standing under a burning sun in the prison courtyard.

The typical monk, as we generally see him depicted, is in the majority of cases of short but broad figure, with a shaven head, a double chin, and generous paunch, tied about the middle with an old rope; but, if these particular "padres" had ever been encumbered with too much surplus flesh, they had long since gotten rid of it. Shaven heads the majority had, and some still wore old blue gowns with capacious cowls attached to the nape, but many had been obliged to cover their nakedness with the cast-off uniforms of the cazadores. Several were smooth-faced boys still in their teens, but the others had allowed their beards to sweep their breast, until they resembled what we out West call a "mountain pard." Some of them, in fact, did remind me of returned mining prospectors out of luck.

On this same evening of their arrival we happened to give one of our "John Brown's Body" concerts, and the friars gathered around the door to listen. During one of the intervals, O'Brien, who wished to do the polite thing, as he termed it, stepped to the door with the invitation: "Come inside, hombres, come inside; sit down on the bed and be comfortable." "Hombre" is only used when addressing inferiors or intimate friends, but O'Brien's knowledge of Spanish, like that of the rest of us, did not reach into details, and he was quite unaware of not having spoken with due courtesy. The friars drew themselves up, while one of them retorted impressively: "Nosotros somos padres!" (We are padres!) For the moment O'Brien was taken aback. For a few seconds he seemed to reflect, then he replied in his best Spanish: "Ah, yes, yes, we know that — we understand — but no importance — we don't mind that — come in anyhow — you're welcome all the same!" But the padres went away and left our English friend wondering for some time how he had offended them. They departed again next morning, but we were destined to meet again.

As the 15th drew near we became anxious, for, still having full faith in the existence of an armistice, we felt that the decision of the Insurgent leaders concerned us deeply.

Of late, however, we had received no definite information upon which to build any further hopes. We heard no more of the forces to the southward, much less of those reported to the northward. Our own families in distant America could probably have given us a great deal of information on the situation right about ourselves, of which we were practically ignorant. News was the much desired premium. "No hay noticias?" we hurled at every passing Spaniard, the answer generally being a sad shake of the head. But on the 15th the oppressive gloom hovering over us was pierced by a tiny ray of light from the outside world.

It was late in the afternoon on that date, most of us lying on the bed kicking our heels in the air, discussing the advisability of investing a cent in a new cooking pot to replace the old one which had been cracked by a disastrous fall, when suddenly O'Brien, who had been sitting in the window, gave a shout. We all rushed up beside him and glanced down the street. A squad of soldiers came marching up with fixed bayonets, with a tall, fair-haired man in their midst. But what caused our hearts to leap was the fact that he wore an American soldier's uniform. "Hurrah!" we yelled, as we followed each other in a wild rush for the courtyard. "News at last!"

[1] I have seen and visited a secret underground passageway from the Bishop's palace, in Vigan, to a neighboring nunnery, but have learned that this has since been filled in by the Americans. These subterranean passageways were said to exist in other places!

Chapter Twelve - News from Outside

So wild had our rush been into the yard that the guard stationed at the door failed to check us, this not being the hour for walking, but the onlymanner in which he could have done so successfully would have been with cold steel or bullets, and to these means he did not resort. The truth is, he was hardly less excited than we. But soon we were forced back into the cell, where we stood in the doorway anxiously watching for the new prisoner. At length he was ushered in, and taken up on the veranda of the alcaide's quarters, where he seemed to be subjected to some sort of an examination. Tall, bearded, and fair-haired, he was a typical Anglo-Saxon, but it was the brown uniform that appealed to us. At length he descended the steps, and was conducted across the yard to us. To say that we extended the new arrival a hearty reception is expressing it a trifle mildly. We all endeavored to shake hands with him at once, failing in which we bodily seized and dragged him into the cell and sat him down upon the bed. Our enthusiasm evidently alarmed the stranger somewhat; probably he feared the rigor of prison life had overpowered our minds; so, to give him time to recover himself, we drew back and stood about him in a semicircle. Then commenced a rapid-fire volley of questions, but first of all we inquired, was it known in the American lines that we existed? was it known who we were? and could our families possibly have been informed that we were among the living?

"Yes," he answered, "we saw your names on the wall of the Malolos prison." We all gave a sigh of relief. Thank God those names had been written!

"But how about the armistice?" we again queried. "That ends to-day, doesn't it?"

"Armistice? What armistice?"

"The armistice that commenced on the first day of the month, of course, and ends to-day. We do know a little of the outside world, even if we don't keep the morning papers."

"I haven't heard of any armistice. Wouldn't hardly have captured me during an armistice — would they? Been some pretty heavy fighting going on since the first of this month."

"What, no armistice? Holy smoke, what a disappointment! But why don't the troops at Dagupan march down and close in on us?"

"Troops at Dagupan? No troops there. A small gun-boat cruises about in the Lingayen Gulf, but no troops have disembarked."

This was too much for us. We were struck dumb and stood stupidly staring at one another, our fondest hopes dashed to the ground and crushed. Again we ventured:

"But why in the name of Jupiter don't they advance? Where is the army? For God's sake, tell us quickly, have they met with any reverses? Don't keep us in suspense!"

"Reverses! The Filipinos beat us? No! the army is now at Calumpit resting after that terrible advance on Malolos. I tell you, we came a ripping and a tearing up that railroad track on the double quick, and covered that whole distance in six days. We just kept the amigos on the run the whole time, and they ran so fast that we didn't see but very few of them after leaving Caloocan, until we got to Malolos, and there we arrived just in time to see a train pulling out of the station. But we couldn't catch it with the battery guns, and it got away safely. With the exception of a few Chinamen the town was deserted and partly burnt. To get into our good graces the Chinos showed us where three big Krupp guns were buried, and the prison where you had been confined and where your names were still plainly written on the wall. After resting a few days we marched on to Calumpit, or to the river at least, for we couldn't cross it, as the railroad bridge was partly destroyed. The boys were crazy to go on, but we received orders to rest. They said we needed it. So we lay down and watched the insurgents build trenches on the other side of the river, as we did at Caloocan for nearly two months, but when those trenches are finished and can't be made any stronger, the boys will just sweep right on and take them too. There's no glory taking trenches unless they're finished, and lots of bloodshed, and dead Filipinos lying about."

The pleasure we felt in meeting Albert Bishop, as our new fellow-prisoner called himself, with news from the American lines but four days old, could hardly offset the bitterness of having our dearest hopes so entirely crushed! No armistice! No conference! No troops at Dagupan! Where could such stories originate? The Spaniards had given them as affirmed facts. Life seemed to us just then a hollow mockery!

Nevertheless, we continued pumping our new companion, and, nothing loath, he sat down on the bed, his back against the wall, and talked until way into the night. His story was to us intensely interesting. As nearly as possible I give it in his own words:

"Shortly after the capture of Malolos, Battery K of the Third Artillery, of which I am a member, was ordered out to hold a town close to Malolos, and called Paombong. This place is situated on the south bank of a small river, but on the opposite side stands a stone church.

"On the night of the 11th I was on outpost duty. Usually the outposts were stationed on our side of the river, along the bank, but on this particular night we were sent over to occupy the church. As I was not to go on post until four in the morning, together with the rest of my relief, I lay down to sleep inside the church. In all we numbered fifteen, with a sergeant in command.

"I had been soundly sleeping when a great uproar woke me up. Our light had been extinguished, my companions were stumbling about in the darkness trying to find the door, and above all this confusion came the rattling of regular volleys being fired outside, followed by the crashing and splintering of the shell windows about us. Jumping up I reached for my Krag, having stood it in a window-sill just above me, but it was gone. Believing that it might have fallen to the floor I groped about in the darkness hoping to find it, but soon realized that somebody had taken it. Giving up all hope of recovering my gun, I started to follow my companions, but, on coming outside, found that the Insurgents had cut me off from the river and driven the outposts back to the main camp. In the darkness I became completely lost, for I heard the Remingtons going off on all sides of me, so I lay down in a ditch, hoping the boys would drive the Insurgents back before daylight. I must have been lying in the mud there for several hours, when the horizon in the East began to lighten, and still the Filipinos were between me and the camp. Hoping that the boys were but waiting for daylight to drive them back, I waited until the sun rose over the distant mountains, but, with the exception of an occasional shot, all remained quiet. Becoming at length impatient, I determined to make an effort to crawl through the enemy's lines. Raising my head above the sides of the ditch, I saw the Insurgent soldiers stretched out in skirmish order along the bank. In one place there seemed to be quite a break, and toward this I began to crawl in the rice-stubble on my hands and knees. Suddenly I heard a shout behind me, and, turning, found I had been discovered by three bolomen, who came rushing toward me with uplifted weapons. Jumping up I made a dash for the river, but the soldiers, hearing the cries of the bolomen, rushed in between and opened fire on me. A young officer commanded me to halt, which I then did, when the firing ceased. The captain then detailed a corporal and three men to take charge of me, and I was conducted to the rear.

"In the afternoon I was brought to Calumpit, part of which, on the north side of the river, is still in the hands of the Insurgents. I was taken into the convent, and well received by a number of high officials, some of whom addressed me in English. Later on I was invited to seat myself at the table with them, to a supper such as I had never eaten since leaving the States. At the head of the table sat a dark little Filipino dressed in black civilian clothes — this was Aguinaldo. During the supper the President, in half Spanish and half-broken English, asked me all sorts of questions regarding the next election, and what chances I thought Bryan had for the Presidential chair of the great United States. He seemed to know as much of American politics as I did. With his own hands he poured me out a glass of cool beer.

"That night I slept in a better bed than I had seen since coming to the island. My opinion of the Insurgents had undergone a wonderful change.

"The following morning I saw Aguinaldo again, who gave me a Mexican peso to remember him by. He told me that I would be taken to San Isidro, where I would meet six of my countrymen.

"From Calumpit to San Fernando I was taken in the train, and from there to here I came on foot by easy stages, well treated on the whole route."

When Bishop had concluded his story, we told him that he had better prepare himself for a change, as beer did not form any part of our diet, although quite willing to do the pouring out ourselves, nor were we on calling terms with Don Emilio or his staff.

For two days we left poor Bishop but little peace with our questions, but patiently and with great good nature he answered them all to the best of his ability. Arnold also had his curiosity aroused and paid us a visit, bringing with him a copy of *La Independencia*, containing an account of Bishop's arrival, as follows:

"We have just had an interview with the newly arrived prisoner who was captured by our army at Paombong, which, although short, was none the less interesting. He informs us that the reports circulated among us of the great cruelties and tortures inflicted by the Americans on the Filipino prisoners have no foundation and are entirely false. On the contrary, they are well treated, he says. Undoubtedly such reports are likewise circulated among the Americans about us. The prisoner gives his name as Alberto O'Bishop; he is large, well built, and has whiskers like a horse! His knowledge of Spanish could be improved."

Alberto O'Bishop, the man with whiskers like a horse! That joke clung to him ever afterward, and nobody enjoyed it more than he did himself. Although he was not more than thirty, his beard reached almost to his belt, and this no doubt greatly amused the smooth-faced Filipinos. However, it is highly within the limits of probability that the editor of *La Independencia* meant a goat instead of a horse.

In a few days we had once more settled down into the usual tedious stagnancy. We should have liked one prisoner to arrive every day, a sort of a human newspaper to keep us up with passing events. Probably it would not have been as agreeable to those captured as to ourselves.

Once we heard our guards state that a large American cruiser had been captured, and the crew, numbering over three hundred, taken prisoners. Such wild rumors we had heard often before, and they had ceased to amuse us. Next day, however, the rumor took more definite form, though greatly modified. A small gunboat had been captured on the Pacific (Eastern) coast of the island and fifty prisoners taken. This was supposed to be by telegram. Finally on the 21st we were told that the prisoners would arrive within twenty-four hours, now reduced to one officer and thirty men. We began now to grow interested.

By the afternoon of the succeeding day we had forgotten all about these vague prisoners, when the shouts of a crowd of people outside on the plaza aroused our curiosity and brought us all to the window. Both sides of the street, as far as we could see, were black with people, the middle being kept clear by soldiers and police. Great excitement seemed to prevail. Finally from the distance the strains of a brass band playing the "Marseillaise" reached us, and gradually grew more distinct.

"Viva! viva!" shouted hundreds of voices. "They are coming, they are coming!" At length a squad of soldiers with fixed bayonets and military step marched into view. Then, about twenty yards behind, followed the band, the members of which were ragged and barefooted, but almost bursting with pent-up melody. The people cheered and screamed, and those that had hats tossed them in the air. Next came a squad of police, and after them, and followed by a second squad of police, seven limping, dirty, ragged, half-dead-looking creatures, who looked as if they at some time might have been Americans.

These were the long-expected prisoners, seven of them, with half a company of armed men to guard them. At the gate they were formally turned over to the alcaide, and marched into the yard where we already stood to receive them. The hand-shaking and jumbling of questions that followed can hardly be adequately described. The new-comers were taken into the cell where they at once dropped down on the bed from sheer fatigue, having marched all that day and the night before. They should have numbered eight in all, but their officer had remained with the Governor in the presidency. Only two had shoes, the rest were barefooted and their feet in a bleeding condition. The clothes they wore, or rather what was left of them, told us they were navy blue-jackets, so we surmised them to be the crew of the captured cruiser.

Chapter Thirteen - Off for The North

No doubt the reader has already guessed the identity of these new arrivals. Lieutenant Gillmore and his party need no introduction. These seven wayworn sufferers were indeed the survivors of that unfortunate affair at Baler, the particulars of which have repeatedly been given to the public. We did not see the lieutenant himself until next morning, when he appeared on the alcaide's veranda. He appeared to be a rather heavy-set man of middle age, slightly under medium height. He still wore his dark blue undress uniform coat and pants, but instead of a cap a large broad-brimmed straw hat edged with red tape. He did not come down to see us that day, but several of our party were called up to converse with him, telling him our past experience.

Little by little they told us their terrible story, how, fifteen in number, they had left the Yorktown in a boat to reconnoitre at the mouth of Baler River, how they had gone just a little too far and fallen into an ambush, seven of the fifteen to drop before the fire of an invisible enemy.

With the exception of T. Ellsworth, coxswain of the captured boat; W. Walton, chief quartermaster of the Yorktown, and P. Vaudoit, sailmaker's mate, three old sailors of many years' experience, the rest were but boys on their first cruise.

Besides L. Edwards, landsman, a native of Indiana, there were A. Peterson and T. Anderson, the former a Californian, the latter from Buffalo, N. Y., both apprentices, seventeen and nineteen respectively, and S. Brisolese, ordinary seaman, a San Franciscan of eighteen years.

On account of the great increase in our numbers the cell had become too small, so the alcaide had us removed to one adjoining, twice the size, where we were obliged to use the bare floor as a couch. The only furniture contained in our new lodgings was two pairs of stocks. Gillmore was quartered in the alcaide's rooms, where he ate and slept.

The succeeding day brought us the agreeable surprise of an augmentation of our daily rations from five to ten cents, or eight motas each. Lieutenant Gillmore was given one peseta, double that of ours.

This enabled us to live in comparative affluence. Each gave six motas toward the common mess fund, retaining two motas for private expenses or desserts, such as cigars, bananas, mangoes, or pancakes made of fermented corn and rice flour mixed. The latter deserves mention as a universal dish among the Filipinos, and is called "bebinka."

Every morning early, the bebinka bakers, generally women, may be seen squatting on their heels in the village plaza, baking "bebinka" in a small pan over a charcoal fire. Instead of greasing the pan, they cover the bottom with a piece of banana leaf, which prevents the dough from adhering. Then another leaf is placed on top and covered by the bottom of another pan in which is another charcoal fire, on Dutch-oven principle.

Even the high-class natives, if no white friends are present, will squat down beside the baker and eat a few of her bebinkas, covered with shredded cocoanut. The universal price of them, all over Luzon, is one mota, but I have seldom seen them sold in Manila.

A small fruit-store or canteen was kept by an old woman inside the prison yard, just outside our door, and here the extra two motas were generally spent. This woman made delicious soups of catfish, pigs' blood, and snails, but it was a tremendously expensive dish. One of our mess tins full cost four motas. Thinking it would be more advantageous to buy wholesale, we clubbed together once and bought thirteen motas' worth. The result was only two platefuls. Experience soon taught us that retail was the cheapest method, so when next we clubbed together we made thirteen separate trips to the store, purchasing one mota's worth each time. This brought us four platefuls, or a gain of one hundred per cent, over the wholesale method. Domestic economy demanded close study and attention in those days.

To pass away time I now commenced to write up a sort of account or record of events of my past experience, in diary form, spending a mota each day for paper. I remember I had finished it up to date, when, dissatisfied with a certain portion of it, I tore out several leaves in order to rewrite them. These leaves contained an account of the retreat from Malolos, commencing with the words: "Men, women, and children are fleeing before the advancing

Americans!" Having rewritten them, I crumpled up the old pages and threw them under the wooden floor of our cell. Those poor, soiled, and torn pages were the only lines of my diary ever to reach American eyes. A month later they were found by some of the Minnesota Volunteers, and in due time appeared in the American papers, but, being unsigned, the writer was, of course, unknown. Had I known how soon that paper would fall into the hands of friends, what would I not have written on it? To think that we all could have sent word home by simply throwing messages down into that hole, when they would have reached their destination as safely as Uncle Sam's mails could have taken them — what a chance missed! Still, they might have fallen under the strict censorship of General Otis.

That reminds me of a letter that I really did write in the hope it would go through. Our old friend and benefactor, Señor Ramon Rey, appeared one day among us. Being a civilian, he received no rations, but the alcaide permitted him to shelter himself under the prison roof with his countrymen. Poor old Ramon, now a prisoner, in former times once had been governor or alcaide of this same prison. I went personally over to thank the old man for his former kindness, and he received me with an effusiveness truly Spanish, which I believe in this case was sincere. He was so sick that he could hardly walk. Supporting himself by grasping my arm, and a cane in the other hand, he hobbled out into a small outhouse, where, he said, he wished to speak a few words with me. Imagine my surprise when the old gentleman suddenly dropped the cane, and, loosening his hold on my arm, straightened up fully six inches and went through the steps of a Spanish fandango. In a moment he explained all. "I am feigning sickness," he went on, "so that when the Americans advance I shall be left behind. If you wish to send a few lines through, intrust them to me, and I will see that they are delivered."

Returning to the cell I wrote a short note addressed to the Commander of the American forces in the Philippines, giving a list of our names, our treatment, and an appeal for an effort to exchange us, as the alcaide intimated that the Insurgent leaders certainly would give their consent. Then going up on the veranda I informed Lieutenant Gillmore of this opportunity. Coming down into our cell to escape observation, he wrote a list of our names, adding that he was well, addressing his letter to his brother-in-law, Major Price, in Manila. Both these letters I gave to Ramon Rey.

The old Spaniard's clever trick was successful. He was subsequently left behind, when upon the approach of the Americans we had to set out on our long and weary march to the north. He delivered the letters into the hands of an American officer, who in his turn gave them to General Lawton. Both were forwarded to General Otis, who did not make mine public. Copies of both letters, however, had been taken and sent by a newspaper correspondent to the papers he represented, and a month later were published in a number of American dailies. Ramon Rey was rewarded for his kindness to us, being made official guide and interpreter, first to General Lawton and afterward to General Young in the northern campaign.

One day fifty Negritos were added to the constantly growing number of native prisoners. These Negritos are a race of small negroes that inhabit the wild mountain regions of some parts of Luzon. They are supposed to be the remnants of the aborigines that were conquered by the Malays and driven from the lowlands into the mountains.

These new arrivals had been persuaded to join the Insurgent army as a company armed with spears and arrows. They had evidently not damaged the United States army to the same extent that they had suffered themselves, for, discouraged at shooting arrows at people they couldn't hurt, and not being able to ward off those big four-inch shells with their shields made of carabao hide, they simply told Aguinaldo that the Tagalogs might continue the war if so inclined, but fighting people that couldn't even be seen was not to their liking, so they requested the Honorable President to accept their resignation. But the Honorable President didn't see it in that light: if they wouldn't fight, he would send them to the calaboose, which he did.

I had, never seen a Negrito before, so was much interested. They were not well built and almost dwarfish in stature. Their skins were coal black and their hair crisp and kinky like that of an African negro, but their heads were better formed, I think, not being so egg-shaped. They are practically primitive savages, their only approach to clothing being a cloth round their loins. Their teeth they file to sharp points.

We made the acquaintance of their chief, whom we distinguished as such by two corporal's stripes being tied round his bare arm and a dilapidated high stovepipe hat tilted on one side of his woolly head. He paid us an official visit accompanied by his two lieutenants or sub-chiefs, evidently considering us the representatives of the great American nation. As plenipotentiary of the great Negrito tribe he informed us that his people would receive the American Government with satisfaction, and wished only the most friendly relations to exist between them. All this he told us by signs, our conversation being somewhat hampered by the fact that the chief spoke no Spanish and very little Tagalog, and we, speaking but poor Spanish and no Tagalog, didn't even know how to laugh in his native dialect.

This, of course, prevented us from going into any deep political discussions, such as the representatives of two such mighty people otherwise would have done; but the best of feelings prevailed, peace was declared once more between the United States and the Negritos of Luzon. We shook hands on that, and the swarthy diplomat took his leave with one of our ten-for-a-cent cigars between his teeth.

On May 3d the long-dreaded orders came; we were to march! The Americans were misbehaving themselves again at the front, and we were obliged to move on. But before leaving, knowing the good that had resulted from doing so in Malolos, Huber once more wrote our names on the wall, now fourteen in number, and there they remained to be seen by the advancing Americans.

Early in the morning we each received four days' rations, and together with the Spaniards were lined up and marched out into the street, the first time we had passed through the prison gates since our arrival. Evidently they had received an earlier warning than at Malolos, for the confusion there prevalent was not visible here. But the inhabitants were, nevertheless, making preparations to leave.

Guarded by Aguinaldo's own body-guards, we were by them escorted as far as the river (Rio Grande), a short distance from the town where a squad of twenty regulars took charge of us and ferried us across. Gillmore went ahead in a carromata with a Filipino captain. Then, after jumping ashore on the other bank, we started forward at the old familiar command, "sigue," on our march, not knowing for how long or where to, only realizing that our backs were turned toward friends and liberty, and our faces toward an unknown region and captivity!

Chapter Fourteen - On the March

IT was ten o'clock in the morning when the church tower of San Isidro disappeared from our view behind the fluffy tops of the bamboo jungles, and, excepting an hour's rest at noon in a small town called Lopez on the map, we tramped the muddy roads all day.

The rainy season had now set in, transforming the fields into swamps and lakes. In places large lagoons stretched across the road, through which we were obliged to wade, the water sometimes up to our shoulders. All but the officer who had us in charge, and Lieutenant Gillmore (they being mounted on native ponies), were on foot, even the guards who passed through the same hardships side by side with us, having no advantage over the prisoners — all day, tramp, tramp, through rain and slush. We crossed through marshy jungles darkened by the thick, tropical foliage overhead, the inky pools through which we waded suggesting alligators too vividly to be pleasant. From the limbs overhead long creepers hung down which seemed at times to change into writhing pythons ready to drop on us. Above the pattering of the rain on the leaves overhead we heard the shrill cries of monkeys, seeming to jeer at us. Boats would decidedly have been more suitable for these parts than our mode of travelling.

Night overtook us in the jungle, and we were obliged to seek shelter under the old nipa roof of an unfinished hut. Besides this there was another bamboo hut, inhabited by a family. Here the Filipino officer found quarters for the night, inviting Gillmore to share them with him.

The old nipa roof was not an unqualified success as a shelter from the heavy tropical rain. A steady little stream pouring down on my chest managed also in some miraculous way to trickle around the back of my neck and down my spinal column. All sorts of insects had sought shelter about my person, and seemed to be fighting among themselves for the best places. And that was the evening of my twenty-first birthday. Thus did I celebrate my coming of age.

Before dawn next morning reveille sounded, calling us up to resume the struggle against water, slush, and mud. On we toiled, with no other object than to increase the distance between ourselves and friends. Our hearts were as heavy as the mud that clung to our bodies.

Many times we were obliged to give Blondin performances over swollen streams on bamboo poles, substitutes for bridges, and at other times, when wading through lagoons of mud and water a man would slip and entirely disappear from view, to reappear again a moment later with a brown coating all over his body like a chocolate tart.

Finally our troubles terminated on our arrival at a town called Aliaga. We were kindly received by the local authorities, who sheltered us from the weather in the best room of the presidency.

On the morning of May 5th the rain had ceased and we made a four-hours' march over a flat country, following a trail through a coarse species of wire grass ten feet high in some places. So dense was this grass that, had it not been for the narrow trail cut through, headway would have been impossible. At noon we reached Santo Domingo, remaining there for the rest of the day.

May 6th we left Santo Domingo early and travelled all day. This was not on account of the distance covered, but on account of the slow gait of the two carretones that accompanied us, one containing Lieutenant Gillmore and young Edwards, the latter showing symptoms of dysentery. The other was loaded with the baggage of the fifty Spaniards, such as cooking pots, blankets, etc. These carts, the wheels of which are of solid wood, resembling giant ginger-snaps, were drawn by two water-buffaloes, or, as called by the Filipinos, carabaos. They are a species of cattle with very little hair on their bodies. Whether the climate of the Philippines was made for the carabao, or the carabao was made for the climate, I cannot say, but the fact is they are wonderfully adapted for each other. Those mud lakes and swampy puddles, so abundant in the rainy season, are the source of much comfort to the water-buffalo, who delights in lying in them for hours, nothing but his head visible. Then when he rises, the sun dries the mud on his elephantine hide into a thick coating, serving as a protection from flies and mosquitoes. The natives use the carabao as a draught animal, but he soon drops from fatigue unless allowed to roll in a puddle at least once in two hours. Being permitted to do this for ten minutes, he rises again and resumes his labor with original strength.

On account of these frequent baths of our two carabaos our progress was slow, but as the road lay through a majestic forest of gigantic trees, the walk was neither hot nor unpleasant. We spent the night in a small town called Obispo, on the edge of the foot-hills.

We continued on the morning of the 7th over a range of rugged foot-hills. In several places we passed trenches built across the road by the Filipinos in the insurrection of 1897. We saw at times charred timbers protruding from the low underbrush, all that remained of whole villages to which the Spaniards had applied the torch.

Stopping for two hours at San José, a small mountain village on the edge of the hills, we resumed our march in the afternoon, reaching Humingan at dusk, once more on the plain.

May 8th at dawn we left Humingan, and, marching two hours, reached San Quintin. The municipal authorities here received us coldly, giving us nothing to eat. At Humingan the soldiers, who had until then acted as our escort, turned us over to the local president, they themselves returning to the front, southward. We were from now on entirely in the hands of the local presidents, each one sending us on to the next town on the line of travel, with the police, who turned us over to the next president, and so on. We were no longer in the hands of the military.

As we passed through the different towns we had been joined by new prisoners every day until now, upon arriving at San Quintin, we found at least seven hundred prisoners concentrated. But the Filipinos came near regretting this. Emboldened by their numbers, and half desperate with hunger, the Spaniards rushed upon the presidency of San Quintin the day after our arrival, overpowered the police, and took possession of a carreton of rice. A Spanish officer, knowing the consequences of an uprising, cowed the cazadores down by his authority, and ordered them to return the captured arms and rice. The former they sheepishly returned to the discomfited police, but the latter they retained; on that point they remained firm. In the evening a large force of bolomen came into town, and the President, meek as a child during the day, resumed his former insolent bearing.

At that time we considered that Spanish officer a coward, but since then I have changed my judgment. Supposing the Spaniards had succeeded in banding themselves together in a body, armed with half a dozen Remingtons and a few bolos, what could they have accomplished? To reach the nearest American forces we should have been obliged to march back to San Isidro and fight our way through the Insurgent lines. We should have had to traverse the entire width of Nueva Ecija, an enemy's country. It was a hopeless undertaking, and that officer acted wisely and for the best.

We spent four days in San Quintin, which were four days of hunger. Fortunately we were not confined, but allowed to wander about the streets during the day, and, although we did not actually beg, accepted offerings of bananas, com, and bebinkas from those of the inhabitants whose pity became aroused at our miserable condition. In this place Lieutenant Gillmore was forced to sleep on a table, the rest of us stretched about on the floor. This was singular, as the lieutenant had until then always been treated with due courtesy.

While here I witnessed a marriage ceremony between a boy of eleven and a girl of ten. The parents were superintending the whole affair, for it was evidently not according to the wishes of either bride or groom, who both wept dismally while the Filipino priest spliced the holy knot.

Native priests were to be seen in all the towns. Hearing so much said against the friars I inquired why they were tolerated, but was informed that they were not friars, simply ministers of the Catholic religion. They had, the majority of them, at one time been sacristans to the Spanish friars, but now took the friars' places, living on the small marriage fees, gratuities for mass, etc. Many of them were good and pious men, and those that were hypocrites could at least do no serious harm.

We were beginning to believe that San Quintin was to be our home for some time, but on the morning of the 12th, reveille called us out early to prepare for the march again. Once more we formed in the plaza, but to our amazement, instead of continuing to the northward, the police, taking the lead, escorted us out of town by the same road we had entered, toward the south — and friends. Cheer after cheer arose. "Viva la Libertad!" the Spaniards cried. The war was over, they said, and we were to be delivered to the Americans! Viva! viva!

Arriving at Humingan, we rested but a short time; the Spaniards could hardly he restrained. Songs floated up in the air, and our steps were as light as our hearts.

We had just about gone half way to San Jose when an officer on horseback dashed up to the head of the column, and, coming to a sudden halt, he roared out at the top of his voice, "Alto!" All came to a halt. Songs and laughter died suddenly out, while wonder and amazement showed on each face. Then, rising in his stirrups, he cried out again, "Media vuelta!" Slowly, heavily, the cazadores turned about; faces gloomy; all silent. Evening found us again at San Quintin.

Many times afterward we discussed that half-day's backward march, but could never find a proper solution to it. Some believed that negotiations to deliver us up had really been entered into, others again that they had wanted to switch us off into the pass somewhere close to San José, leading up into the mountains to Bayombong.

Early in the morning of the 14th we left San Quintin the second time, but bound northward. The road lay parallel to a range of mountains close by on our right, through a densely timbered country. From limbs of lofty trees we noticed many bats suspended of the size of chickens. Two hours' march brought us to Tayug, a town notable for the size and grandeur of its church and convent. We had now left the province of Nueva Ecija and were in Pangasinan, the natives of which province speak a dialect entirely different from Tagalog.

From now on our march was an uneventful one for some time. Each day we walked the distance from one town to the next, always escorted by the police. The Spaniards had been broken up into small bands, some of which went ahead, while others lagged behind a day or even two. We spent a night successively in the towns of Ansingan, Binalonan, Pozorrubio, Alava, and Rosario, arriving at the latter town on May 18th. This brought us across the province of Pangasinan. We were now to cross over into Union, the first of the Ilocos provinces of which we had heard so much from the Spaniards, where the natives were said to be kindly disposed toward the white race.

Since leaving San Quintin we had always travelled along the foot of the mountain range on our right, as close as possible, without actually entering it; consequently we saw many of the Igorrotes, as the wild tribes inhabiting this part of the mountains of Luzon are called.

The Igorrotes are by no means similar to the Negritos, except in the absence of all manner of superfluity of dress, barring a breech-clout of the most economical dimensions. Their straight blue-black hair is long and coiled up loosely on the top of the head. Their color is of a light coffee-brown, and differs but slightly from the average Tagalog. Most of them are tattooed, some even in their faces. In physical appearance they are small, but well shaped, every muscle developed in symmetrical proportions, and compare favorably with the Negritos, whose legs seem to have an almost uniform thickness from hip to calf. What caused us to wonder was the fact that we seldom observed an Igorrote who was not leading a string of dogs. Inquiry revealed the fact that dog forms the favorite dish in an Igorrote bill of fare, and, to obtain a sufficiency, they often come down to the low-lands to trade horses, calves, goats, copper ore, and even gold dust for curs that would hardly be permitted to exist in our country.

The religious belief of these Igorrotes is of the vaguest order, tainted with gross superstitions of seemingly Mohammedan origin, and all the efforts of the friars to convert them have signally failed. I am told that the monks who went up into the mountains for this purpose had a nasty habit of disappearing. Finally the friars decided to leave them entirely alone. These people live in small villages, each governed by the oldest male inhabitant. The villages are familiarly known by the Spanish name "rancherias" throughout the islands.

On the morning of the 19th we left Rosario and struck into a little range of foot-hills. On reaching the ridge an exclamation of joyous surprise escaped from many throats as we beheld the blue waters of the China Sea in the distance, but, on descending into a valley soon after, we lost sight of it again. The beauty of this little valley still lingers fondly in my memory. On both sides rose up green but steep and densely wooded hills, while through the centre rushed a sparkling river, here and there dashing over bowlders or struggling through rocky narrows with great noise and corresponding foam. Extending from the hills to the banks, on either side of the river, we observed highly cultivated fields of rice, corn, sugar-cane, tobacco, and banana-trees, subdivided here and there by hedges of the maguey plant. A number of little villages dotted this beautiful landscape, and those through which we passed had a more thriving aspect than those of the Tagalog country. We were now among the Ilocanos, and I confess that the impression of superior thriftiness remains with me still.

As we passed, the "tauis" came out on the road from their fields and offered us sugar-cane and tobacco leaves. Again the dialect had changed. A mota was now a "ciping," and a banana, which in Tagalog is "saaging," was now only to be had by asking for "saaba." When stopping at the huts for water, the Tagalog word "toobig" was no longer understood; it was now "danom." And so with the whole dialect, entirely different; and a Tagalog taui and an Ilocano of the same class, meeting, and unacquainted with Spanish, would understand one another as well as a Laplander and a native of the Samoan Islands.

Before sunset we reached a small town nestled between the ridges and sheltered by stately trees; this was Kabao. Here was stationed a garrison that showed us but scant courtesy. At evening, on the following day, we left Kabao, and by the light of the full moon continued our march along a road that followed the banks of the river. Softened by the moonlight, the scenery became like one of fairyland. The foliage met overhead, and through the trees we could distinguish the spray leaping into the air, as if impatient at encountering the stony obstacles in the numerous cascades, and sparkling like diamonds in the magic light of the moon. All this might possibly have inspired me into a poetic effusion on the spot, had I been given to the courting of the Muses; but the day before I had been obliged to abandon the last remnant of my shoes, and the aesthetic pleasure I felt at the beauty of the scenery was seriously impaired by a hidden dread of stepping too hard upon the glorious landscape, thereby causing to course through my mind thoughts decidedly unpoetic.

In a couple of hours we arrived at Aringay, where we were conducted by the police to the usual large convent of the town. Here we were delivered into the hands of the local police sergeant, and taken upstairs into what had formerly been the padres' dormitory. Hardly had we seated ourselves, when a tall, stalwart, and well-built Filipino, evidently a mestizo, entered, the first real Ilocano presidente we had met on our line of march, and of whom the Spaniards had spoken to us in terms of praise. There was nothing of Spanish polish, which too often borders on the hypocritical, in his manner, but the impression made by the sincere friendliness of his greeting could not have been produced by a million bows and soft words. If Don Juan Baltazar is a fair representative of the Ilocanos, then they are indeed a noble race!

Chapter Fifteen - The People of Ilocos

NEVER in all our experiences had we been treated as in Aringay, with such hospitality and generosity. Baltazar was highly indignant on learning how we had fared since leaving San Isidro.

"Aguinaldo," he exclaimed, "is a good man, and did he know the truth, would be as angry as I am. His orders are that you be well cared for, and treated with all due consideration by all the municipal presidents through whose towns you pass. It is not his fault that his orders are not obeyed to the letter, but, hereafter, you will fare better since you are now in the Ilocano country."

Baltazar insisted upon our resting a day in his town, and this we were only too glad to do. All of the next day we wandered freely about the town in twos and threes, entering native huts on the numerous invitations of their occupants. We were the honored guests of the town, as such the President had declared us, and the simple "tauis" considered his word as law.

By this time those of us who had been captured before the outbreak of hostilities spoke Spanish fairly well, and this seemed to highly please Baltazar. As I asked him a great many questions on resources and products of the country, customs of the people, etc., he became interested in me and ended up by offering to retain me that I might live with him and teach him English. So persistent was he in his persuasions that I could not doubt his sincerity. Several of my companions advised me to stay, as I thus later might gain an opportunity to escape, but, as I could not then honorably do so, I preferred not to be separated from the main party. It was a great temptation, and only the fear of having my motive misconstrued at some future day kept me from accepting Baltazar's generous offer.

The President was very talkative, however, and, sitting in reclining chairs under the trees in front of the convent after the siesta, smoking and conversing, he told me his history. His father had been a well-to-do French planter, his mother a native; thus Don Juan himself was a French mestizo. At an early age he had gone to sea, consequently knew something of the outside world. Returning home some years later he found himself an orphan, the owner of a large plantation. Since then he had devoted himself exclusively to the raising of tobacco, coffee, indigo, sugar-cane, and the manufacture of a peculiar kind of wine made of sugar-cane and other ingredients, his own invention, and for which he had been awarded a medal at the Paris Exposition. I tasted this wine, and to my judgment it seemed to be a liqueur of fine flavor.

During the insurrection of 1897 he had been arrested as a rebel at the instigation of the friars, whose enmity he had engendered by daring to compete with them in the sugar trade, shipping his goods direct to foreign ports instead of selling to them. For ten months he had been confined in Bilibid Prison in Manila, until, by paying a large sum of money, he secured his release.

He had on his plantation two sugar-mills, one worked by steam, the other by horse-power. Annually he shipped tons of the crude sugar to Manila. He also explained the process of the manufacture of indigo, of which he produced considerable. The indigo plant resembles in general appearance our alfalfa clover. When of about three months' growth the first crop can already be cut, for the plant sprouts again, yielding two or three crops a year. The green tops are then thrown into a vat and covered with about three inches of water, the leaves being held down by weights to prevent them from floating. In about two days this water becomes green, and is then run off into a second vat. The leaves are again covered with water until it also is green. The discolored water is then beaten and stirred with sticks until it becomes full of little blue granular lumps, which settle to the bottom after the stirring has ceased. The water becomes now almost clear again, and is then carefully drained off, leaving the pure indigo sediment in the bottom, to be taken out and dried.

Baltazar also had several coffee-plantations back in the mountains, as the coffee-tree is not successfully grown in the low lands, requiring a dry soil and a certain altitude. "We do not understand the proper cultivation here," said Baltazar; "if we did, our soil would produce a bean equal to that of Java."

Taking me out into the middle of the plaza, the President pointed to a distant mountain-peak. "From that hill," he informed me, "I myself have taken out large lumps of coal. A little beyond I have picked up rich copper ore. Gold also is found in fair quantities by the Igorrotes. I assure you," he continued, confidentially, as we seated ourselves under the trees, "I am anxious to see the American Government established here. The liberal laws of the United States will enable us to develop the immense resources of the country to our own benefit. A government by ourselves would never encourage the investment of large capital, and on a small scale we shall never succeed. With modern implements and American capital the Philippines promise a glorious future for both natives and American colonists. But the only basis on which peace can ever be firmly established, between us and the Americans, is the total abolition of monasterial fraternities, and representation in your Congress with self home government. On no other terms will the Insurgents ever surrender, and, although they may be conquered by superior forces, the spark of rebellion will always remain ready to burst into flame at every opportunity. I feel convinced that the Americans will give us a good government, and would be in favor of unconditional surrender, but these Tagalogs are a stubborn race, and we have few sympathies in common. With a native government they would rule us as the Spaniards ruled them. To reconcile us with the cause, they have appointed an Ilocano to the chief command of the army, but peace once established, we would be ground under the Tagalog heel. Even now the Military Governor of the Ilocano provinces, General Tiño, is a Tagalog."

I felt much interested in Señor Baltazar's conversation, but here we were interrupted by the arrival of a visitor, a well-built, dark, but handsome full-blood native. His countenance seemed familiar to me, but, when Baltazar introduced him to us as Dr. Jose Luna, I remembered the features of his brother Antonio who was pointed out to us in the Malolos gymnasium. Dr. Luna appeared and acted as though every inch a gentleman, asking us all sorts of curious but not rude questions about our own people. Like his brother, he wore a heavy mustache, rather unusual for a native.

But this dream could not last forever, so on the morning of the 22d our northward march was again resumed. Besides supplying us with food, Baltazar had given us a daily ration of twenty cents, one peseta, and Gillmore forty cents. This, he told us, we would hereafter receive every day wherever we stopped, and so we really did until the end of our journey.

It was with deep regret that we bade our generous friend farewell. The last we saw of him, he was standing at the convent door waving his hat to us.

We had been about half an hour on our march, when an abrupt bend in the road suddenly brought into view the ever-welcome sight of the blue sea again, at which we cheered loudly. Far out we could discern the white sails of the fishermen's boats, but we eagerly scanned the horizon in the hope of seeing what was not there, an American war-vessel.

Resting at noon an hour near a cluster of huts close to the beach, we continued in the afternoon along the road always parallel to the sea-shore, arriving at Bauang after sunset. The town was small, but our reception was all that could be expected.

The morning of the 23d we made an early start, still continuing on or near the sandy beach, with our bare feet sometimes washed by the frothing sea-foam. We had quite a little excitement during the day. In passing close to a fishermen's village we saw a large boat aground in the shallow water close to the beach. The sails were set in order to dry, the wind was favorable, and nobody seemed to be aboard. Not one of our four guards had a rifle, and nobody appeared to be within a mile. Bruce and O'Brien cried out, simultaneously, "Boys, here's our chance!"

This inflamed some of the younger members of the party, and, had Lieutenant Gillmore not restrained them, that boat would probably have been taken possession of. Of course, it would have been a risky adventure, putting out to sea and all chances in favor of suffering hunger and thirst before meeting a vessel, so, probably. Lieutenant Gillmore's action in holding down the fiery spirits of the young members saved them from committing an act for which they afterward might have been sorry. I believe that it was the assertion of his calmer judgment that prevented the attempt being made.

At noon we reached San Fernando, where two days of close confinement in the local prison was spent. Here Lieutenant Gillmore was confined together with us, being obliged to occupy the same cell with us. This was rather unusual, as the native officials seemed to have a deep respect for gilt braid and shoulder straps. From San Isidro to the end of our journey, with very few exceptions, the lieutenant had always been treated with consideration, and never allowed to go hungry. A horse, or a carromata, or at the worst a carreton was always at his disposal, and, considering the circumstances, he never had any reason to complain. Being almost always invited to dine with the local officials he was not obliged to spend his ration allowance of two pesetas daily, being able to save up quite a neat little sum. We also laid by a little capital, not knowing how long these good times would last.

On the afternoon of the 25th we took a mere two hours' stroll to San Juan, where we spent the night. From San Juan we departed early next morning, and, resting for an hour at noon at the town of Dagnotan, continued our weary march until nine o'clock that evening, travelling over twenty kilometres that day, which, considering the condition of our bare feet, was a feat of wonderful endurance, especially as the road was covered with sharp rocks, shells, and broken coral. But, upon reaching our destination, Namacpacan, we forgot all our misery in the friendliness of the reception extended to us.

Instead of being housed in the convent or presidency as usual, we were taken into a private house, becoming the guests of Colonel Santa Romana of the local militia. He had already almost a full house, there being besides us the two dozen friars we had seen pass at San Isidro, now on their way to the province of Lepanto, where the main body of the captive monks was kept.

Our host (I cannot bring myself to call him our keeper or jailer) was a fine-looking mestizo of middle age, with a heavy white mustache and still whiter hair. Troubles had prematurely aged him. A casual observer would have taken him for a Spaniard, but he was one-quarter native. His wife, also a mestizo, was much darker than her husband. He was the father of a dozen handsome children ranging from a little toddler of four to a young man of twenty. Hospitality seemed to amount almost to a religion in this household, for during our stay the Señora infused such a sense of sincere welcome in her manner toward us that I may safely assert each member of our wayworn little band forgot for the time being that he was a prisoner. So anxious was she to please that she even took me aside and wanted to know if the lieutenant would be offended if seated at the same table with his men. She was so ignorant of our "costumbres," she explained, and the thought of giving offence to anybody pained her.

But Santa Romana had a history, as I learned from one of the friars with whom I entered into conversation. He was the son of a well-known Spanish general and a native mother. Dying in the Philippines, his father left him heir to a vast estate in Namacpacan, and, having married, the young man settled down to pass a quiet home life in comfortable circumstances.

At the outbreak of the present insurrection misfortunes came. Antonio Rosario, who had been elected "presidente locale" upon the establishment of the revolutionary government, was a bitter enemy of the mestizo planter, on account of some law-suit they had had between them, and seeing an opportunity to revenge himself, he did so. Accusing Santa Romana of being an "Americanista," he caused him and his two eldest sons to be thrown into prison, and his property confiscated, the wife and smaller children being cast out on public charity.

Such was the state of affairs when the well-known Insurgent leader, General Buencamino, passed through the town on a journey to the northern provinces. Buencamino and Santa Romana had attended the Military Academy of Manila together, and, although they held different political opinions, were, nevertheless, warm personal friends. Consequently, upon reaching Namacpacan, Buencamino's first inquiry of Rosario, the local President, was: "But where is my friend Santa Romana? His house used as soldiers' quarters — how is this?" The result was that Santa Romana was released, his house and property returned, and had Buencamino had any power over the civil authorities, Rosario would certainly have suffered. But to place him out of reach of his enemy's power, he appointed his friend colonel of militia, practically a sinecure, since he had no troops to command. Being a military officer, Rosario dared not again molest him; in fact, Romana in some matters had higher authority than the President, which fact was illustrated the day after our arrival, when Rosario insisted that we be marched around the plaza that the people all might see us. Romana's reply was: "The Americans are not a troop of actors, and, while under my roof, they shall receive all the respect due to helpless prisoners."

It may not be inappropriate here to mention an after event of this story. The local President, whom I have called Rosario, since I have forgotten his real name, was, upon the establishment of an American garrison in the town of Namacpacan, six months later, arrested and confined in the convent by post-commander Captain Johnson of the Thirty-third United States Volunteers, on complaint of the citizens, who accused him of extortion and robbery. That he was a scamp and a tyrant in his small way was evident, but the robbery could not be proved. Still Captain Johnson held him for some time on the entreaties of the populace. It was about this time that the writer, some time free already, passed through the town on his way to Manila and once more enjoyed the hospitality of Señor Romana, then elected local President under the American Government. On the same evening of my arrival, while Romana and I were seated talking about incidents at our former meeting, the wife of Rosario entered, threw herself on her knees before Romana and begged him to speak a word for Antonio to the post commander. The tears coursed down the cheeks of my host, and, gently raising the old woman, he escorted her to the door, promising that he would do all in his power to comply with her request. Returning, he took me by the arm, and, passing me my hat, said: "Come, you must act as my interpreter. I wish to speak to the Señor Capitan." Crossing the plaza to where Captain Johnson's company was quartered, we found the captain himself in his quarters. Through me, as interpreter, Romana begged the American officer to release Rosario and permit him to return to his family. "Not for his sake," he explained, "but for his wife, who is old and helpless." Captain Johnson promised to comply, and together we went over to the convent where Rosario was confined. The old ex-President was then told that he might return to his home, "but," the captain insisted on explaining, "you have not me to thank. I only liberate you at the recommendation of Señor Romana, the man whom I understand you once did a great wrong. May you learn a lesson in true nobility of heart from him!"

Begging the reader's pardon for thus leaping half a year ahead of my narrative, we shall once more return to the time of our first acquaintance with this noble gentleman.

The colonel would not consent to the resumption of our march next day, and insisted upon resting our fatigued limbs until the morning of the 28th. I was thus enabled to enter into long conversations with several of the friars, and, having heard so much said against them, determined to listen to what they might have to say in their own defence. He to whom I spoke was a Dominican, and, nothing loath, he came to the point at once. "The people here do not like us," he admitted, "but, while willing to enjoy the benefits the Church gives them, they refuse to pay for them in return. We have not given them the more advanced forms of education because they are not yet fit for it. Give a child a knife to play with and he cuts himself. Yet a grown person may use the same knife as a valuable tool. No sooner do we give a Filipino a good education, when he turns upon us and uses the knowledge derived from us to do us harm."

"But," I inquired, "cannot the Filipino be made fit to receive the higher forms of education?"

"No," he replied, "they are a stupid race. It will require centuries so to educate them. They lack intelligence, and, unless ruled by an iron hand, will never learn. Pity is lost upon the average native; they understand only fear, and only by inspiring them with dread of the white race can they be governed."

This friar, furthermore, informed me that his order, at least, had had enough of the Filipinos, and would not remain under any circumstances: "Probably we shall go to Bolivia or to some other of the South or Central American republics."

On the morning of May 28th, accompanied by the friars, we marched to Bangar, five kilometres distant. We remained here until the afternoon, but the friars went on, striking up into the mountains at this point through the pass of Tagudin up to the Igorrote country in the province of Lepanto. Here they were surrounded only by the "unbelievers," and it is my conviction that Aguinaldo had a purpose in this, for here they were safer than down in the Christian provinces. It was not the President's wish to have them murdered by enraged mobs, so, as soon as practicable, he had them removed up into the Igorrote districts, where they ran no risks from the garrison of disciplined regulars.

During the afternoon we left Bangar and travelled a distance of three kilometres over a delta country, crossing no less than four branches of one river that emptied into the sea close by. This river forms the boundary between the provinces of Union and Ilocos Sur. Having crossed the last fork, we entered the town of Tagudin, where three companies of soldiers, armed with nothing more than wooden guns, escorted us into the plaza to the presidency with much ceremony. The treatment we here received still upheld the good impression we had of the Ilocanos. Each of us, besides our ration, received a present of twenty cents, and Lieutenant Gillmore received five pesos. In doing this the President had an object, for he requested Gillmore to write him a letter of recommendation, addressed to American officers in general. The President was far-sighted and invested the five pesos to good purpose, although I admit he deserved it as far as we were concerned.

A Chinese merchant of the town sent us a goat by a Spaniard, asking also for a similar letter of recommendation, and, as the lieutenant refused to comply with the Chino's wishes, Honeyman and myself paid him a visit in his "tienda" across the plaza, and wrote the required document.

During the following few days we passed through the small and uninteresting towns of Sevilla, Santa Cruz, and Santa Lucia, arriving in the rather more important town of Candon on the morning of May 31st. The old President, Pedro Legaspi, who to this day retains that position, treated us in a manner only equalled by the hospitality of Baltazar and Santa Romana.

A banquet was here given in our honor, where on a snowy table-cloth a dinner was spread equal to any to be had in the best Manila hotels. Afterward came black coffee and cigars, served out on the balcony while we leaned back in cane reclining chairs, our bare feet raised to a level with our heads on the balcony railing, and while we puffed away at our cheroots the municipal brass band serenaded us below in the plaza. In spite of our rags being infested with vermin, we exclaimed to each other, "Who wouldn't be a prisoner?" That treat was repeated three times, in the evening, the following noon, and night. Chocolate was served after the siestas.

We now learned that our final destination was to be Vigan, the capital of the province, and, as we were told, the second city in size in the island of Luzon, next to Manila. On the morning of June 2d we were once more on the road. The rest of our journey was uneventful. We were treated more like guests than prisoners in all the towns we passed through, enjoying the hospitality of Santiago, San Esteban, Santa Maria, and Narbacan, until the evening of June 4th, a month and a day since leaving San Isidro, found us in the town of Santa, on the banks of the river Abra. On the other side was situated Vigan, so we knew that the morrow would end our travels, for some time at least.

The President of Santa was courteous to Gillmore, but the rest of us were lodged in a filthy stable, then used as a depository for all sorts of refuse. Instead of giving us our ration money, he compelled us to pay twenty cents for a meal. Evidently he had imbibed the Spanish idea that an officer should be treated as a gentleman and the common soldiers as mere animals. I took particular pains to remember him, and long afterward we met again. I believe that I was at least part of the cause of his downfall.

On the morning of the 5th we were ferried over the Abra River on bamboo rafts. The river here comes down from the mountains through a large gap or pass known as "La Bocana." Owing to heavy rains it had swollen into a roaring torrent, but the dexterity those raftsmen displayed in ferrying us across was something really admirable.

Half an hour's march brought us into the suburbs of a large town. This was Vigan. Conducting us through what seemed a labyrinth of narrow streets, accompanied by a dense throng of the inhabitants, we at length reached the plaza and were taken into a handsome large building used as the presidency. Large buildings lined the plaza on all sides, which at one time must have been a beautiful park, with two band-stands in the centre and a drive around them.

At length a stalwart Ilocano, the provincial President, made his appearance, and, having counted us, turned us over in charge of a squad of soldiers. Once more we were in the hands of the military. A short walk down a narrow street found us before a long rambling brick building, almost the counterpart of the San Isidro prison. Our guards conducted us through the gloomy entrance into a courtyard. The heavy iron gate clanged after us, and we knew our journey was over! "Once more behind the bars."

Chapter Sixteen - Vigan

THE prison of Vigan was laid out similar to that of San Isidro, but much larger, being divided into two sections, with two separate courtyards. One wing was used as barracks by part of the local garrison, the other, in which we now found ourselves, was the military prison and municipal jail together. In the centre over the entrance was built a large square tower, in the upper story of which Gillmore was now quartered with the alcaide and his family. We others were confined in what had apparently at one time been the prison chapel, for at one end was built an altar, on which sat a much-discolored wooden saint staring fixedly up at the rafters. Again we had been fortunate with regard to room, for our cell, facing the street, was at least fifty feet long by twenty wide. Six large but heavily iron-barred windows pierced the eastern wall of our quarters, allowing the sun to enter freely every morning. But the view from these windows was depressing, for nothing more than a high stone wall came into sight on the opposite side of the street, and to look either up or down the thoroughfare was impossible, owing to the distance of the bars from the outside sill.

The alcaide was inclined to be kind to us, for his mental vision saw into the future, and he was wise. As I write this he is still alcaide of the Vigan prison for the American Government.

At first Lieutenant Gillmore had been confined with the rest of us, but so strenuously had he insisted upon being separate, that the alcaide had obtained permission from the proper authority to take him up into his own rooms, where the lieutenant was given an entire apartment to himself. Here he could sit on a small balcony and survey the surrounding country from the Abra Pass or La Bocana to the sea.

Our rations were now cut down to ten cents, or eight motas; even the lieutenant was not supposed to receive more. Ten cents without rice allowed of no luxuries, but, fortunately, every one of us had saved at least one peso from the road, and this helped us along the first week. The alcaide did not issue the money to us, but retained it, and twice a day gave us a meal of rice and paw-paw soup, which we named banana-stalk soup, as for a considerable time we labored under the delusion that such it really was. That the alcaide retained his commission we never doubted, but he was uniformly kind, and that counted also. The "teniente," as he called Gillmore, was his idol, however. Nothing was too good for "el teniente." He even gave him breakfast every morning at his own expense, and often supplied him with cigars. Meat, bread, eggs, chicken, and sausages formed his chief diet every day, and as this alone would cost over twenty cents, the alcaide must certainly have paid the difference from his own private purse. Sly dog, this alcaide!

It can, of course, easily be imagined in what condition our clothes were after a month's march. With the exception of the lieutenant, who had received numerous presents on the road, we were all either bareheaded, barefooted, or tattered. Most of us deserved all these adjectives, I among them, besides disabled by a running ulcer on my right foot that refused to heal. Edwards had suffered dreadfully from diarrhea, or rather mild dysentery, but was now a trifle improved, and all of us looked gaunt and hollow-eyed. This, together with the ragged state of our wardrobe, gave us the appearance of an advance guard of famine, or we might have been of the crew of that ship in which the "Ancient Mariner" made his eventful voyage. Again the Ilocanos came to the rescue.

One day the alcaide entered accompanied by a mestizo of the upper class, whom he introduced to us as Senior Pedro Rivera, a Vigan merchant, the wealthiest man of the province, as we later learned. Behind them came a servant, his arms full of clothes, which he deposited in the middle of the floor. "Help yourselves," said Señor Rivera, and we did so. There were coats, shirts, pants, and pajamas of all sizes, colors, styles, and cuts, and we each found a suit of clothes at least. Señor Rivera had gathered them from his friends, adding a good many himself. We thanked him in the choicest words of our united Spanish vocabulary, but our true feelings of gratitude would have been difficult of expression even in English. Before leaving, Señor Rivera promised to return on the next day with shoes, hats, underclothes, and more cigars, though each of us had already received a package of ten of the latter article. But we never saw Señor Rivera again.

The same evening after this visit, General Tiño, the commanding officer of the Insurgent forces in the Ilocano provinces, who had his head-quarters in Vigan, summoned Señor Rivera into his presence. "I understand that you have given the American prisoners clothes and cigars, Don Pedro," he began, as we afterward learned. "If your philanthropical inclinations are so strong, bring them to bear on our own soldiers, who are barefooted and ragged also, and are fighting for our independence. Should you once more give the Americans so much as a mota, you run a great risk of joining them permanently."

Thus did this Tagalog general, a lad of twenty-one, destroy all our prospects of relief from the friendly Ilocanos. Not satisfied with this, he cut our rations down to ten cents and declared us "incomunicados," that is, we were to have no communication with the outside world. Guards were stationed overlooking our windows, so that no passing Spaniard or native might speak to us. Tiño was evidently taking the old Bastile as his model.

We were, nevertheless, permitted to retain the clothes already given to us, and, after washing ourselves at the well in the yard, each donned a clean suit, giving us a more respectable appearance, although the cuts were not made for our figures.

For a time the restrictions were scrupulously enforced, but, encouraged by the alcaide, the soldiers grew lax and closed their eyes to an occasional chat with passing Spaniards at the windows. In this manner rumors reached us of more conferences and prospects of speedy liberation, but our confidence in Spanish veracity had been sadly shaken by the armistice stories of San Isidro and the phantom army landed at Dagupan. From the roof of the tower, we were told, vessels could often be seen passing so close to the shore that the American flag could be distinguished flying from the mast-heads, and often we saw the soldiers there gazing seaward. Several times during the nights the small patch of sky, to be seen from our windows, was illuminated by flashes of brilliant light, and we could distinctly see the rays of the search-light sweeping across the limited field. Meanwhile only one company of Insurgents with one hundred old-fashioned Remingtons guarded the town and several hundred prisoners.

Although I still believe that the alcaide was not inspired by pure philanthropy, he nevertheless made our existence as endurable as lay in his power. His own life was not a bed of roses either; he had a large family to support, and his pay for the past six months, fifteen pesos monthly, was still due him. But he was really kind, and on one occasion he displayed his friendship in a practical and rather forcible manner.

Brisolese, one of the sailor boys, was seated in the window one day, his back leaning against the iron bars. A passing "taui" saw this, and, unable to resist the temptation, crept up under the window unperceived, and jabbed the point of his bolo into the boy's back, who immediately gave a scream of pain. The alcaide happened to be near, and, attracted to the spot by the noise, took in the situation at a glance. Snatching the gun out of the hands of a sleepy sentry, he rushed out, and before the taui had time to escape he stretched his own length on the ground. The guards then dragged the fellow into our cell, where, after punching him considerably about the head, the alcaide had him placed in the stocks, where he would remain, he was told, until he kissed Brisolese's hand and begged his pardon. This he really accomplished after having been in the stocks for half an hour. He was then allowed to depart, wiser, perhaps, but sore about the body, for the alcaide was no weakling. This little incident had a healthy influence on other would-be "valientes."

So poor was the prison diet, served out to us but twice a day, that at the end of the month several of us became ill, looked wasted and gaunt and hollow-eyed as many of the Spaniards had appeared. For a time no attention was paid to our miserable condition, but, fortunately, Tiño's adjutant. Colonel Bias Villamor, came around on a tour of inspection about this time, and on our appeal to him he promised to send a medico around from the hospital to inspect us.

This was about July 2d. The day before Lieutenant Gillmore had written a letter to the local authorities, begging to have his rations, as an officer, doubled to twenty cents. A reply came in due time, and, on opening it, the lieutenant read with surprise the following in English, written in a graceful Spencerian hand, such as no Spaniard or Filipino ever uses:

Lieutenant Gillmore.
Sir: Your request has been received, filed, and granted.
The Provincial Governor.

And we had spoken to the provincial governor on the day of our arrival, and knew that his English was limited to the one word "Good-by." Who, then, could have written it?

Chapter Seventeen - An Insurgent Hospital

COLONEL BLAS VILLAMOR proved to be a man of his word, for, on the afternoon of July 3d, the day after his visit, two Spanish hospital stewards or "practicantes," as they here were called, appeared, sent from the hospital established in one of the Government buildings on the plaza, the roof of which could be viewed from our windows. As I was probably in a worse condition than any of the rest, having had dysentery for over a week, it was decided to remove me to the hospital building for treatment.

Bidding my companions farewell, I left the prison accompanied by the two practicantes and an armed escort of four men. It was only with the greatest exertion that I could walk at all, yet those four soldiers watched me with a vigilance that would have led one to believe there was some danger of my making a desperate break for the American lines, two hundred miles distant, or that I might suddenly throw off my shirt, develop a pair of wings, and with a grand flap soar up into the blue sky.

To the plaza was but a few steps, and soon we found ourselves before the "Hospital Militar de Vigan," a Red Cross flag fluttering above on a bamboo staff. Having formerly been the Spanish Governor's residence, the building was not a small one. About the entrance stood groups of Spaniards, whose appearance was strongly suggestive of the nature of the establishment.

Passing a sentry at the doorway, we next ascended a broad staircase to the floor above, where the two Spaniards conducted me into a large apartment so darkened that it was with difficulty I could see any object at all. They seated me on the edge of an iron bedstead, where I remained for some time trying to pierce the gloom, but, as my eyes gradually grew accustomed to it, the objects about me became gradually more visible. Around against the walls stood some two dozen beds similar to mine, all occupied by reclining forms. A silence as oppressive as the gloom pervaded the entire establishment, broken only by an occasional sigh or a stifled groan.

Almost exhausted by the walk, I threw myself on the cot against a pillow. There was a movement on the bed next to mine, and its occupant rose slowly into a sitting posture. A faint light from the open door happened to fall full upon him — my God, what a sight! A feeling of intense horror sank into my very soul at what I saw. A Spaniard it evidently was, but never had I thought it possible for a human being to be in such physical condition and still live. Two round, black hollows, wherein the eyes were no longer visible, stared at me; the lips had shrunk back, displaying protruding teeth; the head had sagged weakly on one shoulder, being connected to the body by a stem not thicker than a man's wrist. The arm at the shoulder and the wrist was of an equal thickness, the elbow giving the arm the appearance of a rope knotted in the middle! I closed my eyes, trying to keep out this awful apparition of tortured man, but it seemed to burn to my very eyelids. How I wished myself away, yes, even back in the gloomy prison

It was not long before my bed was surrounded by a number of officers and attendants, all of whom wore on their sleeves the Red Cross brazzards of the Insurgent hospital corps. One of them, a fine-looking mestizo, who appeared to be the surgeon in charge, felt my forehead and pulse, but said nothing more than that I must keep quiet, though I was not conscious of creating any disturbance. Shortly after an attendant administered a dose of brown powders to me, and almost immediately I dozed away.

My first night in the Vigan Hospital was an ordeal that has convinced me thoroughly that the hair on a man's head does not turn gray in one night: if that was true, mine would certainly have done so. The powders had thrown me into a lethargy, during which, while unable to move a muscle, I was still half-conscious of my surroundings. Suffering intense physical pain, I was also afflicted with terrible visions that arose before the eyes of my feverish imagination, but which I could not separate from reality. I lay on my side, my eyes glued on that Thing on the other cot. It seemed to rise and chatter its horrible teeth in my face at times, but, try as I would, it was impossible to turn my head away or utter a sound. By a dim light I saw the nurses standing about the bed, while from time to time wild screams would echo a thousand times in distant rooms. At length, in a more lucid interval, I distinctly saw that Thing arise, throw its arms toward the ceiling, and with a loud gurgle fall back motionless. I closed my eyes, and, when I opened them again, a white cloth covered that wasted form on the other cot from head to foot.

For several consecutive days I lay either entirely unconscious or staring in a listless stupor at the painted figures on the ceiling, uninterested in my surroundings. Sometimes it seemed to me that a woman's face bent over me, but my senses were too vague and confused to feel surprised. Had winged angels floated by me, I should have accepted that as the most natural feature in the world.

In less than a week, however, my condition began to improve, and once more my mind became clear and normal. The doctor explained that he had dosed me with opium, which partly accounted for my previous state. Once more I was able to take an interest in what took place around me, but, strange as it seems to me now, the horror and indescribable fear first experienced had altogether left.

The particular ward of which I was now one of the inmates, was a spacious apartment well suited for the purpose for which it served. Four doors opened out on an outside balcony, where the patients might sit and breathe the fresh air coming in on the ocean breeze.

With the exception of three or four native soldiers suffering from slight wounds, the rest of the patients in this ward were all Spanish prisoners, the majority of them in the last stages of disease. These were the grave cases, I was told, waiting their turn for the almost daily trips to the "campo santo," the gates of which were visible from the balcony.

There was about a score of them, some forming painful illustrations of the tenacity with which the soul sometimes clings to its shattered, rapidly decaying frame. Some of these patients, I am certain, did not weigh fifty pounds — living skeletons in the true sense of the word. Downstairs were seventy more, called convalescents, but that word was misapplied, for they all were candidates for the vacant cots which the dead left behind in the room above. These poor fellows slept on the floor. In another room next to ours, on the same floor, were quartered a dozen Spanish officers; they all seemed in pretty fair health, spending their time playing monte and walking up and down a gallery in the rear part of the building. From here, the upper story of the prison tower where Gillmore was quartered was plainly visible, and often when I came out there we could see each other and wave our hands.

The surgeon in charge, Capitan Victorino Chrisolojo, came to visit me daily, apparently anxious that I should recover. His appearance was that of a real gentleman; at first glance I rather "took" to him, nor never afterward had reason to change my opinion of him during our long subsequent acquaintance.

But his wife commanded my most profound respect and admiration. She, too, was a mestiza, showing but faint traces of the native blood in her appearance. With true womanly sympathy and tenderness she did all that lay in her power to alleviate the sufferings of the sick under her husband's care, though her powers were limited, the Government allowing the hospital no more than ten cents daily for each patient — not a great deal for dying wretches.

Chrisolojo also had an old mother who occasionally came to visit us, and together these two ladies made the lot of the poor sufferers the least trifle less bitter.

Next to the doctor in charge came Lieutenant Abasilla, ranking as second lieutenant. He was a little, fat, good-natured, full-blood Ilocano, a former practicante in the Spanish hospitals, now a full-fledged medico. The first acquaintance I had with him was when one day he came to my bedside and, with a broad smile on his face, seated himself comfortably in a chair. Feeling my pulse, he smiled still more broadly, and, with a repeated "Bien, bien!" handed me a cigar at the same time. "How are you now?" he inquired. "Better," I answered. Again came a "bien, bien!" and with that another cigar, he having apparently forgotten that he had already given me one. For some time he sat there, evidently well pleased with the world in general and my case in particular. "What do you think of the Ilocanos?" he asked me again. "Good people," I replied with sincerity. This brought out three more "biens" from the contented little doctor, with a third cigar. Every time he pronounced things "bien" I received a cigar, so that when at length he departed I had just half a dozen fine Cagayan cheroots under my pillow. But, unfortunately, a few days later this agreeable little individual left Vigan for Bangued, the capital of the province of Abra, twenty miles up the river that came down through "La Bocana," where he established a branch hospital for the soldiers and prisoners there stationed.

Next in rank came the two practicantes, Perez and Manuel, the two Spaniards who had brought me over from the prison. Although prisoners themselves, their experience in the Spanish hospitals in this capacity made their services valuable here, and for a couple of pesos monthly salary they undertook the duties and held the rank of non-commissioned officers in the Insurgent hospital corps, at the same time being prisoners of war. They were constantly busy, administering medicines, bandaging sores and wounds, and mixing compounds in the doctor's laboratory.

The nurses were two native boys, Perico and Leon, both relatives of the doctor. Their ambition was to learn and in time become students in the Medical College of Manila, where Chrisolojo had graduated, but, as that was now impossible, they were taking practical lessons in the capacity of nurses or "sanitarios."

Besides these there were half a dozen well Spaniards, called "infermeros," clumsy fellows whose greatest ambition was to shirk their duties, consisting in aiding the helpless to rise from their cots, bring water, wash the sick and their clothes, and in other ways assist the practicantes. They were in their turn also assisted by a squad of soldiers stationed downstairs, called "camareros" (literally litter-bearers), who mounted guard, carried out the dead, and swept up the floors, keeping the premises clean in general.

This formed the whole hospital corps of Vigan, and so far all was well. The doctor did all he reasonably could be expected to do, but without the proper means was practically helpless. His laboratory contained but few medicines, and, what was there, had probably formed part of Magellan's medicine-chest. Some powders, iodoform that had lost its penetrating smell, emetics, salves, and a very few other chemicals completed the outfit. There were not even the necessary instruments for amputating a limb, had such an operation been found necessary, and in many cases paper was substituted for bandages, with cotton batting underneath, this latter being present in abundance as a home product. Linen was used only in the most serious cases. As Chrisolojo himself often remarked, he needed everything and had nothing.

I was at first a great curiosity in the hospital, and, as visitors were allowed to enter every afternoon between the hours of three and six, many of the Vigan citizens availed themselves of this privilege in order to see upon what plan an American was really built. They were, however, never offensive, and even gave me presents of cigars and cigarettes, until I soon had enough to distribute among my Spanish companions, less fortunate than I in not being rarities. But one day I received a visit something out of the ordinary.

It was a week after my arrival that Perico one afternoon came in, and shaking my arm — I was sleeping at the time — said that a "Señor" was desirous of seeing me. Sounds of footsteps caused me to turn my head, and there at my bedside stood David Arnold, whom none of us had ever seen since leaving San Isidro. For a moment we stared into each other's eyes, neither speaking a word. At length he extended his hand to me, saying: "Well, I thought I would come up to tell you the news."

Since leaving the prison I hadn't heard a word of English spoken; I was lonely, sickness had weakened me mentally as well as physically, and his words caused my hand, almost before I knew it, to go out and meet his. For the first time since February 13th we now spoke to one another. I had resolved never again to speak to Arnold with other words than those of an enemy, but I admit that I broke that resolution here. Perhaps he secretly laughed at my weakness, but, if so, his words didn't show it, and almost unconsciously I found myself conversing with him as freely as if nothing had ever happened between us. Perico, Leon, and several Spanish officers from the next room stood around to listen to the strange accents of the English language, but, paying no heed to them, Arnold commenced to relate his experience since leaving San Isidro.

He had been in Vigan already over a week, he told me, but Tiño had forbidden him to visit the prison. It was he that had written the mysterious answer to Lieutenant Gillmore's application, the provincial governor having requested him to do so. He was now residing in what had formerly been the Bishop's Palace, as it was still called by the Spaniards. This was situated on the opposite side of the plaza from the hospital, and there Tiño and his staff had established their head-quarters. Arnold was now acting as the General's English teacher, as he had done for the Governor of Nueva Ecija.

In spite of the efforts of his former patron to retain him in San Isidro, the higher officials had nevertheless insisted upon his going north, evidently not deeming it safe to have him so close to the front. In company with our old friend Captain Espiña he had come to Vigan by easy stages, taking just two months to cover the same distance over the same road we had travelled in half that time.

While in San José he saw two carretones loaded with tinned goods, flour, potatoes, bottled lemonades, coffee, sugar, and tobacco, sent through the lines by the Red Cross Society for the fourteen American prisoners. He admitted having applied for and received one-fifteenth part of the stores, and in return gave his receipt. The probability of these stores ever reaching Vigan seemed indeed slim. Arnold likewise told me that he had learned from authentic sources that originally there had been thirty cases, but he saw only fifteen. General Luna's secretary had also confidentially informed him that on the General's table had appeared American preserved fruits, tinned meats, devilled ham, condensed milk, and lemonades. This was not so surprising as the fact that fifteen cases had reached San José, and this again as a miracle was eclipsed when three months later half of one of these fifteen cases really reached us, weather-beaten and with tins much rusted and dented. One-half a case of thirty!

Besides the above, Arnold had another interesting incident to relate, which well illustrates the mutual antipathy existing between Tagalog and Ilocano. While he was at Caudon this affair had taken place in a neighboring barrio. Six Tagalog soldiers had entered a private dwelling, as soldiers of all nationalities will do, commencing to loot and insult its occupants. A male member of the outraged family escaped, and, once clear of the house, raised his fingers to his lips, blowing a shrill whistle. In a few moments a dozen stalwart Ilocanos appeared on the scene, and atonce attacked the Tagalogs with their bolos. The result was three dead and three wounded soldiers, the latter seeking safety in flight, leaving their Remingtons in possession of the Ilocanos. This affair had caused quite a stir in military circles, and several of the participants were arrested and given long terms of imprisonment.

It was almost sunset when Arnold took his departure, promising to visit me every afternoon. After he was gone I discovered a package of fine Cagayan cigars beside my pillow, but I gave them all to the Spaniards,

Arnold came almost daily after this, until one day I received a note from him written in Spanish, stating that Tiño had forbidden him to continue his visits, and that he must obey. But often I saw him gallop by the hospital on a handsome pony, waving his hand to me as he passed.

Soon I was joined by another companion from the prison. Petersen, one of the Yorktown's apprentice boys, was brought over suffering from dysentery. He had changed so much since I saw him at the prison that I hardly recognized him. For a long time I thought the boy would not pull through, but having been a prisoner only three months he still retained enough of his original vitality to pass over the dangerline, yet hardly again will he stare death so closely in the face without being carried off.

With the Spaniards it was different. Many of them had been in the country for three and four years, campaigning in the rainy season, overworked, underfed, and poorly clad, consequently they were less able to withstand such debilitating diseases as dysentery, fever, anaemia, and beri-beri. Almost every day they succumbed around us to these complaints, enfeebled by want of proper nourishment such as rice and "vianda" could not afford. This would have been worth more than all the medicines in Chrisolojo's laboratory, but what could be done with ten cents!

Meanwhile, as Arnold and the Spaniards told me, Tiño sat in the "Club de Vigan," gambling at monte, winning as much as five hundred pesos daily for a long run.

On the first night of my arrival a man had died in terrible agonies on the bed next to mine, but the Vacancy was the next day filled by a young cazador from below. This was a mere boy of eighteen, a recruit who had arrived in the Islands but shortly before the war. His appearance and manner led me to believe that he belonged to a better class family, and this made his fate all the sadder. As we were neighbors he and I became very intimate, and would sometimes lie for hours chatting with one another. He told me that he had been drafted twice for the army, and each time his father had paid the price of a substitute, but the third time his family could no longer meet the demand, and he was obliged to leave a promising position as assistant scenic artist in a Madrid theatre, to serve his king in the colonies.

At first his illness had not appeared so very serious to me, as he was able to walk about and even seemed in good spirits, but long before Chrisolojo told me that he would never see Spain again, I had noticed how rapidly he was sinking from day to day. What the sickness was, the doctor did not tell me, but Perez said significantly "hambre," and somehow I could not but believe him. The boy grew weaker and thinner, unable to eat the sickening paste placed before him every day. The eternal rice gave him fits of dry vomiting at the mere sight of it. "Take it away! Take it away!" he would exclaim. "Morosqueta! [1] How I hate it!" Raw eggs were given him, but one dozen cost two days' rations. Milk was three motas a pint, and a small chicken was priced at one peseta, so nothing remained but rice, it being the cheapest. As Perez said, if the rations had been doubled, deaths would probably have decreased fifty per cent.

At length my neighbor could no longer rise from his cot without assistance. Often he called on me and I would help him, for he might have lain there all day before the infermeros would have come to his assistance. Often after this I heard him quietly crying to himself at nights, stifling his sobs in the pillow — he now realized the truth. I did not know how near the end was, until one evening a black-robed priest entered, followed by a servant, the latter carrying a large wooden box which he deposited on the floor.

The padre seated himself at the boy's bedside, bending over and speaking to him in a low voice. Meanwhile, the servant opened the box. When I saw its contents my heart sank within me, for the boy and I were friends.

Having donned a white silk gown, the priest began the ceremony, reading an incomprehensible Latin prayer from a book, and holding a small ivory crucifix to the lips of the dying youth. Before he could finish, however, the latter gave a loud shriek of agony, and with a convulsive jerk turned over on his side, burying his face in the bed-clothes, sobbing and calling on his mother. The priest laid aside the book and crucifix with a trembling hand; the tears were coursing down his dusky cheeks, and his chest heaved spasmodically. Then he turned and bent over the dying cazador, hiding his face from my view. Whether he prayed or spoke to the boy I could not tell, but, gradually, the sobbing ceased, and the two figures might have been of stone, so still were they. Presently the priest rose again, took off his white gown, drew the cowl of his black cloak over his head, and quietly left the room, his hands clasped before him. But, before leaving, he had covered the young face with a white handkerchief.

Many times since have I fancied this scene again before my eyes, only to awake with terror and find it a dream. It was not the rarity of the case that caused such an impression on my mind, for similar scenes could be witnessed every day, but — the boy and I had been friends.

Death was a frequent visitor at the hospital of Vigan in those days, nor did he confine himself to the set hours of the establishment, and no sentry's bayonet would keep him out. Fourteen times did he swoop down to bear off a victim during my stay of two months. Some were quietly taken off during the night, their bodies found cold and rigid in the morning; others resisted the bony grasp with shrieks and screams before finally giving in. There were others who simply wasted away until the soul no longer found room in its clay dwelling, and quietly slipped out. The worst sufferers of all were the victims of beri-beri.

This disease is peculiar to tropical Asia, and unknown in America. Out of several cases I witnessed here I will describe one. A cazador, whom I had noticed upon arrival ss being apparently in tolerably good physical condition, lay on a cot on the opposite side of the room from me. Gradually he grew thinner until he seemed to be on the verge, but soon began to pick up again, and was daily gaining in flesh, though not in strength. Each day he grew stouter, and the hollow cheeks filled out once more, still retaining a ghastly yellow complexion, however. I remarked to Perez one day: "That man seems to be doing remarkably well." The practicante shook his head, saying: "No, no, I have seen such before. The best physicians in the world could not save him now — he has beri-beri." For a few days more this unnatural swelling increased, and the patient seemed in great pain. His legs now puffed up to the thickness of his thighs, and he lay on his cot paralyzed from the hips down. Then he was carried out on the balcony and laid on a mat.

The following day, hearing him cry out as if in great bodily pain, I stepped out to see what might be the cause, and if the sufferer possibly could be relieved in some way. The sight that met my eyes sent a shudder through my body, notwithstanding that for the last three weeks I had been compelled to witness suffering daily. The man was naked, and over his bloated body stood Perez and Manuel, the two practicantes, cutting small incisions in the diseased legs and arms, from which trickled a whitish, sticky-looking fluid, which had gathered in a large pool as it dripped on the floor. The pupils of his eyes were barely visible, though the lids were wide open, and from the whole emanated a sickening stench. An hour later, on going out again, I found him alone in a pool of the horrible liquid, half his former dimensions gone, but dead.

But what horrified me most was the neglect with which the very Spaniards treated their own dying countrymen. Perico and Leon were but mere boys, and were on duty only one at a time, still I liked them _ better than the Spanish infermeros for the kindness they showed the sick. At night, however, when these two boys and Chrisolojo were asleep in a distant part of the house, the fiendishness of the Spaniards became most apparent. The helpless might then call for water or assistance to go out on the balcony, but their cries were not only not complied with, but mocked.

One day, in answer to the piteous appeals for help from one of the poor wretches, I arose and went over to his bedside. A nurse, lying sleepily in a corner of the room, shouted to me: "Don't trouble yourself about that fellow, he only cries out to spite us." Just then the doctor's wife, having heard the noise, appeared in the doorway, and the fellow leaped to his feet, pretending to be busily engaged with his duties in general.

The worst example we witnessed one night long after taps had sounded in the barracks across the way. Did I not have two witnesses to testify to the truth of this incident I would hesitate to mention it. Petersen had returned to prison, but Edwards and Bruce were now my companions, and we three saw this act committed.

A patient in the last agonies was screaming at the top of his voice, all attempts at quieting him proving useless. At last, with an oath one of the nurses sprang to his feet, and, going up to the dying man's bedside, he buried his fingers in his neck, thus effectually silencing him. There were no more screams, for the poor wretch suffered no longer; but a murder had been committed.

[1] The name by which rice in a cooked state is universally known throughout the Philippines, derived from the word "moro," or "moros," the Mohammedan natives, who were the only ones that used rice before the advent of the friars.

Chapter Eighteen - Lieutenant Castro

AS before stated, Petersen had recovered and been sent back to prison, but, although I also was cured of dysentery, another ailment came to prevent my return. My legs from the hips down became swelled to almost double their size and covered with ugly ulcers, some so large and deep as to be able to contain a hen's egg. These ulcers are very common even among our own soldiers in the Philippines, but mine was an aggravated case. Chrisolojo informed me that they were the result of bare feet, improper diet, want of physical exercise, and hardships in general, and that he had seen cases where these eating ulcers had laid bare the bone of leg and foot, so as to render amputation necessary. This latter statement the doctor had the tact and consideration not to tell me then, but after my recovery. Many of the Spaniards suffered from them.

Bruce and Edwards were now my companions, the former, as Chrisolojo one day told me aside, in the first stages of consumption, the latter suffering from general debility. Poor Bruce, had he been able to receive proper treatment then, all might have been well, but Chrisolojo was helpless, as he asserted himself.

Time passed more rapidly now, for, besides studying Spanish several hours daily, and teaching English to Chrisolojo, who proved an apt pupil, I now commenced to write out a detailed statement of my experiences, on the backs of old Spanish documents and records which lay stacked almost to the ceiling in the room once the Spanish Governor's office, now the doctor's laboratory. My diary written in San Isidro was lost, so I was obliged to start afresh.

The doctor seemed to have taken a liking to me, for several times he assured me that so long as he could prevent it I should not return to the prison. After all, I liked it better here, for, not only did I have writing paper in abundance, and access to the doctor's books, among which were several Spanish and English grammars, but here also could I read *La Independencia*, which arrived by mail twice a week. The Insurgents had a mail system sadly inferior to ours. The news was, of course, much distorted, but we were at liberty to draw our own deductions from what we read.

We also kept up a continual correspondence with our companions in the prison, either by means of notes which Perez would throw in through the bars wrapped about a stone, while passing, or by signals. We had all learned the Navy Signal Code while over in the jail, to pass away the time, and now the knowledge became useful. From the rear veranda of the hospital the tower of the prison was plainly visible, and from the window of Gillmore's room, Vaudoit, the lieutenant's interpreter, could see our signals with white rags on the end of sticks, or sometimes with the arm alone. Walton, chief quartermaster of the Yorktown, was the master hand at signalling, however, and whenever he was allowed in the lieutenant's quarters, could send us the happenings of a week in a few minutes. At length Gillmore, not considering it safe, ordered his men to desist, so we only communicated by means of notes.

Seeing that the lieutenant's request to have his own rations doubled had met with success, his men requested him again to try in their behalf, and this he did, but with no success. At length, having learned that Arnold was in town, the lieutenant wrote to him, requesting him to secretly visit Señor Rivera, the native merchant who already had been kind to us, and negotiate for the loan of a certain sum of money. Arnold did so, with the result that Señor Rivera sent the lieutenant fifteen pesos. Notwithstanding the secrecy with which this transaction had been carried on, Tino heard of it, and, as will appear later, Rivera suffered severely. But how did this reach the Tagalog general's ears? We can only surmise.

But one day brought the boys in the jail a visit from our old friend and benefactor of Santa Isabela, Captain Espina, who had been sent up here to build trenches. Through his influence they were allowed several hours' daily exercise in the street before the prison building, well-guarded, though. Rations remained the same.

But to return to the hospital. Not only were we more comfortable here, but the many pleasant acquaintances we made with both Spaniards and Filipinos caused our imprisonment to be less irksome than it had been before. Although familiarity does not always breed contempt, the scenes of suffering daily witnessed made not the impression now they had done before.

One Sunday Dr. Chrisolojo was notified by the Ladies' Red Cross Society of Vigan that they would inspect the hospital that same afternoon. The rooms were nicely swept and everything placed in the best possible order. Shortly after the siesta they came, about twenty young mestiza ladies. A couple of weeks later we read an account of this visit in *La Independencia*, a copy of which I have before me now, and, therefore, I will give a literal translation of the article, which was entitled

Deeds of Charity

"There are deeds done which, on account of the good example they set the public, it would be a great pity to keep in obscurity, so that men knowing of these soft touches of human nature may not become sceptics.

"One of these acts took place in the hospital of this district, of which I was a witness, revealing the noble sentiments of woman, and distinguishing charity as one of the most cultivated virtues in our country. Through the kindness of the Director of the Vigan Hospital I am enabled to send you the facts of this incident, risking the displeasure of the young ladies in question, who, owing to their natural modesty, would undoubtedly prefer less publicity.

"On the afternoon of Sunday, the 16th inst., the ladies of the most prominent families of this community, as: Señoras Ignacio and Bernardo Villamor, Señora de Espina, Señora and Señorita de Querol, the Señoritas de Singson, Señoritas de Donate, Señora and Señorita de Formosa, and Señoritas de Avila, paid the hospital a visit.

"After visiting the different wards, giving words of comfort and consolation as only women can do, they at length returned to the reception room, where this wreath of living flowers, as we may well call them, decided to leave behind them something more substantial than the mere pleasant recollection of their visit. At the proposal of Señora de Villamor, a collection was taken up, large enough to give to each of those suffering beings, who together, Filipinos, Spaniards, and Americans, numbered almost one hundred, the sum of thirty cents, no distinction of nationality being made. Sufficient funds were left over for an extraordinary dinner on the following day.

"And those ladies, inspired by the warmth of charity, a virtue binding together all humanity, drowning all petty hatreds, were not even content with distributing their money, but also had brought with them underclothes and linen for the most needy, besides an abundant supply of cigars and cigarettes!

"The patients received the presents and the actions of kindness not only with thanks, but with tears of gratitude, and those that were able followed the kind ladies to the door on their departure, with exclamations of gratitude.

"May the blessed virtue of charity live forever in the heart of woman!

"Raimundo Querol."

"Vigan, July 21, 1899."

For once *La Independencia* did not prevaricate, not even exaggerate, for such were the facts in the case.

But let me now tell of another instance where we were the objects of many such acts of kindly feeling and compassion, and their author never became known beyond the narrow limits of our ward.

At the beginning of the month of August the hospital became so crowded that Chrisolojo applied for an assistant. A young doctor, Gabino Castro, stationed in a northern town where sickness was rare on account of the absence of prisoners, was sent down to Vigan in reply to Chrisolojo's application. We all liked him on first sight.

Lieutenant Castro was a rather handsome young mestizo, tall for a Filipino, and, but that his eyes pointed straight across his face, might have been taken for a Japanese of the higher class. I believe that constant association with suffering had on him the opposite effect to what it usually has on others, it being well understood that young medical students gradually become callous and indifferent to physical suffering of others, to a certain extent. Not so with Castro: his heart was as soft as a woman's. At his suggestion many beneficial changes were made in the management of the hospital, and with his own private means he often bought medicines from the three pharmacies in Vigan, such as the laboratory at the hospital did not contain. His pay as first lieutenant was but twenty pesos monthly, and with this he had to support his family, a wife and three children. Still we often found a basket of bread in our ward, of mornings, to be distributed, and the "lechero" came frequently around to pour half a pint of milk into the bowl of each patient. We soon learned that Castro was at the bottom of all these little acts of kindness. Often would he take one of us aside and slip a peseta into the lucky one's hand. And how quietly he did it — dear, kind Castro. Even the Spaniards spoke of him with respect and even love, and when a Spaniard speaks well of a native, he must indeed be good. As I afterward learned, the young lieutenant would go about and personally solicit pecuniary aid in our behalf from the well-to-do citizens of Vigan, for with his scant salary he could never have done as much as he did.

Still, Castro was a red-hot Insurgent. It was "Viva Aguinaldo!" and "Viva Filipinas!" with him, always. Down with the Spaniards and the Americans, were his sentiments, of which he made no secret to us, and I respected him all the more for it. In the heat of one of his political discourses, in which he often recklessly annihilated whole Spanish or American armies, I would suddenly exclaim: "But, Castro, if you hold such blood-thirsty views, as you profess to do, why did you send the 'lechero' around this morning with milk for each of us?"

"I sent no lechero round," he would say.

"But Perez saw you give the fellow half a peso to do so."

"Well, that is so, this morning, but the money was not mine; the cura sent it for the purpose."

As a fraud Castro was not a success. The local priest, or cura, often came to make us small presents, but *he* never sent them. He would not have done it secretly anyhow, so we did not believe Castro when he tried to put it off on the padre. Besides, the priest, at that time cura, has since assured me that this was not the case.

God bless Castro! As the years roll by, the misery of those long and weary days may gradually fade from my memory, but he will forever stand forth as a ray of light in that dreary period of my life, shedding a glow over my recollections of that gloomy period with a grateful warmth.

Another friend I made in the Vigan Hospital was a young Ilocano lieutenant, Bernardo Villamor, a nephew to Bias Villamor, at that time Tiño's adjutant. Although not more than twenty-three, he had already graduated from the highest colleges of Manila, and was a fine specimen of an intelligent pure-blooded young Filipino, proving that the original native is by no means inferior to the mestizo. He had been wounded in the foot by the accidental discharge of a gun, for which reason he also was an inmate of the hospital, although not of our ward, being quartered with the Spanish officers. He often came to converse with me, showing a familiarity with the outside world that almost led me to believe that he had travelled, but such was not the case. His sympathy with the revolutionary cause was mild, but his admiration for Aguinaldo evident.

Shortly before I had listened to rumors of Luna's assassination by Aguinaldo's orders circulating among the Spaniards, and now I requested the young lieutenant, whom I certainly put down as a sympathizer with the Ilocano general, for the particulars and his opinion of the murder,

"No, no," he protested, "Aguinaldo is not responsible for Luna's death. I happen to know the true details of the whole affair from personal friends of mine, also Ilocanos, who were in Cabanatuan at the time the crime was committed.

"Luna, you must know, while a man of rare abilities, was harsh to his inferiors, and altogether a strict disciplinarian. An officer or soldier who shirked his duty or showed cowardice on the battle-field could expect no mercy from him, and on several occasions he had culprits executed or otherwise severely punished for such offences. This severity, combined with the fact of his being an Ilocano, caused a certain faction of young Tagalog officers to entertain a deadly hatred for him, as many of them had already felt the weight of his iron hand.

"One evening, at Cabanatuan, and while that place just then formed the temporary head-quarters of Aguinaldo and his staff, Luna called upon the President for a consultation in the convent. With him was Colonel Francisco Roman, his chief of staff and warm personal friend. It was this officer who on February 24th last led that disastrous night attack on Manila from the bay, wherein his whole force nearly became annihilated, he barely escaping with his own life.

"At this meeting Aguinaldo and Luna had an altercation about some subject on which they held diverse opinions, but other officers present say that it amounted to no more than a friendly argument. Shortly after this Luna and Roman departed to return to their quarters. Hardly had they passed the convent door when several shots rang out. The two friends were found lying side by side, Luna with his empty revolver in one hand, Roman grasping the hilt of his broken sword, both dead. About them lay three of the assassins, also dead. Two had been shot by Luna's revolver, the third had been run through by Roman's sword.

"We, as Ilocanos, have lost a good deal of sympathy for the cause since then, but none of us have ever accused Aguinaldo of being the cause of Antonio Luna's death."

Such was young Villamor's account of Luna's assassination, which agrees in all principal parts with what has since been told me by other Filipinos, both Tagalogs and Ilocanos. Never have I heard Aguinaldo blamed for that crime.

It was not long after this, when, having recovered sufficiently from his wound to leave the hospital, Lieutenant Villamor made preparations to ascend the river Abra to his home in Bangued, to finish his recovery there. Here he asked me if I would be willing to accompany him on parole, as his companion, provided he could obtain the necessary permission from Tiño. Of course, I expressed myself as only too glad to accept such a privilege.

In the evening of that same day he returned from his visit to Tiño's headquarters, but not only had the Tagalog chieftain refused to grant him the favor he asked, but at the same time advised him that it would not be to his advantage to form any intimacy with the American prisoners.

Next day he bade me good-by, departing for Bangued, where two of my acquaintances now were — he and Dr. Abasilla.

For some time past we had heard rumors of a peace conference again. Chrisolojo appeared a good deal excited, and several times while at his English in his private office he would suddenly exclaim: "I must study hard, so that when the Americans come here I can speak to them," Upon questioning him I furthermore learned that they (the Insurgents) were but waiting for the Americans to give them a definite description of the government to be established, and they would lay down their arms. "A government like that of Canada, and we will be satisfied, but these uncertain promises we now receive are not satisfactory. We want a written agreement signed by both parties. As long as the Americans persist in treating the Filipinos as savage tribes, they will refuse to surrender. We consider ourselves worthy of being treated as a people, and so long as the American Government persists in ignoring Aguinaldo as our representative, so long will we all, Ilocanos and Tagalogs alike, feel that we are being oppressed."

One day a cry from one of the Spaniards attracted us all out to the balcony, and, looking toward the seashore, we saw in the harbor the smoke of a steamer rising above the intervening treetops. The ports had been opened, we were told, and communication was established between Vigan and Manila. Whatever doubts we may have had on the subject were effectually removed the next day, when two-thirds of the Spaniards received letters from Manila and Spain. Chrisolojo showed us a letter from his brother in Cavite, also a surgeon, but employed in the American hospital. It bore the old familiar two-cent postage-stamp with George Washington's profile, so we knew it was genuine.

Naturally we felt deeply disappointed at what appeared to us strange neglect. "What!" Chrisolojo exclaimed, "you have received no letters? That is not our fault. Your Government authorities could have forwarded you any amount of mail, as well as to the Spaniards. Why don't they send you books to read? Undoubtedly you all have letters awaiting you in the Manila post-office. Why don't they forward them to you?"

Many times after that we saw American war-vessels pass on the distant horizon. "If they only knew," we thought, "that the town is garrisoned by less than a hundred poorly trained soldiers, each armed with an old-fashioned Remington, and refilled ammunition scarce, with no retreat into the mountains within twenty miles save the Abra Pass up a swollen mountain torrent, what could they not do for us?"

Little did we then dream that every school child in the United States capable of reading the daily papers not only knew of our presence in Vigan, but the number of us in the hospital and even the amount of our daily rations!

Of course, we often discussed the possibilities of an escape, though that only brought the helplessness of our situation the more vividly to our minds. By land the Americans were over two hundred miles distant, since we knew that after taking San Isidro they had once more retreated. To reach the ships would be equally impossible, without aid from some person acquainted with the location of a boat, the nature of the three miles of country between the hospital and the beach, and the ability to obtain some provisions. Many Spaniards had really escaped on the march, but as they were seldom guarded, this was comparatively an easy matter. Under similar circumstances we Americans would not remain prisoners very long, and to judge by the vigilance with which we had been guarded the officials evidently thought likewise. On various occasions I had been approached by cazadores contemplating escape, inviting me to accompany them, but each time some unforeseen hitch had occurred, feet became sore, new guards, or patrols stationed, etc., and those schemes never materialized. Every Spaniard had conceived an original plan for escape, but he never wished to put it into execution himself; he gave you the idea gratis, and you were welcome to make use of it. However, there occurred an incident that stirred my hope in a successful accomplishment of a scheme of this nature.

One evening, after taps had been sounded, Perez, the practicante, came to my bedside, and, bending over me, whispered softly, "Inside of five minutes you come out on the veranda." When it seemed to me that time had passed, I arose and tiptoed softly out on the balcony, where in an obscure corner I found Perez, Manuel, two practicantes from below, and a sergeant, the latter a patient from the officers' quarters, all seated on the floor and conversing in low whispers. I was pulled down beside them, and Perez said: "Promise that to no one, not even your two comrades, you will repeat a word of what passes between us here tonight." I gave my word, and then they unfolded a plan for escaping that certainly seemed plausible enough. By bribing a fisherman they had secured his aid in finding a boat hidden in a small lagoon opening out into the sea. With a few pesos saved from their earnings they could buy enough provisions to last six of us several days. This was Tuesday. On the following night a little before the rise of the moon we would all steal out into the grounds in the rear of the hospital, scale the practically unguarded back wall, and by a road familiar to them reach the boat and launch her. Knowing me to be a seaman, they had decided to invite me to join them, as they themselves were entirely ignorant of the manipulation of a boat, and once out upon the water I was to have entire charge of the expedition. So feasible did this plan appear, that I at once became intensely interested. Besides, the quiet and determined manner in which they spoke, all of them intelligent young men, impressed me with confidence in the sincerity of their intentions.

At first I felt some compunction at leaving Bruce and Edwards out of our number, both of whom would, I knew, not have hesitated a moment, but Perez so strenuously insisted that we must not include them on account of the scarcity of provisions and water that I had no choice. I must either leave them or give up all chances of escaping. By following the latter course I did not benefit them — I chose the former.

When Wednesday evening came it was found necessary to postpone our departure until Thursday night, as the bamboos of water, more necessary even than the provisions already there, had not yet been brought down to the boat. A large mat and some rope, to be used respectively as sail and rigging, also remained to be carried down, and that could not be procured until the morning.

Thursday morning I saw nothing of the five Spaniards until almost noon, when Perez made his appearance, his clothes torn, muddy, and wet. Rushing to the cot where he slept he hurriedly changed his garments for clean ones, hiding the soiled suit under his mat. As he then went out on the balcony, I followed to learn the cause of this strange behavior. "Dios moi!" he cried, breathlessly, "all our plans destroyed! Barely did we ourselves escape; the patrol fired on us as we were carrying down the water. Last night a Spanish lieutenant with four men escaped in a boat, and now they have stretched a cordon of soldiers and bolomen along the beach, with orders to fire on any Spaniard that approaches within rifle range. Not knowing what had taken place, we went down this morning with the sail and the water, and as we approached the boat we were fired on. We scattered and fled, fortunately finding shelter in the jungle."

This was, of course, a death-blow to all our hopes. The boat and provisions seized, escape became as impossible as if we had been bound with chains, and we fully realized it. However, I had occasion to remember this failure long after, and, although it had now come to naught, it served its purpose, for me at least.

The Spanish officer who had made good his escape was a Lieutenant Repol, a young Porto Rican. He and his four companions were recaptured two days later, the want of water driving them ashore ten kilometres above Vigan. Before they could procure the necessary water, however, a patrol of bolomen discovered them, taking them down to Vigan again, where they were thrown into the prison with our American comrades. O'Brien wrote us an account of their arrival and their punishment, and sent it to us in the hospital through Perez.

Tiño was away at this time, as was also Bias Villamor, his adjutant, the latter having been appointed post-commander of San Fernando de Union. A certain Captain Reyes had been left in charge, whose hatred of the Spaniards amounted almost to a mania. He had Repol and his four men strapped down to a bench and publicly flogged, giving each one fifty lashes, the lieutenant the same as his men.

Two days later Tiño returned, and learned what had taken place during his absence. Witnesses who were present afterward told me that the youthful general flew into a violent passion, almost venturing to strike Captain Reyes, whom he placed under arrest for some time. "I detest the Spaniards as much as you do," he is reported to have exclaimed, "but to punish an act like this, which we ourselves under like circumstances would commit, is downright cowardice!"

This Tiño was a strange character. He had many admirers as well as enemies, some of the former being also of the latter. Although not twenty years of age at the time, he came into command of a brigade in the insurrection of 1896 and 1897; going to Hong-Kong with Aguinaldo after the treaty of Biacnabato, and returning with him again in 1898 as an ally of the Americans. While Aguinaldo remained in Cavite to superintend operations against the Spaniards in Manila and the other Tagalog provinces, Tiño with less than five hundred men marched north, driving the Dons before him. The latter, double the number of the Insurgents, retreated fighting, gathering up garrisons on their way until reaching Tagudin, where they made their last stand. Here, I am told by Spaniards themselves, they numbered fifteen hundred; Tiño's force about eight hundred. The latter attacked the Spanish trenches, Tiño personally leading the charge, and, after two hours' fierce fighting, the Spaniards fled, leaving the Tagalogs in possession.

Before going further on with this boyish general's victorious advance on an invasion of the Ilocano provinces, it is worthwhile noticing that almost at this same place, that is, in San Fernando, Tiño, fifteen months later, with about an equal force, possibly a little less, was in the same position as the Spaniards, and unable to resist the charge of thirty American cavalrymen. This seems hard to believe, but such are, nevertheless, the facts as I gathered from authentic sources.

On August 13, 1898, the same day that Manila capitulated, Tiño entered Vigan and raised the Insurgent flag over the Bishop's Palace. Leaving a small garrison, he continued his pursuit of the retreating cazadores, who finally surrendered to him in Ilocos Norte, placing into the hands of the Insurgents two thousand stand of arms and untold quantities of ammunition.

It was on this occasion that Tiño captured the Bishop of Vigan and over one hundred friars. I will repeat a story told me by different persons claiming to be witnesses of an incident which occurred at this time, which I consider undoubtedly true.

Upon fleeing from Vigan the friars carried with them a treasure of several thousand pesos in silver. When realizing that capture was inevitable, the bishop had the bags of silver thrown into a hole dug for the reception of a number of drains. Covered by the filth and slush of this cesspool, his reverence evidently thought the treasure safe until at some future day he could recover it. Some native must have seen this done, for it reached Tiño's ears, and calling upon the bishop in person, who was confined in the convent, he requested him to reveal the hiding-place of the treasure, promising to give him a fair percentage as reward, and also to treat him with all the courtesy due to his station. The bishop professed profound ignorance of any hidden treasure. Tiño had the Spanish prelate brought to the brink of the pool. "If that silver is not forthcoming within five minutes," he told him, "your reverence bodily enters." The bishop was then obliged to kneel on the very brink, and with his own hands he fished for and finally pulled out the bags of silver, one by one. Fortunately the pool was not deep, so he soiled no more than the entire length of the sleeves of his episcopal gown, but it was said that so great had been the shock to his nervous system that for months he was confined to his couch, whether caused by the humiliation or the loss of the money is not known, however.

On another occasion, shortly after that related, while in Vigan, Tiño learned that the captive friars were living well on money sent them from Manila, while the poor cazadores were obliged to subsist on their meagre rations. Before they could hide it, the young Tagalog had their money seized, and, having all the soldier prisoners assembled in the plaza, he divided the pesos of the friars equally among them, the cazadores cheering the Tagalog general lustily.

But the story of Tiño that has amused me more than others, and the truth of which I am also more positive of, is one that my friend Villamor told me, and the principal actor of which I also learned to know rather intimately afterward.

There lived in Vigan, in the time of the Spanish Government, a gentleman of proud old Castile, who held a high position in the Civil Service. As this same gentleman, as I now write, still lives in Vigan, and still holds the same position under the American Government that he held before, I will call him

Don Francisco, to avoid wounding any feelings, which the connection of his true name with this story might occasion. But, should any of my friends in Vigan have learned sufficient English to read these lines, they will recognize the man — and smile.

Well, Don Francisco was a very haughty gentleman, and demanded homage from all his inferiors in social standing, especially from natives. Any Filipino that dared to pass him without first saluting soon learned to rue his neglect. Don Francisco, being a proud man, was also very strong. Thus with his muscles did he teach the natives the respect due his person. Considering all this, it is really not surprising that the worthy Don was not especially beloved by the people. Everybody must salute him — it was with him a mania.

But the insurrection came, and, along with the rest of his countrymen, Don Francisco was taken prisoner by Tiño's forces. Now the tables were turned, and the people cried for the blood of their quondam oppressor. "Death to Don Francisco!" they shouted at the prison gates. "No," answered Tiño, "he shall not be killed in cold blood. We are not savages." "Then give us satisfaction," the people cried again, "give us satisfaction for the wrong this man has done us."

Tiño now issued a proclamation, calling upon all who felt themselves wronged by this Spaniard to assemble on the plaza the following morning, when satisfaction would be given to each one. All Vigan was agog to know what the proud aristocrat's punishment for his former arrogance would be.

When morning came, the plaza was thronged. Tiño made his appearance, and after him came Don Francisco, escorted by four soldiers, armed, not with guns or bolos, but with rattan canes. Then all those who had any grievance against the prisoner were told to form into line, and one by one they filed past Don Francisco, who was ordered to salute each native as he passed. Each time a man passed, and he failed to salute him, the soldiers cut him across the small of his back with their rattans, so he soon concluded to salute each man. All day long, from early morning until night, that endless file marched by, and to each one the now humbled Spaniard repaid a salute which at some time past he had demanded by force. Many, having once passed, returned to the rear and fell into line again, willing to stand patiently waiting for their turn to once more receive their fallen enemy's enforced salutation. It was said that so many times did Don Francisco work his hand up and down on that day that for a long time afterward, when enjoying his liberty, he would occasionally be seen standing on the street, absentmindedly bringing his hand up to his forehead in a military salute, although there might be no person within a hundred yards of him.

It was now drawing on close to the end of August, but what between the doctor, his wife, the two boys, Perico and Leon, and Castro, our time passed rapidly, considering, of course, the impatience consequent upon our imprisonment. Everybody connected with the hospital was kind and considerate to us, and, therefore, our confined situation was far less irksome than it might have been. Castro brought us a chess game, and every evening played with some one of us, and proved himself an expert player. He would choose the black figures and leave us the white, and, then, when he had his opponent checkmated, would joyously declare that so would the greater game end, the chess-board of which was the Philippine Islands, and the chessmen black and white regiments of soldiers. But soon a change came!

It was nearing the change of the monsoons and the end of the rainy season, when on a certain afternoon toward the end of August we were all lying down on our cots, the unusual fine weather making us all feel drowsy. The sky was a deep blue, not a cloud to be seen. A light breeze floated gently up from the south. All of a sudden, several of the nurses, being on the balcony, appeared in the doorway, and excitedly called out: "Vamos! vamos! Cañonazos!" In a moment all of us that could move, were out there leaning over the railing. We listened. Sure enough, that same familiar angry hum, like bumble-bees. The Spaniards were almost frantic with excitement, and we ourselves, although not so demonstrative, hardly less expectant.

Several days after this Tiño left the town with all the troops he could spare, hardly half a company remaining to do garrison duty. We then heard that the Insurgents had captured, looted, and partly destroyed the steamer Saturnus of the Compañia Maritima of Manila at San Fernando, and in revenge an American war-vessel had bombarded the town. On the same day of Tiño's departure all the Spanish officers quartered in the town were sent up to Abra. Evidently Vigan was no longer considered safe.

It was on the morning of September 4th, just as we had finished our meagre breakfast, that Chrisolojo entered with a solemn face. "I am afraid you must go," he told us. "I have orders from military headquarters to send you all over there preparatory to leaving for Bangued." We three at once commenced to roll up mats, pillows, and bedclothes on which we had slept, and which Chrisolojo now gave to us. A corporal stood at the door, ready to take charge of us. The doctor looked on as if sorry to have us depart. Presently an idea seemed to strike him. "Do you wish to stay behind?" he asked me. For a moment I hesitated, but Bruce whispering in my ear, "Fool, if you don't," decided me. "Yes," I answered. "Then lie down," he said, "and feign serious sickness. I will report that you are in a critical condition and unable to travel."

So, bidding good-by, Bruce and Edwards left me, confident that within a short time I should be within the American lines. The Americans having bombarded and landed at San Fernando, we thought, Vigan would next be attacked. In the general retreat the sick would be left behind. I felt certain that in such a case Chrisolojo and Castro would have forgotten me — they would have taken particular pains to do so.

Three hours later a message came from the palace, as head-quarters was familiarly called, containing the following:

"Señor Director del Hospital Militar de Vigan: Send that American on, even if he must be carried.

"Capitan Reyes."

Dr. Chrisolojo showed me the note, and once more I packed up my bundle. The doctor's mother and wife came in, the former slipping into the pocket of my ragged blouse a package of home-made cakes, the latter a small bundle of cigars. Tears were visible in their eyes. Castro was gone and would not return until morning. I felt sorry to leave without seeing him. Having bid everybody "adios" I started down the stairs accompanied by a guard and Perico. The doctor came down, and, calling on us to stop, slipped a silver peso into my hand. I felt heavy of heart, for now I realized how kind these people had been to me.

Chapter Nineteen - Up the River Abra

LEAVING the hospital, my single guard and Perico conducted me across the plaza to the palace, where Captain Reyes, seeing that my condition was not as bad as he had been given to understand, became exceedingly wroth, but a few words that Perico spoke to him in Ilocano seemed to mollify him. I found my companions, with the exception of Lieutenant Gillmore and O'Brien, confined in a room in a back part of the building. The Englishman had been separated from the rest for the last week for striking a guard. Here we remained until the afternoon, when we were lined up outside, O'Brien and Gillmore joining us. A carreton stood ready, and in this Captain Reyes directed me to be seated, along with the lieutenant. "You will not need to walk one step until Bangued is reached," he informed me in a gentler voice than I had at first thought he could command. Suddenly, to our surprise, Arnold appeared, and also crowded into the carreton, and off we went through the narrow streets of Vigan, followed by an escort of twenty soldiers, and all the small boys of the town.

Following the same road by which we had come, we at length reached the banks of the river Abra, where a halt was called, and preparations made to camp for the night. A fire was built, and around this we stretched ourselves out to sleep, but even so, the cold toward morning was intense. Long before dawn reveille was sounded, and we arose to prepare for the day's journey.

The Insurgent reveille, original with them, is very different from the brassy blare that disturbs the morning sleep of our American soldiers. The Insurgents occasionally made use of the Spanish reveille, something equally disagreeable as ours, but their own was a complete melody, which, when played by a good performer, as most Filipinos are, is really a pleasure to listen to. It can, in fact, not be rendered on a bugle; it requires a cornet. So softly does it commence that the first notes are hardly audible, but gradually they swell into more volume, like a skylark descending from on high down toward the earth, its warbling growing louder and louder. Again it sinks to a low mellow strain seeming about to die out, when, with a wild leap, it once more bursts out into a melodious crash that sends a thousand echoes back from the neighboring hills which still continue resounding long after the last notes of the cornet itself have died out. So did the reveille sound on that morning of September 5th.

The Filipinos are naturally born musicians; few of them but what can perform well on some instrument. Each town, no matter how small, has its brass band, and these otherwise ignorant "tauis," barefooted and ragged, will place the brass instruments to their lips and launch forth into difficult operatic airs, which, after having heard performed but once or twice, they can repeat without losing a note.

I forgot to mention a little incident that occurred to us on the march once, and which was highly amusing. We had entered a town, and were marched in great state to the presidency, escorted by all the local police and a brass band. To an American, new from home, the scene would have been a strange one — hundreds of dusky half-clad natives on all sides of us, naked, long-haired Igorrotes intermingling in the crowd, hoarse cries and shouts in a strange guttural dialect, the old Spanish convent of ancient architecture with a background of tropical foliage, all suggestive of a remote and unenlightened corner of the earth, whose inhabitants evidently thought their own narrow sphere of existence the centre of the universe. Presently, however, the big bass drum ahead of us received two resounding whacks, and we found ourselves marching to the familiar air, "There'll be a hot time in the old town to-night." The shouts on all sides now only helped to suggest a parade on election night.

These musicians had heard the air as played by one of the American regimental bands on the Luneta in Manila, and, after practising awhile, could go through it as well as those they had heard it from.

But let us once more return to the banks of the Abra River.

Shortly after reveille, dawn broke, and a number of natives appeared who at once set to work at launching three large bamboo rafts that had been hauled up high and dry on the bank. As soon as they were afloat a small wicker cabin, or enclosure, was placed on each and the baggage stored inside. We were now divided into three groups, soldiers and prisoners alike, each division embarking on one of the three rafts. There were three raftsmen to each, and they at once, by means of pushing with stout poles or hauling by long ropes of rattan, sent us up against the current, through whirlpools and up rapids. On they went without once stopping, knowing just when and where to take advantage of a back eddy and how to cut around bends with the least exertion. Sometimes they poled, sometimes they jumped overboard and pushed, at other times they would paddle or pull with a will, and when the wind was fair they would hoist a sail, but, whatever obstacles presented themselves, they would know how to overcome them.

By eight o'clock we were entering "La Bocana," and, although up to now it had been calm, a terrific gale of wind now swept down on us through this mountain gorge or gap, which gradually died out, however, as we kept on ascending the river and entered the pass. On both sides of us majestic cliffs rose abruptly from the water, leaving no possible path by which a traveller on foot might have passed. In one place a long rattan rope stretched from a small sand-spit along the bottom of a perpendicular rock wall to another pebbly beach. Here an old native lived who made an existence by rafting travellers from the one sand-spit to the other, pulling his bamboo raft the distance of several hundred yards by means of the rope. Only in this manner could "La Bocana" be passed by travellers on foot.

As we continued penetrating into these mountains the scenery became even more wild and impressive. Far up from out jutting rocks goats gazed down upon us, which, had they fallen, might almost have dropped on the rafts. Small spurts of water shot out from ledges hundreds of feet above us, and fell in white ribbons of spray, squirming in the wind like silvered snakes, while along the banks countless little rivulets and cascades emptied into the main river to help swell its volume. Nestling among these imposing peaks and ridges were little cañons, sometimes broadening into small valleys, from some of which the nipa roof of a lonely hut peeped out from the broad leaves of a banana grove. Each bend in the river opened up a new scene, a constantly changing panorama.

At noon we stopped at a small town built on the brow of a cliff overlooking the river. This was San Quintin, and here we disembarked, ascending a steep path to the top. For several hours we were confined in the presidency, patiently waiting for a promised dinner to break our twenty-four hours' fast. At last it appeared in the shape of a plate of blue-looking rice for each and a tin cup full of paw-paw soup, the latter strongly suggestive of boiled watermelon rind, but, as our guards fared no better than we did, we had no right to complain.

At about 3 P.M. we again embarked, at liberty to recline at our ease on the rafts, to smoke and to admire the scenery. The river now seemed to change into a winding chain of broad lakes, in which the high peaks of the surrounding mountains were plainly reflected, so calm was the water. Strange birds of brilliant plumage skimmed over the surface, uttering wild cries as if angry at our intrusion into their domain, while some cattle we observed here and there on the low banks, staring at us, would suddenly turn about, throw up their tails, and quickly disappear in the thicket.

These cattle were not carabaos, but resembled rather fine Jersey cows, and are generally confined to the mountain regions of Northern Luzon. At first I thought that they at some time had been imported from America or Australia, but a hump on the shoulders, just behind the neck, very prominent in some, and almost imperceptible in others, would rather lead one to believe them of East Indian origin. The natives often use them to draw light vehicles, as quilez or carromatas, for they have the advantage over horses that they are cheaper. They are also sometimes used in the carretones, for carabaos are scarce in these parts, and, while not so powerful, the "vacuno," as the natives call him, is quicker of movement, and does not need those frequent baths or mud wallows, consequently has more resistive power. Their meat is excellent, while that of the carabao is tough and leathery, and their milk is equal to that of our American cattle in both quantity and quality.

There were also half-naked men gazing at us from the banks, their flowing hair sometimes hanging down their backs, and sometimes done up in a coil on the tops of their heads, in Chinese fashion. Some had long spears in their hands, giving them a fiercer appearance than they really deserved, for these, the Tinguianes, a wild tribe similar to the Igorrotes, are a very peaceful people. A white man need have no fear in trusting himself entirely alone and unarmed among them, for they have all the virtues of Christians without their vices. In appearance they are small of stature, but well formed, with muscles wonderfully well developed, especially those of the legs. Their color is perceptibly lighter than that of the Tagalogs, and many have a decided Mongolian cast of features.

History informs us that Chinese pirates established colonies in these parts of Luzon two centuries ago, and the Spanish, sending out an expedition against them, drove them back into the mountains, where they settled down among the Tinguianes. This undoubtedly explains what appears to be a strain of Chinese blood in them.

Although the rivers in other parts of Luzon, as I am credibly informed, teem with crocodiles or caymen, they do not exist in the Abra River, for the natives bathe freely in its waters, and many do not even know what a crocodile is. For the night we camped on a broad sand-spit, but the cold toward morning deprived us of sleep.

Before dawn we resumed our journey, and for five hours continued steadily to ascend the river, which now became narrow and swift again. At length we entered a broad valley, and at about ten o'clock disembarked at a small landing. Gillmore, Arnold, and I were given a seat in a carreton, and, the rest on foot, we commenced to follow up a muddy road which ran in a straight line through rice-paddies, cane-brakes, and corn-fields.

At the end of half an hour we reached Bangued, the capital of the Province of Abra, a town of not half the size of Vigan, but very picturesquely situated at the foot of a range of high hills. We were brought to the presidency, where a large crowd of natives and Spanish prisoners gathered about to inspect us, but none of them behaved in a rude manner. I was sitting in the rear of the carreton, my back toward the main part of the crowd, when behind me I heard a familiar voice: "Bien, bien, hombre, how are you?" Turning I beheld Abasilla's fat, good-natured face beside me. "And how are you?" he inquired. "Much better, thank you!" I replied, shaking hands with him. "Bien, bien!" he exclaimed, his face beaming with a broad smile, "have a cigar." I accepted a fine cheroot, such as were not ordinarily bought. "Why are you riding?" he continued. I showed him my bandaged legs. "Ah!" he retorted, "ulcers; we will soon cure them here. Good-by, I will see you again!" and shaking hands with me he disappeared in the crowd.

In a little while the local President appeared and ordered us to be conducted to the jail, a small, cramped, and gloomy brick and stone building. Here we all entered with the exception of Arnold and O'Brien, the former being given quarters in the convent with the cura, the latter leaving town altogether for parts unknown. His action of striking a guard had earned for him the reputation of being a dangerous character.

With these two exceptions we were once more reunited under the roof of the jail of Bangued.

Chapter Twenty - Filipino Friends

ALTHOUGH our new prison was cramped, the alcaide was kind and considerate, trying in every way to make us as comfortable as circumstances would permit. On account of my condition I had been placed in the same quarters with Lieutenant Gillmore, the two of us occupying a room in the front part of the building overlooking the plaza. The others were confined in a large but gloomy cell in the rear.

Abasilla came to visit us in the afternoon, telling me that he had received a letter from Chrisolojo, advising him to have me removed to the Bangued Hospital for further treatment. Edwards had entirely recovered, and Bruce also looked so much better that I thought Chrisolojo had been mistaken when diagnosing his case. The doctor told me to write an application for my transfer to the hospital, address it to the local President, and give it to the alcaide, who would see it delivered. It was a mere matter of form, he said.

In the evening I received a visit from my old acquaintance Bernardo Villamor, who came in spite of Tiño's warning to have no intercourse with American prisoners. He was on duty again as one of the garrison officers.

The following day I wrote a letter to the local President in my best Spanish, as the doctor had advised me to do. In the afternoon two policemen appeared who escorted me across the plaza to the hospital building, where Abasilla received me at the door and conducted me upstairs. This establishment was in reality not entitled to the name of a hospital, being classed only as an "infermeria," the building not being half the size of the one in Vigan, but the number of prisoners did not demand a regular hospital.

Arriving on the top floor the doctor led the way into an extensive room where about a dozen Spanish officers were quartered. Passing through this we entered into a smaller room beyond, wherein stood several chairs, a table, and two bedsteads. On one of the latter lay an elderly Spaniard, reading, but as we entered he rose and greeted us. Abasilla introduced us to each other, telling me that we were to be roommates, as the other bedstead was for me. The elderly Spaniard was Captain Hiado of the Ninth Battalion of Cazadores, also a patient in the hospital, but what his illness consisted in always remained a mystery — even to himself, I may add.

The room was large and sunny, with three sliding blinds or windows, one overlooking the plaza, the other two affording a view of the neighboring hills.

I now spoke to Abasilla of Bruce, hoping to have him brought over as a companion, but he had examined him, and his less experienced eye had failed to detect what Chrisolojo had seen.

My existence now glided tranquilly but monotonously on for some time. I had brought my manuscript with me up from Vigan, besides a quantity of old documents blank on one side, suitable for writing, and for several hours daily I found employment with my pen, or the doctor's pen, to be more exact, for from him it was borrowed together with the ink.

Young Villamor came to visit me frequently, bringing Spanish novels for me, to learn from and amuse myself with at the same time.

There were in reality no sick in the hospital, the only patients being Spanish officers who might have been ailing at some time, but were all in good health now. They invited me to join their mess, and many a pleasant hour have I spent in their company. The imprisonment had somewhat roughened them but not made them coarser. For the first time since my capture I was able to sit daily down to a table, and eat my meal from a plate with knife and fork. Each officer had his own private attendant or "assistente," as he was called, a soldier which the Spanish army rules assign to each commissioned officer as his servant. Captain Hiado and myself got on especially well together.

On the second afternoon after my arrival at the infirmary Abasilla sent one of his servants to escort me to his private home in the neighborhood, for the doctor did not live in the hospital building. His house, but a few steps down a side street from the plaza, though small, had a very respectable appearance, being built of wood, with a nipa roof. The latter is not always a sign of poverty, for even the well-to-do sometimes have such roofs over their fine houses, they being cooler than tiles or galvanized iron.

I found the doctor in his front parlor almost buried in the depths of a spacious cane reclining chair. As I entered he motioned to me to follow his example, so I dropped into a similar chair. It seemed his object in sending for me was only for the purpose of having a friendly chat, and, puffing away at his cigars, we discussed politics. Later his wife entered and joined in the conversation. She was a young, pure-blooded, typical Filipino woman, her features rather dark but remarkably intelligent looking. Her dress was that of all the middle-class native women, a low-necked chemisette of maguey cloth, with very wide sleeves only to the elbows, and a calico skirt. Over her shoulders she wore a fine shawl of real piña cloth, manufactured from the delicate fibres of the pineapple plant, and embroidered with silk. On her feet she wore silk "chinelas," a heelless slipper which gives to the Filipino woman's step the sound of a shambling gait.

I was invited to stay for dinner that evening, returning to the hospital at nine, o'clock, escorted by the servant again.

It soon became the custom for me to drop around on the doctor's family every afternoon, and they made me feel very much at home. For half an hour each day I taught his wife the rudiments of English, while she for an equal length of time expounded to me the mysteries of Spanish grammar, which she was well capable of doing, having a thorough convent education. Almost every evening I lingered until nine or ten o'clock, as they gave me to understand that the invitation to supper was a standing one.

I have forgotten to mention that the hospital was guarded by a single policeman, who was most of the time asleep. He it was who sometimes escorted me around to the doctor's house and return. Upon the first day of my arrival Abasilla had said to me: "The building is practically unguarded, but you must not venture outside unattended; you might compromise me by so doing." This I considered as binding as a whole company of guards, consequently I never allowed myself to be seen in the street alone.

Now it often happened that after I had spent the evening with Abasilla and his family, and the time had come to return to my room, this solitary policeman, instead of waiting for me, had crawled into some corner and fallen asleep. Then the doctor was obliged to conduct me over to the hospital himself. As I have already remarked, he was fat, and walking had long ceased to be a recreation to him, so he didn't like it. One evening, when I was on the point of returning, the policeman was again conspicuous by his absence. After cursing him for some time, the doctor, who was wedged in between the arms of his reclining chair, grunted out: "Never mind; steal around to your room alone, but let no one see you." I did as he told me. The next night I did so again. Thus this soon became a habit, and the policeman was not even looked for.

One day I asked the doctor's permission to visit the prison. The policeman, as usual, was absent, but it was broad daylight. Abasilla looked helplessly about, but at length said: "Run across the plaza, but be quick; I shall place that miserable fellow in the stocks when he returns." But Abasilla was not the man to have anybody placed in stocks, and nobody knew this better than the policeman himself, who soon reduced his duties as watchman to an occasional tour of inspection about the premises.

One afternoon young Villamor appeared and asked me to accompany him to his house. As Abasilla was present he requested his permission, although he really outranked him. Villamor's house was some distance away, on the other side of the town, in fact. He introduced me to his family, consisting of his great-aunt, sister, one brother, and cousin. Villamor was married, but his wife on this occasion was absent on a visit to her mother in Bucay, a town about twenty miles farther in the interior. All the male members of the family, five in number, were graduates of the highest colleges of Manila. They had a library of several thousand books, from deep scientific works to light literature, and I was given to understand that, whenever I felt inclined to read, his books were at my disposal. Upon my leaving, Villamor accompanied me to the corner of the street and then bid me "adios." "But am I to return unguarded?" I asked him. "Oh, what nonsense," he exclaimed, "I will be responsible."

Upon arriving at the hospital, Abasilla saw that I came alone. I explained to him the reason, but he only smiled and said, "So long as you don't go outside the limits of the town, no harm will result." This practically removed the last restraint on my movements.

Being able to obtain sufficient bodily exercise, health soon returned, and the ulcers on my body gradually disappeared. It soon became pretty well known that the illness on account of which I was in the hospital no longer existed, not even in my imagination, and, but for Abasilla's friendship, I should have been sent back to the prison.

I now visited my comrades in the prison daily; in fact I wrote several hours each day on my manuscript in Gillmore's room, at his table, for my blank paper had disappeared so rapidly in the hospital that I had begged the lieutenant to keep it for me in his room, where the clean white sheets would tempt nobody. Several times he had written to the local President, and even to the provincial governor, for the liberty of the town, but rarely were they even answered. Once, however, the local President had sent word stating that he did not wish to take the responsibility; if the doctor in the hospital was willing to allow the American in his charge to wander about unguarded, why, that was his own look-out. Thus it appeared that my comrades were in the hands of the municipal authorities, and I still in the charge of the military.

On several occasions the Spanish officers had taken me with them on morning walks to a spring a short distance outside of town. It was an ideal walk, through avenues of tamarind and banana trees, long hedges of the maguey cactus bordering the road on both sides. The spring itself gushed out from the side of the mountain, its source buried in a perfect jungle of ferns, bamboo, and a dense variety of tropical plants. The water, pure as the atmosphere itself, ran through a number of consecutive cement basins, built in imitation of some ancient Roman baths. Into one of these basins we could plunge; the rest were filled with water-lilies and other aquatic plants. On all sides, in wild confusion, grew bamboo, rattan, cocoa trees, coffee-bushes, areca palms, tamarinds, mango, and banana-trees. The overhead foliage completely shut out the sunlight, and even at midday this nook was deeply shaded and cool. Here I often brought out a book to lie down and read in the shade.

On one occasion I met the alcaide of the prison in a neighboring tienda, and treating him to a cent's worth of vino, which placed us on the most friendly footing, I asked him as a favor to allow one of my comrades under his charge to accompany me each morning to the spring for a bath, and between his natural good-nature and the vino he consented. The very next morning I took Bruce with me, and we remained there under the trees for two hours. On another morning I was accompanied by Edwards. These two needed a change badly, and it did one good to see how they enjoyed that invigorating walk. At length the alcaide relaxed to the extent of allowing Lieutenant Gillmore also to accompany us on these morning trips.

Our condition kept gradually improving. A telegram came from Aguinaldo, who at that time was in Tarlac, ordering the "presidente provincial" to allow all his American prisoners the liberty of the town between the hours of six in the morning and eight in the evening. I have since learned from authentic sources that this same order also provided for the increase of our ration money to one peseta each. Why that part of the order was never carried out, probably the provincial authorities only can tell.

La Independencia of September 21st contained an interesting and highly magnified account of our treatment, which, considering that we were closely confined at that time (at least all my comrades were), it was exasperating to think Americans in Manila should read and perhaps believe. Below I give a literal translation of this article:

"Treatment of the Yankee Prisoners."

"The humanity and consideration which the Filipinos feel for those in misfortune are well known and admitted by those capable of judging us with impartiality and justice. Our culture and our civilization are doubted, but, nevertheless, our actions have proved us to be on a level with those nations that claim to be our superiors. But what matter these insults and this injustice to us, if we but comply with our duty and follow the dictates of our own conscience?

"To these noble characteristics of the Filipinos the Yankee prisoners can well testify. They can tell whether, since falling into our hands, they have been treated according to the customs of savages, or by the rules of international law. Fighting for an ignoble and anti-humane cause, assassins of liberty, they have been neither mutilated nor tortured by our so-called hordes of bandits; they have not even been confined to a prison.

"All this we say on the authority of a friend of ours who visited the house where these prisoners reside. Each one receives a daily allowance of two pesos, which he expends for his food and other small necessities. Their meals are excellent, almost luxurious, consisting of bread, wine, and a regular variety of dishes. For breakfast they have eggs and milk. Bananas, of which they are so fond, are supplied to them in abundance. They are in need of nothing, not even cigars and cigarettes. At their orders they have a servant constantly in attendance.

"It is said that every morning the president inquires after their health by telegraph, recommending them to the officer in charge for good treatment. Their servant sees to it that their clothes are constantly clean and in good order; a barber is always within their call. In no ways are they restricted, being at liberty to wander about the country as they please. They show a marked aversion to speaking on the war. They admit that they fought with no enthusiasm and that their cause is both inhumane and unjust, promising to write to their friends on the fraternal treatment they receive, and how the American officers have deceived their men in representing us as cruel, savage, and sanguinary.

"All these details we submit to the public, that it may understand the noble sentiments of the government, which wishes to comply with the international-al laws of war, although not obliged to do so, in favor of those of the enemy that fate has placed in our hands. The noble hearts of the Filipino people rise above all petty desire for revenge, and they see in a prisoner not an object of abuse, but an unhappy fellow-being that deserves pity and compassion.

"We do not doubt but what all our enemies will in time be convinced of their error in believing us savages and cannibals, little above the level of the tribes of Central Africa, and that our treatment of a fallen enemy is not equal to that shown by other nations in similar conditions, including the Americans themselves. Do they treat the Filipinos in their power as well?"

So wrote the fertile pen of the editor of *La Independencia*. Whether the gentleman really believed all this himself, or only followed the flights of his vivid imagination, we cannot say, but it is also possible that this article was written more for American than Filipino eyes. It was about this time that, having collected fourteen other American prisoners, Aguinaldo had them well cared for, giving each a daily allowance equal to a general's pay, and, having kept them in this style for a few weeks, delivered them over to General Lawton on September 30th at Angeles. None of these men had been captive over a couple of months, and, naturally, after such treatment, their praises of the Filipinos ran high. This was a clever ruse on Aguinaldo's part to gain sympathy, but was, nevertheless, seen through.

The fact that they would not even allow us to communicate with our friends showed plainly that they feared our testimony might not be of the most flattering. The article referred to was evidently written to accompany these fourteen "guests" that were turned over as above.

Given the liberty of the town the men made good use of it, but the greatest trouble was that Arnold, to ingratiate himself with them, kept them constantly supplied with vino, of which several, especially the sailors, took undue advantage. This at length caused the priest to have Arnold's quarters changed from the convent to the presidency. One day one of our men, in a state of intoxication, struck a sentry before the barracks, forcing his way past his post some distance before he was finally got under control by the soldiers. I may well ask what an American sentry would have done under like circumstances! Yet the offender in this case was not punished.

The men now did their own cooking in the jail, each one taking his turn. Bruce and Edwards, however, had different ideas of domestic economy from the rest, and the two formed a mess of their own, which Gillmore also joined later on. Corn-meal was cheap, and every morning they had corn-meal mush and occasionally corn-bread. Every Sunday they could afford a chicken, and so well did they manage, that meat, vegetables, eggs, and coffee formed their daily bill of fare. Rice never appeared on their "table." But then again for vino they never spent a cent — they detested the vile liquor.

As for us in the hospital, rice in some shape or other appeared at each meal

— for breakfast cooked rice and weak coffee; dinner, rice soup, or vegetable soup of some sort with a small piece of meat each, and one banana for dessert; supper the same as dinner, with coffee and cigars. One day, however, a restaurant was opened in town close by the hospital, and our mess was broken up, the Spanish officers preferring to eat in this restaurant. But I took advantage of this opportunity to join Bruce and Edwards's mess in the prison, which was more to my liking. I retained my quarters in the hospital, however, although sometimes I was absent from there all day. We four now messed together, Gillmore, Bruce, Edwards, and myself, and, considering our means, we lived fairly well.

I now made quite a number of friends among the natives, thus finding my patient study of the Spanish language well repaid. One afternoon I met at Abasilla's house an Insurgent officer, Comandante Peña, from whose acquaintance I have derived much pleasure and information. José Peña was a wonderful man in his own sphere. He was a Spanish mestizo, not much over thirty, and bore a strange resemblance to Antonio Luna in many ways. The Insurgent Government had sent him up to Bangued to take charge of a "maestranza" or arsenal to be established here. As a manufacturer of ammunition he was a valuable man to Aguinaldo, his deep knowledge of physics, and profound learning in general, gained under great difficulties, earning him the respect of even the Spaniards.

To begin with, Comandante Peña was a freethinker, which, considering the country he was brought up in, was in itself extraordinary. He had read and studied Voltaire and was familiar with the speeches of Robert Ingersoll. Seeing how I had become deeply interested in his conversation, he told me his whole life's history.

In his early youth he had been a student at the Jesuit College of Manila, where he formed a lasting friendship with a French friar. Padre Fauvre. Leaving the college, he opened a chemical laboratory to pursue his researches, but was obliged to teach fencing to earn the means wherewith to continue his studies. Later he was arrested as a suspected Insurgent, at the instigation of the Recollets, and condemned to be shot, but here his friend Padre Fauvre came to the rescue by assisting him to escape. This decided him to join the Insurgents in good earnest, applying himself to the manufacture of ammunition, but, as he himself admitted, he was handicapped by lack of proper means, and his productions were inferior.

Peña was well acquainted with all the latest discoveries in chemistry, having been a subscriber to the Spanish edition of the *Scientific American*, and to him Edison and his inventions were as familiar as to any American scientist. When I left him to return to the hospital that night he invited me to visit him in the arsenal the next day, and this I considered an opportunity not to be lost.

At the appointed hour on the following day I went over to the "maestranza" in one of the public buildings on the plaza, and found Peña seated at a table, surrounded by chemical apparatus, bottles, an endless number of vials, etc.

"I am now," he explained to me as I seated myself, "testing a new explosive which I believe is superior to what I so far have been using. With this we will destroy great numbers of your countrymen." On the other side of the room at another table were two assistants refilling old Remington cartridge shells. With a little tin measure they poured in the black powder, and, after wadding this, the bullet was fitted in. The cartridge was then placed in a small machine which pressed the top of the shell tight around the bullet, thus preventing it from falling out. I heard hammering and the clanking of metals in another room, which I was, however, not invited to enter; but through a partly open door caught sight of a half-finished gun carriage.

The comandante then showed me a small rifle which he himself had manufactured. The barrel, of about a twenty-two calibre, he assured me was made from a piece of shell the American vessels had fired into San Fernando when they bombarded that port shortly after the capture of the Saturnus. The stock was a piece of neatly carved native mahogany. We took a walk into the wood outside of town, where he allowed me to shoot at a bird, which I missed, though he later took a shot at another bird and brought it down.

Peña's learning was not confined to chemistry and physics; he was also an adept in natural history in general, and of the human race in particular. He was a firm believer in Darwinism, and I am not ashamed to confess that I learned many things from him of which until then I had been ignorant.

Among other things he contended that the Filipinos, especially the Tagalogs, are recent descendants of the Hindus of East India, assuring me that he himself had compared ancient Tagalog manuscript with Sanskrit, and found a marked resemblance.

Shortly after this I made still another friend through whose influence I was able to raise myself from a state of abject poverty to one of comparative affluence. This was the representative of the province, Señor Isidro Paredes, who had returned to his home in Bangued since the disbandment of Congress. The Paredes family lived in the largest and finest house in town. One day, while out for a stroll, I chanced to meet Arnold before the Paredes' residence, and, as he was just about to enter on a visit, he invited me to accompany him. We ascended to the floor above, where Arnold introduced me to a fine, intelligent-looking, pure-blooded Filipino. This was Don Isidro himself, and I felt that I was in the presence of a gentleman. Although but little over thirty, Don Isidro was already rather stout, but his clear-cut features and bearing in general impressed one with a dignity rare even among the upper classes of Filipinos. Nor did his appearance belie him, for he was a man of superior education. As Peña was an adept in chemistry and general science, so was Don Isidro as deeply versed in arts, literature, and law. For years he had followed the profession of the law in Manila, but at the outbreak of hostilities between Spain and America he had joined the Insurgents, and later was elected a representative of the Province of Abra in the Congress at Malolos. In the course of my visit I was also introduced to the rest of the family, the old father and mother, three brothers, and four sisters. One, Mariano, a boy of nineteen, was a graduate of the Military Academy and School of Agriculture of Manila, and now held a commission as "inspector de montes" under the Insurgent Government, with the rank and pay of captain.

Don Isidro, as he was called by all Bangued, invited me to repeat my visit, which I did, and, before many days had passed, I advanced to him an idea I had conceived of forming a class of children for the study of English, of which plan he at once approved, furthermore promising his support. He kept his word, for in two days he had gathered together fourteen children of the well-to-do families at Bangued, and, thereafter, I spent an hour each morning in the Paredes' residence, teaching the rudiments of English to fourteen little brown imps, who absorbed with remarkable intelligence and quickness all the information I gave them. Their eyes fairly sparkled in their eagerness to outvie each other. One of the brightest was little Jesus, the ten-year-old nephew of Don Isidro. So small was he that often I was obliged to grasp him by the slack of his jacket in the back, as one lifts a kitten, and hold him up to the black-board, where he wrote what he had learned, as clearly and correctly as his taller companions.

However, there was one exception — a little fellow who couldn't learn until he had spent half an hour by himself kneeling in a corner, after which he would generally stumble through half his lesson. This method of hastening the comprehension of the young mind did not originate with me; I was but following the custom of the country, and I found it rather effective.

My only girl pupil was Mercedes, a little bashful miss of thirteen, who, in her quiet way, proved as apt a scholar as noisy little Jesus, who never could keep quiet in spite of sundry whacks across his back applied by both Don Isidro and myself.

I must not forget to mention my youngest pupil, little Pepito, brother to Jesus. He was but four years old, but in those four years he had come to the practical conclusion that life was not worth living without bebinkas.

Don Isidro had at first not enrolled him as a regular member of the class, but one day Pepito appeared himself, and asserted his right to enter the portals of learning as well as the others, and was admitted.

I had been teaching them all to count, "One," I said in a deep bass voice, with a suitable flourish of my rattan. "One," they all repeated in chorus. Suddenly as if from the ceiling came a little piping squeak: "One!" Looking around I could see nobody. "Two!" I continued, with all the dignity of the learned professor. "Two!" roared the class. A moment's silence and then again that distant mysterious squeak from nowhere: "Two-o-o!" This perplexed me. The class tittered, but I considered it beneath my dignity to request them to explain. Just then my attention was attracted to a comparatively dark corner of the room where stood a table, on which were piled a number of books. On the uppermost volume sat a diminutive brown figure hardly larger than one of the little jungle monkeys, contentedly reducing the size of a huge bebinka which it held in two chubby hands. Thus did Pepito acquire the foundation of his knowledge of our language which he at no distant day undoubtedly will be able to use with great fluency.

For teaching these children I received four pesos monthly; moreover my position as teacher also gave me some social standing. All the children of Bangued, whether my pupils or not, greeted me in the street with a neat little military salute and a "Buenas dias, maestro," as they did the official schoolmaster of the town, who was a Government employee.

Every Saturday I had a grand review of the lessons given during the week, and on these occasions the school-room was crowded by the parents of the children. Even Lieutenant Gillmore attended then; and it was really interesting to observe how the pupils progressed from week to week.

Then Don Isidro decided to take lessons himself, and for an hour each afternoon I taught him and his younger brother Quintin, the latter a boy of fifteen, For this I received an additional three pesos, thus giving me a monthly income of ten pesos, including my allowance from the Government.

This enabled me to help the mess along with fifteen cents daily instead of ten. Gillmore also contributed fifteen cents, and together with the two ten-cent pieces of Bruce and Edwards our daily mess-fund for us four amounted to half a peso. On this we lived well.

Since our arrival the cura had sent us each a suit of clothes, and, considering the mildness of the climate, we were not so badly off. Gillmore was well dressed, had a number of changes, and bought himself a pair of fine boots. A Chinese merchant in town had given me a pair of canvas shoes and two pairs of socks for teaching him a number of conventional phrases in English. Villamor had made me a present of a new straw hat, and the doctor's wife had her servants do my washing, so I had no reason to complain, considering I was a prisoner of war, nor had any of my comrades, for that matter. But for whatever little comforts we enjoyed we did not owe any thanks to the Government, but to the good people of Bangued.

One day, while lying on my bed in the hospital conversing with old Captain Hiado, a native entered our room, dropped a bundle on the table, and was gone before we could speak to him. Taking up the bundle, which was done up in a linen handkerchief, I found a slip of paper containing my name in large printed letters attached to it. Upon opening I found a new suit of clothes, a straw hat such as only the better class of natives wore, two pairs of socks, and three handkerchiefs. I could not recognize the handwriting on the slip of paper, but I had caught a glimpse of the boy's face who brought the present, and knew him to be one of Paredes' servants. But that was just their way of giving, and in the same manner they one day sent a whole sheep to the jail.

Chapter Twenty-One - A Wedding in Bangued

IT was in the month of October that a great event took place in the Paredes family. The eldest sister of Don Isidro, Seiiorita Isabela, was to be married. Preparations were made for weeks in advance, and, when finally the invitations were sent around to the friends of the family, Arnold and myself found ourselves among the number. All the guests were to assemble at the church as the sun rose over the hills on that eventful day, at six in the morning, when the marriage ceremony would be performed by the cura.

At the appointed hour, Arnold and I, both of us attired in our best, found ourselves, together with a large crowd of well-dressed natives, awaiting the bridal procession.

Shortly after our arrival the church bells pealed forth as the handsome carriage of the Paredes family, drawn by two milk-white horses, appeared coming up the street, with the bride and her maids inside, all enveloped in gauzy clouds of costly piñas. In their black hair, which hung down over their shoulders loosely, sprays of flowers had been inserted. With the exception of a white veil, depending from the back of her head, as the mantilla is worn by the Spanish women, the bride was dressed exactly like her companions in the carriage, three in number, A second carriage contained the bridegroom, a young local merchant, and three groomsmen, all attired in black dress-suits, which became them well. Following the vehicles came the family and relations on foot, Don Isidro, his three brothers, and father bringing up the rear. At the church-door the bridegroom, having alighted from the carriage, assisted the bride to do likewise, and arm in arm they entered the church, followed by the bridesmaids and the groomsmen in couples. Arnold and I joined Don Isidro, who escorted us inside, but so crowded was the church that we could see but little of the ceremony. The whole occupied not more than fifteen minutes, and then the now married pair returned to the carriages and were seated beside each other. The brass band leading the way with a wedding march, the procession started to return to the bride's house, Don Isidro and we bringing up the rear.

Flowers are not plentiful in the Philippines, but the Paredes house was literally hidden in the green decorations of palm and banana leaves, ferns, and tropical verdure of all sorts. At least one hundred persons sat down to the breakfast-table shortly after our arrival. I tried to count the number of dishes placed before us, but the variety was so great I gave up the effort.

After breakfast the hangings and draperies in front of the doors to the adjoining ball-room were thrown aside and the guests filed in, seating themselves about, against the walls. Lucas, the eldest brother of Don Isidro, performed on the piano, accompanying a violin, and to this music the dancing began. In another and smaller room adjoining, the older guests were seated at small tables, playing cards, chess, and dominoes. Out in the dining-room stood vino and "basit" on tap. This latter is a red wine made of sugar-cane flavored with the bark of a certain indigenous tree, the name of which has escaped my memory. One side of the room was covered by a long table loaded down with all sorts of delicacies, where you might help yourself whenever so inclined.

It was a gay gathering — you stood on no ceremony with anybody. Even if you had never seen your neighbors before, you simply addressed them like old acquaintances. I sat conversing with a young lady, a mestiza, and as fair as the average of American girls, and if she knew me to be a prisoner, of which there could hardly be a doubt, she did not in the least make me aware of it. Many Spanish officers were present, dressed in their best uniforms, shoulder-straps and tinsel. Colonel Cuesta, Spanish Military Governor of the province in former times, appeared with his staff, and had a stranger seen them and then been told that they were prisoners he would have experienced some difficulty in believing it.

Between the dances there were recitations and vocal solos. A young Spanish officer and a mestiza belle danced a fandango together, but what mostly interested me was a debate between two young ladies on the pros and cons of an American Government in the Islands. One took the part of America and was decorated with red, white, and blue ribbons. The other represented the Philippines and wore the Insurgent flag for a sash. Both were handsome girls, and as they stood on the floor facing each other, their large black eyes flashed as they entered into the spirit of the discourse. Señorita America opened up with an argument in favor of annexation, couched in poetical language:

"The American Eagle spreads his wings over the child 'Filipinas' to protect it, which, having lost its cruel and unnatural mother, Spain, cannot understand its new parent and protector, doubts its good intentions," etc. She finished up her arguments amid a dead silence. Then Señorita Filipinas flew in. So rapid and heated was her reply that I could hardly follow, and but imperfectly understood it, but with such force and enthusiasm did she speak, and such spirit did she manage to infuse into her impassioned words, that for the moment I forgot that I was an American and believed myself a Filipino, to such an extent that I almost joined in the burst of applause that followed.

At one o'clock dinner was served, followed by the usual speechmaking. Everybody was called upon to say something, and Arnold and I did not escape. Lucas, however, made the address of the day. After a few introductory remarks on the future happiness of the young couple, he went on: "But let us all be merry this day at least, and let the good feeling of brothers and friends exist among us. We are assembled here, Spaniards, Americans, and Filipinos, representatives of the three factors in the present trouble. We may all be good patriots to our different causes and countries, and fight for our different flags if necessary, but why should the troubles and quarrels of our respective governments be imitated by individuals? Although we be at war with Spain or America, may we not clasp the hand of a Spaniard or an American and call him friend? I think we may. I am a Filipino, and always will be, but when I grasp the hand of a friend I do not ask: Is he also a Filipino? or is he a Spaniard, or a German? That he is my friend suffices, that he is a man and has the good qualities of a true man — therein lies the distinction. Let us then for today forget politics and national prejudices, and meet on the common footing of friendship. To-day we are neither Filipinos, Spaniards, nor Americans, but men, just common, ordinary men — friends."

I did not take a shorthand report of the speech as Don Lucas made it, but the above words are the gist of his discourse, as I remember it. The expression of his face as he uttered it convinced me of his sincerity. He was loudly applauded, and this time I joined in heartily.

After dinner the guests retired for the siesta, but at four o'clock chocolate and cakes were served, and the programme of the morning was continued, Lucas proving that he could sing as well as speak.

Supper was served at eight, by which time all the gentlemen were growing more or less merry, but only enough to make the party a greater success. The bridegroom seemed to be in a continual worry that the "basit" was not being distributed freely enough, but he was really the only one who felt uneasy on that score. At about midnight the party gradually broke up, and Arnold and I returned to our separate quarters with a rather indistinct understanding that we were to return on the next day.

On the succeeding day all the American prisoners were invited to a grand dinner for them alone, and, with the exception of Gillmore, all were present. Arnold made an after-dinner speech in English.

The second day after the wedding saw our lessons once more resumed, for not only did Don Isidro and his brother Quintin study English, but the youngest of the brothers also received tuition in higher mathematics from a Spanish officer who taught him daily.

Our condition continued improving day by day. Those of us who had taken the trouble to study Spanish now found their reward in being able to teach English, for which they all were more or less well paid. Those that had once declared their intention of never learning the "darned lingo" now depended entirely on what their more energetic companions gave them. Bruce found two pupils who paid him four pesos monthly. Vaudoit, the Frenchman, taught one young man French, but if he had not known Spanish he could not have done so. Honeyman also had several pupils, for which he received both money and cigars, and Edwards taught several of the local Chinese merchants.

It was about this time that one-half of a case of the provisions Arnold had seen in San José reached us. There was just one tin of condensed milk and one of preserved fruit for each, and a small bag of ground coffee void of all flavor. But when we considered that these supplies had followed us from San Isidro, it is to the credit of the Filipinos that any at all reached us. We have but to glance at similar cases in our own Civil War, and, comparing them, see if our countrymen would have done better under similar circumstances. I feel convinced that, had we remained at San Isidro, the greater part of these provisions would have reached us. But how we would have appreciated letters from home, waiting for us in the Manila Post office, or even a few cheap novels, in preference to "bottled lemonade" or plug tobacco! Nevertheless, we felt deeply grateful to whoever sent those provisions.

The Spaniards fared better. Each officer received twenty pesos, and each common soldier five. This money was sent through by the Spanish Government, and not a cent was stolen or misappropriated. Some of the Spaniards had the ill manners to flaunt this money in our faces and say: "You see, with all its boasted riches, your Government does not provide for its suffering soldiers. Spain is poor, but she remembers her sons when in distress. Bah, with such a powerful Government as yours, you are worse off than we." We made some lame attempts at arguing with them, but lacked conviction ourselves.

The Spaniards were now able to live in comparative affluence, dining and wining on the best the country could afford, while we still had to cling to corn-meal mush; occasionally, however, we profited by their generosity.

Several times we had received letters from O'Brien by both natives and Spaniards. He was now in Dolores, a small town five miles farther up the river, and, excepting that he felt lonely and not too well fed, was well treated. One day we heard that he was sick, and I went to the Provincial Governor for a pass to visit him, a privilege often granted to the Spaniards, of whom quite a number were quartered in neighboring towns. My request was refused, but the Governor assured me that O'Brien would be sent for. Sure enough, he put in an appearance the following day, ragged and bewhiskered, but not sick. It had been a false report, but he was, nevertheless, allowed to stay, and quartered at the hospital, though not in the same room with me.

Often did we take walks into the surrounding country. Edwards and I frequently went to the river for a swim. The Abra River forms a semicircle about Bangued. We would walk due north, and in half an hour strike the river. Tying our clothes on our backs, we would plunge in, and in less than an hour would be five miles farther down, but not more than two miles south of Bangued. This swim we often took, and frequently the natives, seeing us, would warn us against the rapids and under-currents. Abasilla, too, warned me of the dangers of the Abra River. "You will some day meet with misfortune, and then your countrymen will blame us."

"I am a good swimmer," I replied. "You are probably afraid that I shall escape."

The doctor laughed. "You can't escape," he chuckled. "La Bocana is well guarded, and even an Igorrote couldn't climb the mountains."

"The fear of compromising you would restrain me more than a dozen mountains."

"Bah, don't let that detain you. If ever you take a notion to escape, go ahead. In the beginning it was different, I was then responsible for you, but the moment Aguinaldo ordered that the American prisoners be given the liberty of the town, my responsibility ceased. I am not your jailer."

His tone seemed half-serious, half-jesting. At this time I had no idea of escaping, but, nevertheless, the doctor's words threw a new light on my situation, in which I never before had seen it.

"If you knew that I was going to escape," I continued, affecting a serious tone, "what would you do?"

"Formerly I would have had you returned to the prison. Now I would shrug my shoulders and say: This is not my affair — good-luck to you!"

Chapter Twenty-Two - The Meetings in the Hospital

FOR the past two months our lives had been gliding monotonously, although not unpleasantly, along, but in the beginning of November new events took place, which promised a radical change in our situation.

Colonel Bias Villamor paid Bangued, his native town, a visit about this time, and he was as a matter of course received with fiestas and great rejoicing, for Bangued was proud of him. On this occasion I witnessed my first cock-fight in the Insurgent country. The Americans allow this sport to be carried on with almost no restraint, and officers even encourage the pits by their presence, but in Aguinaldo's territory it was strictly prohibited unless on some great occasion, when especial permits were granted. The higher class and more thoughtful Filipinos are against this national pastime, however, since it discourages labor and ambition.

During Bias Villamor's stay in Bangued rumors became rife of a general advance of the Americans. This did not greatly excite us, since we long ago had lost faith in those advances, but when young Lieutenant Villamor called for me one day, asserting that he was going to the front with his uncle, it became evident that something unusual was taking place. I accompanied my friend to his home, where he introduced me to his uncle, who, however, remembered me as the sick prisoner in Vigan hospital.

I also gave Bernardo a letter addressed to any of my countrymen whose eyes it might meet, requesting him to treat the bearer, Lieutenant Bernardo Villamor, with the kindness and consideration that he had extended to American prisoners, especially the writer, simply signing my name and "An American Prisoner." This was to meet possible contingencies.

Next day he left for Tarlac via Vigan, and I never saw him again.

A few days later Spaniards from Vigan brought the news that an American vessel had bombarded the beach and killed an old man's carabao, also destroying the hut. A few days later prisoners began to arrive by hundreds from Vigan and other coast towns, until almost one thousand cazadores were concentrated at Bangued. Paredes quartered four, Abasilla two, and so each householder was obliged to bear a share of the public burden according to his circumstances. Many were also sent to neighboring villages, and altogether there were in the Province of Abra at this time at least 2,000 Spanish prisoners.

General Peña, the former Military Governor of Cavite, also appeared, almost with all the ceremony and state of a king, being accompanied by his staff and quartered alone in one of the finest residences in town. Considering that he was a prisoner, his display and assumption were laughable. Only eighteen months before, when captured in Cavite, he had been thrown in among his own soldiers and compelled to stand in file with them, answering roll-call with the rest. Money had been sent to him from Manila by his wife, and now he travelled in great state. The treatment he now received at the hands of the Filipinos was almost the same as that extended to one of their own generals.

The arriving Spaniards told us many tales of vessels passing Vigan daily, but of one in particular, a large white-painted battle-ship. When we told Gillmore this, he exclaimed, "I'll bet it's the Oregon."

Although the prisoners now crowded the town, the garrison consisted of but twenty soldiers, the commandante, whose name also was Peña, one lieutenant, and one sergeant, and besides these there was not another Insurgent soldier in the whole Province of Abra. Vigan was garrisoned by a force of fifty men under command of General Natividad, who was a cripple, having been wounded by an American shell in the early part of the war. Tiño was in Tarlac with the main army, and Villamor with four hundred men was on the way down the coast toward Dagupan, where an American landing was reported.

How easily, then, could the 2,000 prisoners in the province have taken possession of Bangued and marched down on Vigan and taken it too. We also had it from authentic sources that in case the Americans disembarked troops at Vigan, Natividad would fall back and drive us all into the mountains.

One evening the subject of rising in revolt was seriously broached among the Spanish officers in the hospital. The hottest of all in its favor was a Lieutenant Bustos, who, on this particular evening, made a fiery speech: "Let us rise like men," he said, "and overpower this handful of monkeys, who guard us as if we were sheep. Then, with twenty Remingtons, and thirty Mausers that I know are in the arsenal, stowed away in boxes, let us march down to Vigan, capture the town, and signal to the American vessels that pass daily." Many were in favor of this, but only a small minority were willing to put General Peña's advice aside, whose policy, as everybody knew, was "paciencia," which, considering that he suffered no hardships, was hardly a virtue. A formal meeting of twenty Spanish officers was held in the hospital two or three evenings after this, and guards placed at doors and windows to warn us of any strangers' approach, as their confidence in me had warranted their invitation to be present on this occasion. Had Lieutenant Gillmore been able to understand Spanish they would have invited him also to attend, but I was instructed to keep him informed, and ask his opinion.

At this first meeting a committee of three was appointed to wait on General Peña the following day, and endeavor to persuade him to give his consent to an active effort on our part to obtain the liberty of 2,000 prisoners. Then we adjourned to assemble again on the succeeding night.

I told Gillmore of our meeting, but so strenuously did he oppose the idea of any violent action that I dropped the subject. "No," he exclaimed, "such an undertaking would end disastrously, and the Insurgents would then have the right to execute us afterward."

When evening came we again assembled, Lieutenant Bustos acting as chairman. The three officers had interviewed General Peña, but he had not only refused his consent, but forbidden them to attempt any overt action. They then asked me Lieutenant Gillmore's opinion, but I said vaguely that the Americans would support any uprising for liberty, and I felt that I spoke the truth of them as a whole.

Some were in favor of entirely disregarding General Peña and taking the garrison the following night, but they were in a minority. Said the majority: "Let us wait until the Americans disembark in Vigan, then with or without the general we will go down to meet them."

"But," contested the minority, "when will the Americans land? It may be months yet. And then Natividad will come up and swell the garrison to seventy men, who cannot be overpowered without much bloodshed and perhaps loss of life. Either that or be led into the mountains like a band of sheep."

This was an undeniable fact, and everybody admitted it. Captain Hiado rose and expressed it as his opinion that the only manner in which to bring the scheme to a successful issue was to communicate with the Americans and seek their co-operation.

"Let a small party land at Narbacan and march up the pass at Tangadan," he continued, "and then, if we knew just when to expect them, we could act at our end and march down to meet them. We must communicate with the Americans, and if they agree to cooperate with us, we can all be saved without the necessity of losing a single life."

This proposition was seconded by all present. I was requested to obtain a letter from Lieutenant Gillmore explaining the situation, and suggesting that a company of marines be landed at Narbacan on some set date. A day before they should quietly, under cover of darkness, set the messenger ashore, who should come up to Bangued to post us, that we might act together. At the exact hour of the landing of the Americans we would rise, take the garrison, and march down to meet them. The Spaniards agreed to find either a native or a cazador to act as messenger.

Early the next morning I saw Gillmore, and he agreed to write the required letter. This he really did, giving it to me, and I in turn delivered it to Lieutenant Bustos.

Evening came and again we assembled in the hospital. As yet nobody had been found willing to undertake the mission of reaching the American vessels, but Lieutenant Bustos knew of a young corporal in a neighboring town, who he felt would be the right man, and on the morrow he would send for him. The general features of the plan were again discussed, and now a cross, grumpy old pessimist arose and declared that he didn't believe the Americans would trouble their heads with any attempt to rescue us. "The past proves it," he continued. "Even if our messenger succeeds in reaching the American ships, he will not be believed, not even with a letter from Lieutenant Gillmore. Did not twenty Spaniards escape from Candon but three months since, and what was the result? Nothing. Not a month has passed but what they have had some news of our situation, and even while we were down in Vigan, on the sea-shore, our arms stretched out to them for help, what was done? With their spy-glasses they could observe us on the roads and beach, and with two boat-loads of marines they could have saved us — but no: we were not worth it! Señores, if the Americans would send us help, they could have done so long ago, and I, for one, do not expect any aid from them now."

I could see that this harangue, uttered with bitter intensity, made quite an impression, and for some time no one spoke.

"Truly," ventured one at length, "our friend, the captain, speaks words of reason. The Americans will never trust a Spaniard sufficiently to act upon any information he may bring."

By the manner in which they all glanced at me, I plainly felt that they expected me to make some answer to these reflections they were casting on my countrymen, but, to save my life, I knew not what to say; nothing that the old gruff captain had stated could be denied.

"I admit," I at last replied, "that the Americans may not place implicit faith in the word of any stray Spaniard, nor can they properly be blamed for that, but I am willing myself to accompany any one of your men that may know the country well enough to act as guide, and I am sure that if we reach the American ships, my countrymen will do anything to co-operate with you."

"No, no!" cried several at once. "You are too well known in Vigan, and would not even be taken for a Spaniard. It is impossible!"

"Hold," exclaimed Bustos, "this can all be arranged. I have a friend in Vigan, where they may hide during the day. In one night they can reach Vigan, and during the day following find shelter in the house of Señor Baldolomar. He will also give them all necessary information regarding boats, which will not be so difficult, since the beach is now practically unguarded."

When we separated that night it was fully decided that I should be one of the messengers, but for me to go alone was out of the question, since I knew neither the country nor the language well enough to pass for a Spaniard. Any intelligent person would have detected my foreign accent in speaking at once, so for several good reasons there must be at least two or even three of us. But the Spaniards would see to the finding of my companions.

That night Captain Hiado and I lay talking until late, on the prospects of my success. He took a hopeful view of the whole affair, and had great expectations of a satisfactory finish.

Next morning saw me in the prison immediately after opening of doors, when I informed Gillmore of the new plan, in which I was to take so important a part. "No, no," he cried at once, "I will never give my consent to that. Your chances would not be one out of twenty. I will have nothing to do with it."

During the forenoon Bustos and his friends made all possible efforts to find a suitable companion for me, but without success. I myself saw no less than ten cazadores called into our room, and there Bustos or Captain Hiado stated the proposition to them. Some agreed, and went out to arrange their clothes, they said, but never returned. Others turned pale and stammered excuses: they did not know the road, or they were sick, etc. By noon still no one had been found. Captain Hiado and Bustos were plainly ashamed, and attempted to explain that eighteen months of hunger and imprisonment had taken all the spirit out of the poor fellows; but I doubted it had ever been there.

When I returned to the prison for the mid-day meal. Lieutenant Gillmore requested me to come for a walk with him after eating, as he had something to say to me. Our dinner was soon finished, and then the lieutenant and I walked out under the shade of the trees in the plaza.

"I have been thinking over your proposition," he commenced, "and have a scheme to submit to you. Should you escape, you would soon be missed, and we should at once lose the few privileges we have. Now, it is well known that you often go down to the river to swim, and I propose that when you escape you leave a suit of your clothes on the bank to give the impression that you are drowned. Before you leave tell everybody that you are about to go down for a swim."

I sanctioned his idea at once, especially as a young Spanish officer had been drowned but a week before. In this manner my comrades would not be compromised, and even I might be safer from recapture. Lieutenant Gillmore then agreed to write a short message to Admiral Dewey, whom we thought still in command of the Asiatic Station.

When evening came, Bustos and his compatriots had not yet met with any success. During the day they had interviewed not less than fifteen cazadores, but neither promises of reward nor promotion could tempt them.

On the following morning I met in the plaza a young Spaniard who had just come up from Vigan. He was a mere boy of nineteen, but I remembered him as one of the "practicantes" from the lower ward in the hospital, implicated in the plot to escape with Perez on the occasion when their provisions were seized and they were fired upon. Immediately I thought: "Here is my man; he will not refuse." Preferring that Lieutenant Bustos should broach the subject to him, as the former's rank would give his words more weight, I pointed Guillermo out to him, and he sent for the latter at once. He was brought into the little room where Hiado and I slept, and there the two officers at once explained the situation to him. As they spoke in whispers I could not hear a word of the conversation, although I lay on my bed, but suddenly Bustos turned and swept by me with an expression of disgust on his face. "No quiere," he simply said, as he passed me. Hiado also left the room, leaving me alone with Guillermo, who stood looking rather sheepishly at me, but, with a look of contempt on my face, I turned over on the bed with my back toward him. Coming over closer to me he commenced: "What the captain proposes is impossible —" but here I interrupted him. "Guillermo, over in the prison are thirteen Americans. Of them I am quite certain that not one would refuse to accompany me, did he know the country and the people as you do. In this town are 1,000 Spaniards, who know the language, customs, and nature of the country. Of that thousand not one will go, not even to save his countrymen from further misery and possible death."

I had made this little speech as flowery and eloquent as my Spanish would permit, and it produced just the effect I desired. Guillermo's sunken yellow cheeks burned crimson and his eyes flashed. "I will go where any American will go," he cried. "Call in Captain Hiado again; I will go. I know the road, and I am not afraid."

Soon I had the old captain and Lieutenant Bustos in the room again, and they made all necessary arrangements. At length Guillermo even grew enthusiastic. He promised to find another companion, and then left us to search for him.

Early the following morning, November 17th, Guillermo appeared in the hospital with a companion, a sergeant of cazadores. This latter knew the country well, having formerly been garrisoned in Vigan. I liked his appearance at first sight; he was a dark, handsome fellow of about thirty-two years, impressed one as a man of some nerve, and was evidently in prime physical condition. He called himself Pedro.

It was decided to leave that same night, so we agreed to meet in a neighboring canteen at five that evening. This being fully understood, we separated. During the day I made all preparations, taking Bruce, Edwards, and Petersen into my confidence. The latter, having been signal-boy on the Yorktown, was thoroughly conversant with the cipher code, and Gillmore having written the message which was to accompany me, it was by Petersen translated into cipher. It read:

"Abra, November 17, 1899.

"To the Senior Naval Officer:

"The bearer, Albert Sonnichsen, has been a prisoner of war with me these last seven months, and has volunteered to make our ships. You can have perfect confidence in what he says.

(Signed) "Gillmore."

Except for Gillmore, Petersen, Bruce, and Edwards (O'Brien having once more been sent back to Dolores) I did not dare to confide in my comrades, since they were on too intimate terms with Arnold, and an inadvertent word uttered unconsciously might have given him a hint. Since the latest rumors of the renewal of American activities he had voluntarily removed to the jail, where he lived with the Americans, he and a few boon companions rarely sober. He now claimed to be an American citizen of St. Paul, Minn., and was even heard to declare that he was born there. Yet I knew that from pure hatred he would betray me did he have an opportunity, and for this reason I dared not confide in those who were on confidential terms with him. He had tried hard to reconcile Bruce and O'Brien with himself by offering them presents of cigars, vino, and even money, but these two of our old Malolos crowd had repulsed all his advances beyond being on mere speaking terms.

That morning, realizing that I was delivering the last lesson to my class, I left heavy of heart, for I had grown to like the children. I told Don Isidro that I would be late for the afternoon lesson, as I was going down to the river for a swim. I felt guilty in thus deceiving him, thinking of his unvarying kindness to me, but knowing him to be a Government official I dared not be frank. Nevertheless, as he himself admitted to me since, he wondered why I shook his hand at leaving that morning.

I also told Abasilla and all my other native acquaintances of my prospective trip to the river, and they, as usual, warned me against the danger. If I felt guilty on account of the deception practised on Don Isidro, I felt doubly so in parting with Abasilla. But I remembered his words: "I would shrug my shoulders and say: 'This is not my affair. Good luck to you!'"

My manuscript, over two hundred pages of closely written matter, I gave to Captain Hiado to take care of until we should meet again. The old captain had procured a bamboo cane, and after wrapping Gillmore's message up in a piece of dried banana leaf, thus rendering it waterproof, bored a hole in one end of my cane, and slipped the roll into the compartment between the two joints, and once more plugged up the hole. The cane now contained the message.

Having been supplied with money by the Spanish officers, I spent some of this on my last supper together with my three messmates, after which we sat talking quietly in Gillmore's room. Edwards had made a small bundle of a Spanish uniform and a cazador's hat, and with these he was to accompany me outside of town, where I would exchange them for the clothes and hat I now wore. At the river-bank I would drop the latter.

The church bell struck five and still I lingered. Outside the rain was pouring down in torrents. Just then a shrill whistle from the plaza in front reminded me that it was time, when Guillermo passed the window. Bruce and Gillmore reached out their hands to me and in silence we parted.

Coming outside, Edwards and I found Guillermo awaiting us in the plaza. But first I had to bid Hiado, Bustos, and their compatriots farewell, and while Guillermo and Edwards remained below, I ascended to the upper floor of the hospital, where they all bid me good-by, recommending me to the care of God! The very last to grasp my hand, with tears in his eyes, was Lieutenant Repol, who had suffered so severely in Vigan. "God protect you; may you have more success than I did," were his last words to me, as I left the room.

In the canteen we found Pedro and two others, who also were to accompany us, two young soldiers. Leaving Pedro and these two to follow later, and meet us outside of town, since we feared it might breed suspicion to leave in a body, Guillermo, Edwards, and I left the town by the road to the landing. We were well out on the country road, when Guillermo said to Edwards: "You must leave us now, it may raise suspicion to be absent too long in such a rain." Edwards handed me the bundle, and, grasping him by the hand, I parted with my last comrade. He returned to Bangued, to escape himself a month later, and, together with Bruce and O'Brien, served as guide to the rescuing party under Colonel Hare.

I now felt that I was a fugitive.

Chapter Twenty-Three - Fugitives

THE rain was pouring down as it can only in the tropics, soon transforming the road into a sea of mud and water, but we two struggled on for another mile, when we crawled under a low tree to wait for Pedro and the other two. To me it seemed that we lay there for an age, but at last, above the low roar of the rain we heard the splashing of approaching footsteps, and as three dark figures trudged by, Guillermo and I fell in behind. On we pushed through the blinding rain, the mud, and the darkness, at a smart pace, almost a trot, an occasional flash of lightning rendering the landscape visible for an instant, and showing the road before us, but my companions evidently knew their way, for they plodded steadily on, Pedro leading, and I after him. In half an hour we had reached a small creek, a branch of the river, and this we prepared to ford, after my first undressing, donning the cazador's suit, and leaving the other on the bank. Just then Pedro uttered a loud oath. Looking around, I saw that we now numbered only four. One already had deserted, his courage having failed him.

Fording the creek we continued following the road, and presently found ourselves walking through the street of a town. This was Pidigan, but we soon passed beyond without meeting a soul. We knew that there was no garrison stationed here. After a while the road began a rather sharp ascent: we were now entering the mountains. On, on we continued at a swinging trot, never stopping for even a moment. We must reach Vigan before daybreak. Overhead a telegraph wire commenced to wail dismally, and at times I almost fancied I heard the syllables of my own name vibrating along those slender threads, but reason convinced me that as yet I would not have been missed. Several times we met prowling Tinguianes, but they did not molest us.

At about eleven o'clock Pedro halted abruptly, and the rest of us gathered around him, knowing he had something to say. In a whisper he informed us that we were now within a stone's throw of San Quintin. On account of the river on one side and a bluff on the other we must pass through the town. Six soldiers were garrisoned here to watch the river and to collect a small toll on each raft that passed. To avoid them we must be cautious. Having warned us Pedro again went on, slower and with almost noiseless steps — we following in single file. Just then the moon came out from behind the clouds, and we saw the nipa roofs before us. Even I knew the town and recognized the gloomy barracks on the brow of the bluff facing the river, where three months before we American prisoners had eaten rice and paw-paw soup.

Silently Pedro led the way through the deserted streets, and we as silently followed. We crept along in the shadows as much as possible, but at times were obliged to cross bright patches of moonlight, and my heart stood almost still with fear, half expecting to hear a sentry's "Alto!" Once we heard a shrill whistle, the "All's well" of the Insurgent sentinel. Gradually we reached the opposite side of the town, and when once more we plunged into the jungle, my breath again came naturally. It would have been such a disgrace to be recaptured so soon!

Once more we pushed on, uttering never a word or a whisper, following a trail that a horse could not have passed, at times climbing impossible-looking cliffs, and again descending into gorges by sliding down creepers. After another three or four hours of this manner of travelling, we at length saw "La Bocana" opening up before us, and felt the moaning currents of air that perpetually float through it, which the ignorant natives call the spirits of the pass, who flit in and out. I could hardly blame them for believing this, for now in the stillness of night it certainly seemed as if phantom bodies flew by; the scene was weird and impressive.

Once more we halted, and now the question arose, "How shall we pass through La Bocana?" But Pedro was prepared for this. Leading the way into a clump of trees close to the river-bank we came upon a Tinguiane hut. Pedro at once called out in the native dialect in low, long-drawn syllables, "Gavino-po-oo-po-oo." This he repeated several times, and at length an answer came from within: "Apo-o-o-o!" The door opened and we entered, the Tinguiane seated on his sleeping-mat, from which he had just risen. He and Pedro spoke for some time in the Tinguiane dialect, which the latter knew well, having been seven years in this part of the country. At last the native rose and went outside, we following him. Leading the way he entered a dense thicket, and, with our help, pulled out a small bamboo raft which was there hidden, and launched it into the river. We all embarked, and, with a shove of a long pole, the native sent the raft gliding out into the river. In ten minutes we had crossed to the opposite bank, and, giving the Tinguiane a peso, we continued following the trail along the shore, but presently found ourselves confronted by an impassable cliff which rose abruptly from the water. A rope was here made fast to a tree and disappeared into the river. "No raft," exclaimed Pedro; "then we must drag ourselves through the water to the sand-spit below by means of this rope. The raft is at the other end."

One by one we entered the water, and, slipping my cane over my wrist by means of a lanyard, I allowed the current to carry me down along the rope to which I clung. We made the mistake of following one another too closely, thus placing our united weight on the cord at once. Suddenly, when we had slipped down about fifty yards, I felt something give way, and a moment later was struggling in the swirling eddies and carried out in the current. Had not my movements been impeded by my clothing, I should not have considered the accident a very serious one, but as it was, with the cane fastened to my wrist, shoes and clothing became hindrances to swimming. How long my struggles lasted I cannot definitely say, but to me it seemed hours, although I have no doubt it was in reality less than ten minutes. Finally my feet struck violently against a rock, and I found myself being swept over a bank. Desperately I clung to my foothold in spite of the current, and eventually succeeded in obtaining a firm footing, enabling me to crawl up on the dry sand-spit. Thank God, I was below that awful bluff.

At first I seemed to be alone; nowhere could I see the Spaniards, but soon they crawled up into the moonlight from different points along the spit; none of us having suffered more than a few bruises and I the loss of my hat.

Resting ten minutes, we pressed on again, for we feared that the break of day would overtake us, and Vigan was still three miles away. An hour later we entered the suburbs, but the sky was lightening to the eastward. Guillermo and Antonio were in favor of retreating again and hiding in the bushes until night, but Pedro advocated entering Vigan, and obtaining shelter in the house of Señor Baldolomar, to whom we bore a letter from Lieutenant Bustos. I voted with Pedro, and we pushed on. Fortunately we could discover no outposts, and soon we were passing through some narrow deserted streets of Vigan, Pedro swinging in and out of alleys and by-passages as if thoroughly familiar with them. Of a sudden he came to a halt, peering cautiously around a corner. "Take care," he whispered back to us; "sentries, follow me." I observed we were close to the plaza, and not two hundred yards distant stood the barracks. Almost before us, and but fifty yards away, stood the home of Baldolomar, but to reach it we should have to cross a patch of moonlight, and a sentry in front of the barracks was pacing his post in full sight. Each time he turned he walked back behind a wall for a few seconds, but the next turn exposed him to view again. Thus did he pace up and down, the moonlight glinting on his gun-barrel, Pedro watching for his chance. Again the sentry was behind the wall — the Spaniard leaped across the street and was securely hidden in the gateway of the Baldolomar house. It was now my turn, and I watched the sentry. Up he came again, turned, and once more disappeared, and I dashed across the open space, Guillermo close at my heels. Two minutes later Antonio joined us, and the danger was over.

Cautiously, lest we should disturb the neighborhood, we crept around to the back door and knocked. In my hand I held the letter Lieutenant Bustos had given me, which, from the rain and the soaking in the river, was little more than pulp. Twice we knocked, listening anxiously for some response. Presently somebody moved inside and a masculine voice demanded, "Quien vive?" "Amigos de Bustos," answered Pedro. The bolt inside was withdrawn and the door opened. "Come in," continued the voice, and we entered.

Inside all was darkness, but now a match was struck, a lamp lit, and our surroundings became visible. We were in a small room, containing a bed, table, dresser, and a few chairs. An elderly Spaniard in white pajamas stood before us, also a woman, a mestiza, with a child in her arms. This man was evidently Baldolomar himself, and to him I gave the letter. He opened it and apparently succeeded in making out its contents, for, reaching out his hand, he said: "You are welcome as friends of Lieutenant Bustos."

Our host, being a civilian and merchant, was not a prisoner, but lived in this small house with his family. His wife, although partly native, was even lighter of complexion than her husband. Such a kind and motherly face — we could feel perfectly safe as far as she was concerned. The child in her arms was her two-year-old son, a little tot with light, golden curls and big blue eyes — yet a Filipino.

When we had fully explained our plans and hopes to our host, he gravely shook his head. The beach was still strictly guarded by a cordon of bolomen, and no Spaniard allowed to approach within a mile. Of the Spaniards, only the sick in the hospital remained; the rest were all gone. Nevertheless, he said he would render us any assistance in his power.

The house was small, in fact consisted of but two rooms, and into one of these a native servant showed us. Poor, indeed, is the family in the Philippines, that cannot afford a servant. Mats were spread, and on these we laid ourselves down, our clothes wringing wet. We had arrived just in time, for outside it was dawning, and the melodious notes of reveille came floating in from the plaza. We soon fell asleep.

When again I awoke, the sun was shining in through an open window. I arose, and, through the boughs of a tree, could overlook the greater portion of the plaza, the barracks, the familiar hospital building, and the soldiers at their morning drill. It was a beautiful calm morning, nothing but the blasts from the bugle breaking the stillness. I watched those rows of brown soldiers and thought how quickly they would have come for me had they observed me as I did them. But the tree screened me from their view.

Baldolomar called us in for breakfast, and while we ate told us what news he had.

No American vessel had been seen off the coast for over a week. General Natividad, the cripple (el cojo) as he was familiarly called, was now in command of the garrison, which, together with six men in San Quintin, ten in Santa, and five in Bantay, all neighboring towns, numbered less than sixty. The Americans were supposed to have landed at San Fernando and cut off the retreat of Aguinaldo, who was at Tarlac.

All this was not particularly encouraging, but we hoped to find a boat, and if we could not meet a war vessel, we might sail down to San Fernando with a fair wind, the northeast monsoons being now prevalent. Once more we sought rest in sleep, for, being on the move the entire night before, and knowing that the coming night would be the same, we needed all the rest we possibly could obtain.

Judging by the rays of the sun it must have been about noon when a murmur of voices from the next room awoke us, but with relief I recognized them as those of Spaniards, not Filipinos. Natives could never have commanded such bass growls as I now heard. Shortly afterward Baldolomar called us in, and we entered. Around the table were seated three Spaniards, also civilians and residents of Vigan. One I knew to be a certain Dr. Martinez, a Spanish physician, having occasionally seen him in the hospital. The other two were merchants. They had come to dine with our host, and he, in anticipation of receiving advice or even assistance, had confided our case to them, and even as we made our appearance was yet explaining our plans and what we hoped to accomplish by reaching the American vessels. Long before he could finish they jumped up from the table, knocking a chair or two over, and pranced about the room as if the floor was growing hot, pawing the air and acting in general like men whose excitement had mastered their reason. What we wished to do was impossible. "Impossible, impossible," they cried in chorus. We had come down only to compromise them. They would be blamed and punished as our accomplices. No — no, we must return to Bangued, give ourselves up, etc. I was disgusted with their egotism and felt sorry that our host had confided in them, and now feared that they might betray us, but, demonstrative as they were with their words and gestures, we really had less reason to fear them than such quiet, underhand hypocrites as Arnold.

Soon afterward they took their departure — they had certainly done their best to discourage us. Baldolomar smiled — the scene had amused him, but not me, for as I glanced at the faces of Guillermo and Antonio I saw they bore expressions of deep alarm and fear. Pedro alone seemed unimpressed.

After dinner we returned to the other room and seated ourselves on the mats, our backs against the wall, and for some time nobody ventured a syllable. At length Antonio repeated the one word, "Impossible." "Impossible!" echoed Guillermo. Pedro was lost in reflection and stared vacantly at the opposite wall.

Now, to return to Bangued would have meant nothing more than the walk there to my companions, as they in all probability never would have been missed; but to me such a proposition had a different meaning. The Provincial Governor was known to be no friend of the white race, and, should I return, I should undoubtedly fall into his hands. Although I knew that such friends as Paredes, Abasilla, and Comandante Peña would never allow me to be so seriously dealt with as was Lieutenant Repol, they could not prevent the Governor from placing me in close and possibly solitary confinement, thus destroying my last hopes of escape. Now I was free, comparatively speaking, and I meant to be harder pressed than we were now before giving myself up. How my comrades would have laughed at seeing me come voluntarily slinking back after an attempt at escape with no success — like a runaway schoolboy, coming home to be good again. I felt sorry, however, that I had not delayed my venture somewhat longer and secured two more such companions as Pedro, instead of the two boys, Guillermo and Antonio.

All my attempts at the task of convincing these two that we had good reason to expect success proved futile for a while. They wept like children, and insisted on returning to Bangued. Pedro himself seemed not too favorably inclined toward continuing the expedition, but evidently his pride prevented him from acknowledging the fact. I felt that he would be ashamed to leave me.

While arguing with the other two, I had been turning the leaves of a small school-book, which had been lying on the floor — a book for children learning to read, issued by the friars. It was entitled "Historia Sagrada," giving short, simple lessons in Bible history. While speaking, my glance happened to fall onto the book, and in conspicuous type I read at the top of a page the title of one of the lessons: "Entre los Peligros hay Seguridad" (Amidst Dangers lies Security). Holding up the book I exclaimed: "Comrades, even God counsels us — we must pass through these dangers to reach true security." These words, which almost seemed to have appeared in the Sacred Book especially to hold out my argument, made a deep impression, I could see. I felt that I had gained my point.

It was decided that Pedro should go out in the town after dusk and buy provisions, a rope, and a mat (to serve for cordage and sail), a clasp-knife, and several other small but necessary articles, as also to obtain any information possible. By bandaging his head he ran small risk of capture; he would be taken for a patient from the hospital.

At about six he left us, apparently hardly able to walk. An hour passed slowly away, but still Pedro did not return. The church bell chimed half-past seven, still he was absent. I was beginning to grow exceedingly nervous, when at last, shortly before eight, he appeared, and, by the expression of his countenance, I saw that he had good news. He told us he had met an old friend, a nurse in the hospital, who volunteered to guide us to a place up the coast where there were boats in plenty and where the beach was not patrolled. We must leave the house at once and join our new companion at another place, for the soldiers had seen Pedro enter, and their suspicions might have been aroused. Should the house be searched we would be arrested and our kind host compromised, so, bidding him and his wife good-by, and thanking them for their hospitality, doubly to be appreciated on account of the conditions under which it had been extended to us, we went out into the yard and scaled the back wall. We now walked boldly down to the main street, Pedro and I hatless and with bandaged heads, the other two limping. As it was not yet eight o'clock, we passed a sentry unchallenged, who said no more to us than, "Sigue, Castile."

We soon reached our destination, which was really close to Baldolomar's house, and on the plaza, but we had taken a roundabout route so that we might not be seen leaving his premises. We entered a large, half-ruined stone building, and at once ascended to an upper floor where a number of natives and one Spaniard were seated in a large room, conversing. Having been in Vigan for three months, I ran some risk of being recognized, so I had also tied a handkerchief about my jaw as though suffering from toothache. The native who received us was a well-to-do, kindly disposed old fellow, an old friend of Pedro's; in fact it was here, with him, that the latter had formerly been lodged.

He explained to him now that he had come down from Bangued with a pass from the Civil Governor for the purpose of purchasing cloth for the Spanish officers, which in Abra costs doubly as much as in Vigan. As this was not an unusual proceeding since the distribution of the money sent by the Spanish Government, the simple native had offered him and his friends the hospitality of his house for the few days of our prospective stay. Pedro introduced the rest of us as "assistentes" of other officers on similar errands.

Our new companion, being a hospital nurse, was allowed the privilege of sleeping outside when off duty, and lodged with this native. He and Pedro were old friends and companions in arms. The others familiarly called him Catalan, meaning a native of the northeastern province of Spain, Catalonia. The moment I entered he came forward and exclaimed, "Ola, paisano!" (Hello, countryman!) Turning to the Filipinos he explained that I also was a Catalan, which was a pretty clever stroke, since that would account for my accent in the language, the Catalonians having a manner of pronouncing their words similar to my peculiar accent. So I posed as a Catalonian.

I was supposed to be very ill, but carried the deception a trifle too far, for our host became sympathetic and commenced to condole with me, and I, of course, was obliged to reply. "Catalan is very sick," said Pedro; "don't speak to him." But when our host in accents of heartfelt sympathy ordered a servant to bathe my head in cold water, I came near betraying myself. Pedro again came to the rescue and remarked that I also suffered from hysterics.

At length supper was served, and the old native insisted on my coming to the table to eat. I was extremely hungry, and the fried sausages tempted me sorely, so, together with our host and the four Spaniards, I seated myself. My appetite did not agree with my apparently delicate condition, and in spite of their fears that I might be discovered, the Spaniards could with difficulty restrain their merriment at the manner in which I helped the victuals to disappear. Fortunately our host was so absorbed in a political discussion that he failed to notice me. For half an hour I was obliged to listen to this man (he chanced to be a Tagalog) denouncing my countrymen as oppressors, tyrants, assassins of liberty, etc., and to keep up appearances by replying with "Si" to all he said. The Spaniards were about choking with laughter and kicked my legs under the table, but suddenly the Filipino turned to me and remarked: "You are very light for a Spaniard; you might almost be taken for an American." I explained to him that all Catalonians were lighter than the majority of Spaniards, and this seemed to satisfy him, but it was a warning to be more careful. Complaining of a violent headache, I asked to be shown to our quarters, and shortly afterward was lying down on a mat in another room, separated from the main part of the building, an outhouse in fact. Half an hour later the rest joined me, and then Pedro explained our next move.

The guide, his friend, was well posted on the country in general, and knew of a small village fourteen kilometres up the coast, a place called Masingal, where the beach was entirely unguarded, and boats were numerous. We had all necessary provisions, ropes, mats, etc., and at eleven o'clock we would quietly slip out and strike for the north. Needless to say, I had no criticism to make on this plan. I could suggest none better.

The church bell had just struck eleven when we arose, and, each of us taking a small bundle, we silently stole out on the now deserted streets. By making a circuit of the whole town we avoided the dreaded sentries, for Catalan knew where each one was stationed, and at length found ourselves on the bank of a small branch of the Abra River on the north side of Vigan. The town is situated on a delta land, this branch practically making Vigan and its suburbs an island. This was easily forded, and, leading the way, Catalan trudged on, we following. Cautiously and silently we crept around the town of Bantay, within a mile of Vigan, altogether a separate municipality, but our guide knew every inch of the country, and successfully avoided barracks and police quarters.

About midnight we passed through a group of houses which on the map is called San Ildefonso, and at about one the larger town of Santo Domingo. It was raining and we met nobody on the lonely and quite deserted road. Two hours later we entered another town. This was Masingal, but we had yet another mile or so to reach the sea-shore beyond. Already I could hear the breakers booming, and shortly afterward we crept out on the beach at the mouth of a small river. The moon came feebly out, and by its light we saw two large boats high and dry on the sand. We were in a small cove, and the launching would not be difficult. My heart beat loudly as we cautiously approached those two black shadows, for now it seemed almost as if liberty was really within our grasp. How must my companions have felt, who were well into their second year of imprisonment! Guillermo was sobbing from nervous excitement.

We could not have been more than fifty yards away from the boats when a bright light flared up before us, and we saw a number of dark figures approaching from an opposite direction. We were too late, the fishermen were about to launch their boats for the day's fishing. They numbered a score or more, and with a bitter feeling of disappointment we beat a hasty retreat. We must cross the river, Catalan said; on the other side were more boats and we might be in time to secure one. The river was too deep to ford, so we made preparations to swim. As the distance across was at least half a mile, we were compelled to leave our shoes behind. In fifteen minutes we crawled up on the opposite bank and commenced an exploration of the beach on that side, but nowhere could we see a boat; if there had been any, they were already launched. In the east the sky was now very much lighter, and, realizing that it would no longer be safe to be abroad, we began searching for shelter in the jungle. We at length found a nook in a thick growth of underbrush close by the beach, and into this we crawled to spend the day in hiding. It rained continually, and there we lay shivering, unable to shelter ourselves from a cold northerly drizzle that seemed to soak us to the very marrow. Here I learned many new words of profanity in Spanish, for my companions seemed to be reviewing their entire vocabulary in that direction.

Toward noon the sun came out and shone down on us through a break in the foliage, brightening our hopes, and seemingly infusing new vitality into our drooping spirits. The sea, too, was growing calmer, and we expected no difficulty in launching a boat that night, nor yet in finding one.

It must have been about two o'clock — we were trying to snatch a few winks of sleep — when in the distance we heard a dog barking. At first we paid no attention to this, but as the bark kept approaching we sat up, becoming uneasy. After some exciting moments the cur brought up in the thicket, within a few yards of us, and there he stayed yapping continuously. We tried to dislodge the brute, but with no success; he simply remained there, invisible but close by, the jungle ringing with his bark. We now distinguished the excited voices of men, and unanimously decided that it was about time to move on. Squirming through the underbrush, we reached the sandy beach, and at once commenced to run. We heard a shout behind us, and saw emerging from the bushes half a dozen natives, all with their bolos. We were commanded to halt, but instead of obeying the summons, continued retreating with more speed than dignity. They had now cut us off from the jungle, and before us lay a clear stretch of rice-field at least two miles broad, but on the other side of this the bamboos and trees again promised a welcome and needed shelter, and with the object of reaching this in time we sped on across the rice-paddies. The bolomen continued their pursuit, though to all appearances their little yelping cur had given out. They apparently had not gained upon us, but their numbers had evidently increased. Men sprang up in the field, and with their ready bolos, but a minute before engaged in reaping rice, joined our pursuers. We were now fast nearing the far edge of the clearing, and so certain of gaining shelter that we even slackened our speed the least trifle, when, just as we crashed in under the lofty trees, two of these peaceful reapers cut in ahead of us, and with gleaming bolos appeared just before us in our path. They were but two, but armed, while we possessed nothing more dangerous than bamboo sticks. "Alto!" they shouted in unison, but Catalan, who ran right into them before he could recover, raised his staff and launched it with all his strength spear-fashion at the foremost one. The native fought the air wildly with his bolo for a few moments, but the staff, fully five feet in length, had hit him severely, and he was knocked back or perhaps jumped back to escape further punishment, although he succeeded in almost severing Catalan's weapon in two. Just then Pedro and I came up, and the second native made a thrust at us. Pedro's move partook so much of lightning rapidity that I failed to observe it properly; I only heard a loud thump, and the boloman dropped like a log, the blood gushing from an ugly wound in his head. His companion turned and fled. Not waiting to investigate the extent of the man's injury, we flew on again, shooting into all sorts of glades and openings at all manner of angles, sometimes almost doubling on our own tracks. Meanwhile we could still hear the cries of our pursuers in the rear, who thus served in enabling us to locate them, and by skilful twisting and turning we soon evaded them until their shouts entirely died away in the distance. Nevertheless we made all possible haste to leave the neighborhood, and by dusk had placed several miles between ourselves and the good people of Masingal.

At last we struck the main road and continued following it in the direction of Vigan. Long before morning we found ourselves in the bamboo thickets between Bantay and Vigan, on the banks of the river.

Here we held a consultation, but it soon became evident to me that all hope was lost, the Spaniards being firm in their decision to return to Abra. All my arguments were in vain, no psalm-book coming to my rescue this time.

They in their turn tried all manner of means of persuading me to return with them, asserting that their General Peña would plead in my behalf in case they attempted to punish me; but I was as firm in my determination not again to ascend the Abra pass voluntarily as they were to do so. So it became evident that we would have to part.

Catalan was going to return to his duties in the hospital at Vigan and explain his day's absence with a tale of too much vino. Perez was still there, so I requested the nurse to tell the practicante that at half past eight that night I would be on the river-bank just below the hospital building. Here was a steep embankment, and at the foot of that I requested Perez to meet me. Catalan promised to deliver my message.

At last the Spaniards rose — they were going. I also arose and walked to the edge of the thicket with them, and this caused them to believe that I was weakening, but at the last bush I halted. There was no hand-shaking; they simply walked on a short distance and then turned to look back. Pedro motioned to me to come on, but I remained where I was. Once more they moved on, and then I realized fully what it was to be alone in an enemy's country.

Feeling now that I must hereafter act according to my own judgment, and be my own guide, I lay down in the bushes, first, to hide, and, secondly, to think over a plan of action.

What could I do alone? Unless I succeeded in enlisting new recruits for my apparently hopeless expedition, I felt that indeed all would be lost. It was in vain that I tried to derive some comfort from the thought that every cloud has a silver lining. The cloud that now hung over me so oppressively seemed dark through and through, I must endeavor to-night to persuade Perez to join me, and as he had been eager once before, he might be willing to try again. At any rate, I felt my last hope rested with him.

It is extremely doubtful that I should have remained hiding in that bush all day, for the monotonous clanging of the bells in Vigan every half-hour almost drove me frantic. But I was not to have the chance to test my own endurance. It was about ten o'clock when I heard approaching footsteps which stopped outside before the bush in which I was hidden. I could not see the person, but, presently, I heard the hacking of a bolo against the bushes. Some native was cutting green brush for his carabao. Nearer and nearer came the cutter until I could see his figure. Then, giving a long-drawn and noisy yawn, I arose. Inwardly I trembled, but I tried to hide my fears. I now saw before me an old "taui," ragged, wrinkled, and toothless, and so feeble and harmless did he appear that I took courage. As I arose he stared at me, eyes and mouth wide open. "Apoo-o," he moaned out in a morning greeting peculiar to the tauis. He understood no Spanish, so, evidently, his dense intellect mistook me for a wandering Spaniard. "Abra," I kept repeating, and I suppose he thought I asked the way, for he pointed toward La Bocana, and thanking him in Ilocano, I started off in that direction.

But now to find another hiding-place. I stepped out into the road and started to follow this along, as I feared the neighborhood was hardly secluded enough for my purpose. Several women passed me with baskets on their heads bound for the Vigan market. I had been walking slowly for about ten minutes, when I heard footsteps behind me, and, as they approached nearer, a voice, "Ola, Castile, donde vas?" Turning around I found myself face to face with a native, but imagine my horror when I recognized him as one who had formerly been Dr. Chrisolojo's coachman, who consequently knew me well. I had even given him several verbal lessons in English. For some moments we stood stupidly staring at one another, but at last he broke into a laugh. Calling me by name, he reached out his hand, which I shook as he greeted me with a "Good-morning, meester," words that I had taught him myself. He asked me no questions, however, for he was an intelligent chap and comprehended the situation. For a short distance we walked silently on, side by side, but when we reached the fork where the road branched toward the ford to Vigan he stopped, inquiring: "Are you going to Vigan?" "No," I answered, "not to Vigan, to America." He laughed once more, shook hands, bid me "good-by" in English, and went on his way toward town. A moment later he stopped once more and called back to me, "Look out — muchos soldados." Two minutes later I saw him fording the river below Vigan.

Having my doubts of this fellow, I pushed on toward the foot-hills. He might notify the soldiers and he might not, but, wishing to be on the safe side, I determined to place some distance between Vigan and myself.

On I went along the road, meeting more market women, and even men, but none molested me. I must have gone at least two miles, when I reached a large field of sugar-cane, through which a narrow path led to a hut somewhere in the interior of it, the nipa roof being just visible above the tops of the cane. A sudden attack of fever convinced me that I could go no further, so I entered here to beg a drink of water. After passing through a labyrinth of paths in the cane-brake, I eventually reached a small clear space, wherein stood the hut, like all native bamboo habitations, raised on stilts, about five feet off the ground. A man was sitting on his heels below, feeding a large rooster tied by one leg to a peg in the ground. Two women above in the house were spinning, and three children rolled about in front of the steps, happy and dirty. It was an ideal home of the lower classes, ignorant but contented.

My appearance caused some excitement. Barefooted, ragged, and bareheaded, I must even to them have looked wild and uncouth. They understood a little Spanish, so I asked for food, and one of the women nodded, inviting me to ascend. I did so, and seated myself on the bamboo floor. They commenced to question me — what was my name, where did I come from, where was I going, how did I come to lose my hat, why had I no companions, and why were my eyes the color of the sky? All these questions I answered to the best of my ability, claiming to be from Vigan and bound for Abra. The women and an old man, who now made his appearance, patted me gently on the head, calling me "pobre Castile." Ten minutes later they spread before me a pot of rice, sliced tomatoes, beans, bananas, and water. I ate all, and then offered to pay, but this they refused. Once more I arose to go, but so weak did I feel, and so feverish, that I sank helplessly back, to rest a little longer. Then the old woman went into another room and returned with a mat and pillow which she spread beside me, motioning me to lie down. What a relief to stretch myself, my head resting in the soft bag of cotton. Before I knew it, I was asleep.

All day I lay there as unconscious of my surroundings as one dead, my body needing to recuperate from the violent exertions of the last three days. When I awoke, the sun was low on the horizon and the shadows were long. As the women saw that I was awake, they placed another meal before me, similar to the previous one, and then sat about on their heels while I satisfied my appetite.

The old man came in, as also the young one, with the children, the whole family now being there. The old woman held a mischievous little youngster of three up for me to admire, and I good-naturedly pulled his little nose, what there was of it at least, and this humorous feat placed the rest of the family on the most friendly footing with me, including the youngster himself, who yelled with delight. I had not yet finished eating when the old man pulled down a straw hat from a peg almost as ancient as himself, and laid it beside me. "For you," he explained, and I accepted it gratefully.

By this time the fever had left me, and my strength returned. It was almost sunset, and, bidding my friends good-by, I descended the steps and started off for the main road.

"The Filipinos respect no law but fear," the padre had assured me at Namacpacan. What fear then could I, a miserable, ragged, and helpless scarecrow, have inspired in these people who had treated me with such kindness — me, whom they thought a Spaniard, one of the race that for centuries had oppressed them, though now vanquished forever, no longer to be feared? "No, padre," I said to myself as I trudged down the path, "you who have been in the country for years understand these people less than I who came but yesterday."

I had almost reached the main road when the notes of a bugle reached my ears, from close by, tooting a march, a regular toot-toot-toot, to which the soldiers keep step in lieu of a drum. I had just time to crouch down in the canes, the approaching dusk helping to hide me, when some two dozen soldiers came marching by, going up toward La Bocana. An officer on horseback headed this little column, but at that time I did not know that this was General Natividad; I only felt more cheerful as I realized that this would reduce the garrison in Vigan at least by one-half. Not that I contemplated an attack on the town by myself, but sentries would be fewer.

I waited until the monotonous notes of the bugle had died out in the distance, and then got up once more and stepped out on the road. It was now dark.

According to the church bell it was seven o'clock when I reached the riverbank opposite the hospital. On the Vigan side of the river a steep bank rises abruptly from the water, the bishop's palace, a nunnery, and the hospital being built almost on the brink of this embankment. It was my intention to reach a small stretch of flat beach directly under the hospital, the place where I had engaged to meet Perez. A path led down the steep bank from the hospital grounds above to this shelf of ground, and would be easy for anybody to reach from that direction, but I now saw that for me to get there was not to be accomplished without difficulty. I tried to creep along the bank by the water's edge, but found it impossible; the ground rose too abruptly from the water, and I dared not resort to swimming, for in this part the river was full of thorny bushes placed there for the propagation of fish. I made an effort to climb the embankment, but slipped and fell with a loud crash. "Alto!" cried a sentry from above, but I lay still. "Alto! quien vive?" came several times, then I heard the report of a gun, and a bullet whistled far to my left. I lay there quietly for some time, and then crawled back.

I now determined to approach the place of meeting by coming up along the bank from the opposite direction, but to reach there I must pass directly through the town. Tying a handkerchief around my head I walked up into the streets of Vigan, directly into the main thoroughfare, where the lamps from the shops brightly illuminated the scene. Taking my hat off I held it before me as did the begging Spaniards, and, limping up in the middle of the street, my cane in one hand, the hat in the other, I made my way through the main part of the town, begging from all I met. Nobody paid any particular attention to me, and soon I was treading the quieter and more deserted streets in the neighborhood of the prison. I took care not to enter the plaza, for I knew that sentries were stationed before the palace, the nunnery, the college (Vigan had a fine college), the presidency, and the barracks. Finally I lost my bearings, as we say aboard ship, and for some time I wandered aimlessly about, fearing to meet the eight o'clock patrol or run into a sentry. Never before had I thought Vigan to be so extensive as it now seemed. Eventually I approached a native pedestrian and inquired the way to the hospital; first I wished him to believe me a belated patient from there, and, secondly, if I had but the lofty roof of the hospital building to guide me, I would soon find my way to that part of the river I was searching for. I regretted, however, having addressed this man when he kindly offered to conduct me there. I limped desperately, but the native placed his arm under mine to support me — he evidently thought me a cripple. I felt small and cheap.

At last I noticed the familiar outlines of the hospital building before me, and then I begged my guide to trouble himself no further, and, fortunately, he left me, for had he really conducted me into the hospital the chances were that I should have had to remain there. Guided now by familiar landmarks, I found myself at length behind the old prison wherein I had already spent a month. From here to the river was but a few steps, and soon I reached the water.

However, I soon discovered that to reach the little beach under the hospital by this bank was equally impossible, for, besides being just as steep, there was not a bush to shelter me.

Once more I retraced my steps, and for a while wandered about the streets in hopes of meeting a Spaniard by whom I might send word to Perez, but it was now too late, as all the patients were supposed to be in by eight.

I was just coming up a small alley and stepping into a larger street, when I found myself in the midst of a patrol of at least a dozen soldiers. So narrow was the thoroughfare, that they passed me on both sides. My heart jumped into my throat, but beyond slapping my back and shouting, "Ola Castile!" they did not molest me.

As it had now struck eight some time ago, I became desperate and determined to swim through the fish-traps. Once more I forded the river, and, going down the opposite bank, stood just across the river from the spot which I was desirous of reaching. The bell struck the appointed hour, half-past eight, and I waded out into the water until beyond my depth. Then, holding the cane in my mouth by its rope lanyard, I started to swim across. Fortunately the current here was sluggish, and I drifted but little. Gradually I approached the opposite shore, but when hardly ten feet more remained I found myself entangled in the thorny bushes. The more I struggled the more I tore myself, and I could not stand still, as the water here was deeper than my height. Frantically I kicked about, when, just as I was about instinctively to cry out for help, I caught an overhanging bush from the bank, and by this endeavored to draw myself up. I found, however, that my strength was not equal to it, and there I hung, half my body under water. Several times I tried, but each effort only served to weaken me the more, and I hung there helplessly.

Suddenly I heard a rustling in the bushes above, something grasped both my hands, and I felt myself drawn steadily up until I lay flat on terra firma. "Hombre! Alberto! Madre de Dios!" I heard a familiar voice exclaim in a loud whisper, and Perez and I were embracing each other, half laughing, half crying. There was no occasion to hide our feelings.

It was with difficulty that I walked. My left leg had been badly torn in the fish bushes, but we went off into an obscure thicket to converse. Perez was more excited than I, and for some time could do no more than give vent to exclamations. At length he regained his composure and I told him my experiences of the last three days, ending up with an explanation of the situation and a proposal that he accompany me on another search for a boat. Then he explained how hopeless such an expedition would be.

First, as a landing by the Americans was feared, every possible place where a boat could be launched was carefully guarded and watched. Secondly, there were no boats equipped; all had been stripped of masts, rigging, or oars, until nothing remained but the naked hulls. And white man seen near these landing places would be fired upon at sight.

These, and many others, were the reasons that Perez held forth as impassable obstacles. My only resource, he said, was to return to Bangued and throw myself on the mercy of the provincial authorities. I had friends there with much influence, who would plead for me, and in all probability I would not be punished at all.

Perez remained with me until a little before ten, when he was obliged to retire, as the doors of the hospital were closed at that hour. Before leaving he made an effort to press a half peso on me, but this I declined, especially as I still had some silver on me.

For some time after he was gone I lay in the bushes gazing at the moon, trying to think of some way out of my troubles, but my situation seemed now as hopeless as it could possibly be. I determined at length to return to the hut where I had spent the greater portion of the day, and remain there until I could decide on some definite plan of action.

On rising I found my left leg stiff and throbbing with pain. Then it occurred to me that I neither could nor would swim that river again. So I did the only thing left for me to do, that is, I climbed the bank and stood in the plaza.

A faint hope that I might elude the sentries possessed me. The thought struck me of once more seeking shelter with Baldolomar, and with considerable reluctance I decided to make an effort in that direction. I felt that it was wrong for me to endanger him and his family with my presence, but it was my last resource.

I passed the hospital on my right, safely. The sentry in front of the nunnery also failed to see me, as I crept along under the trees in the middle of the plaza. I had yet to pass the palace and the presidency, the former on my left, the latter on my right. I had already passed the tall stone monument in the centre of the plaza, when a loud cry rang out: "Alto, quien vive?" With a nervous start I flung the cane into the bushes at my feet, and there I let it lie.

Chapter Twenty-Four - Marines from the Oregon

AGAIN the sentry challenged, and this time I answered, "Castile;" advancing toward the palace gates until within a dozen yards of him, when he commanded me to halt. "Show your pass," he ordered, as he in turn approached me. "I have none," was my reply. Telling me to stay where I was, he returned to his post and called a noncommissioned officer, who came out and commenced questioning me, asking what I was doing out after taps without a pass. "I am an escaped American prisoner from Bangued," I answered. For a moment I thought he would fall down with astonishment. Just then an officer appeared, who demanded to know what it all was about, and to him the non-commissioned officer repeated my words. "Well, come inside out of the rain," was his reply, for it had commenced to drizzle again. The three of us stepped inside of the spacious entrance of the palace. The officer was a young mestizo of about my own age, yet on each shoulder he wore the golden star of a colonel.

"Your name is Alberto, is it not?" he asked as we came into the light of a hanging lantern. "Yes," I replied, surprised that he should know me. "Where have you been since the 17th?" he continued, "and how is it that those fools in Bangued did not telegraph of your escape before this afternoon?"

I told him briefly of my adventures since leaving Bangued, of the trip to Masingal, and how the three Spaniards had deserted me. "The cowards!" he cried, as I finished, "to leave a companion like that. But what can you expect from a Spaniard? My God! how wet you are! What is the matter with your leg? are you wounded?" I told him of my swim across the river. "Ah, it was you the sentry fired at some hours ago. Lucky for you he is a boy and can't shoot. Are you hungry?" "Rather," I replied, in order to prevent further interrogation on the subject. Leaving me for a few minutes, he ran upstairs, returning with a coat and pants. "Here," he said, "throw off those rags, here is one of my own suits, a Filipino uniform." With very little trouble I wriggled out of the cazador's suit, which the fish traps had torn into shreds, and when again I emerged from behind the door I was attired in the uniform of an Insurgent colonel, minus the stars. "Bien, bien," exclaimed the young officer (thus reminding me of Abasilla), "now you look presentable." He then ordered a soldier to bandage my leg with his own handkerchief, which he tore into strips for the purpose. The pockets of my new suit he filled with cigarettes and cigars. Leading me out to the gate, he said: "I will now send you to the hospital with this guard. I am sorry, deeply sorry, that you failed. You deserve your liberty. It is my duty, however, to guard against your escaping again, but I assure you, it is against my own inclinations. Let us hope that your imprisonment may not last much longer, but I am afraid, my friend, that you have yet to undergo some hardships. Would that you could continue under my charge, but I must return you to Bangued. But take this; it will help you on the road." As he said this, he slipped a silver peso into my hand. "No, no," he continued, as I hesitated just a moment. "I do not ask you to accept this as charity, only as a loan; some day you may repay me — I would take it from you under similar circumstances; and now goodby." He reached out his hand, which I grasped. "One thing before we part," I requested: "May I know to whom I owe this more than kind treatment?" "My name is Joaquin Alejandrino," he answered, and then, with a warm shake of the hand, we parted.

It was about midnight when the guard and I entered the hospital. I was at once taken up to the floor above, and in ten minutes it was known that I had arrived, and all the inmates, from the officers to the soldiers, gathered around to greet me, with more noise and effusion than either the hour or the place would seem to warrant. Perez seemed nervous and excited, laughing hysterically, until even the others wondered where he saw the joke. The doctor's wife and mother appeared and at once called the sleeping servants to prepare a meal, but all this kindness only made me feel like a bad little boy who has run away from home and come back to be good. The Señora chided me gently as a mother would her child. Why had I run away from people who had treated me so kindly as they had in Bangued? Alejandrino had sent a written message, stating that I had not eaten, and something must be prepared for me at once, but the message was not necessary. While I ate a hearty meal, I answered a thousand questions from all sides, until, finally, all retired again, and I slept in my old bed that night.

When I awoke in the morning the scene seemed so familiar that I half believed the last three months a dream, but soon I noticed how many of the old faces were missing. Sixteen had gone to the "campo santo" since my departure, making a total of thirty in four and one-half months. In fact, most of those that lay about me now I had either never seen before or known as convalescents downstairs.

Later on Dr. Chrisolojo paid me a morning call. His manner was decidedly cool toward me. Without offering to shake hands he simply greeted me with a "buenas dias." For a moment he stood simply gazing at me, until at length he ventured the remark that I had not acted squarely toward him. "Why?" I asked, "how can you complain of my behavior?"

"I recommended you to the good treatment of Abasilla," he replied, "and he allowed you the liberty of the town on his own responsibility. In this flight you took advantage of a friend by compromising him with the Government."

"How could either you or Abasilla be responsible for me when Aguinaldo himself had ordered the provincial authorities to allow us the liberty of the town?"

"But *you* were not in the hands of the provincial authorities, you were under *our* charge, and we had not received any orders to allow you extra privileges."

"I was not on parole, however."

"Practically you were."

However, as I remembered Abasilla's words on this subject, my conscience did not trouble me. I had never heard of a prisoner begging permission to escape, so Chrisolojo and I differed on this point. Later in the day we met again out on the back gallery. I was sitting there gloomily contemplating the sea, when the doctor slapped me familiarly on the back, saying: "Well, I suppose it is pretty hard to reach out for liberty, to find it almost within your grasp, and then fall back again deeper into the mire than ever?" By evening we were on the same old familiar footing; he had quite forgiven me.

I was standing out on the balcony leaning over the railing, when somebody slapped me across the shoulders with a force to almost deprive me of my breath. Turning around, whom should I see but Castro, the same old Castro. Not one word of reproach from him! He made an effort to comfort me by prophesying my ultimate release within two months, and, although I did not believe him, yet I found comfort in the sympathetic tone of his voice. Imprisonment was, after all, not so terrible with such friends as he to associate with. Every spare moment he had during the day he spent trying to divert my mind from brooding over my failure, either by chess or by telling me funny stories, and he partly succeeded.

Besides the Spaniards, there were also four wounded Insurgent non-commissioned officers in the ward. Next to me, on the cot where I had seen my friend, the young Spanish cazador, die, now lay another boy, a young Filipino sergeant, not more than eighteen years of age. The fact that he was a cousin to Paredes made us friends at once. He had been shot through his right arm at a town called San Jacinto, in a fierce skirmish with the Americans, ten days before.

"Your countrymen," he informed me, "had disembarked at San Fabian, ten to our one. We resisted their landing at the cost of half our men, but, Dios mio! we were helpless; they drove us before them as the wind blows the dust on the road. For numbers they were like ants, and they came screaming and yelling like madmen. Half our shells would not explode. Still our men did not stampede, but retreated in order, firing as they went. At times we were fighting hand to hand, and I placed the muzzle of my gun close to the breast of an American and pulled the trigger. But of what good is our refilled ammunition? My cartridge did not explode, and the American shot me through the arm with his revolver. So big he was, too, towering far above me; his fist would have been as formidable as his revolver. Then they turned those horrible Maxim guns on us, and our men fell like sheaves of rice in reaping time. How we Filipinos dread those machine guns, that awful rattle, more terrible than the bursting of large shells." And so he kept on chatting for several hours, telling me of the many battles he had taken part in. I could not help liking the boy, he prattled away so unsophisticatedly. "How singular," he said, reflectively, "your countrymen and mine are now fighting one another, to see who can kill the most, and, yet, here we two are the best of friends. I am sure if I were to kill you now, I would feel as bad about it as if you were a Filipino. How terrible war is, after all."

All that day and the next I spent in the hospital. Natividad had gone up to Bangued the day before. He it was whom I had seen passing from the canebrake. Alejandrino was in command, and he had telegraphed my recapture to Bangued. In reply an order came to send me on at once with a strong guard of police. This much Chrisolojo had told me, so when on the evening of the 22d a sergeant of police and seven men appeared with an order for me, I was not surprised.

My parting with Chrisolojo and his family was as heartfelt as before. The two ladies wept and filled the pockets of the colonel's uniform that I wore with cigars, cakes, and other home-made delicacies for the road, they told me. Castro accompanied me to the gate below, and shook hands with me four or five times, forgetting after each time that he had done so. He would see me again, he declared, since the whole hospital corps of Vigan was coming up to Bangued also within a few days.

The squad of policemen conducted me over to the presidency close by, where I learned that I was not to go until in the morning early.

I was now in the hands of the Provincial Governor, who had received orders to send me on to the provincial authorities of Abra. Meanwhile, I was confined in a cell in the back part of the building, in total darkness. Several times officers came in to interview me on my escape from Bangued. None blamed me, but all agreed that the expedition had been hopeless from the beginning. Every one of them condemned the Spaniards for deserting me, finishing up with, "But what can you expect from such people?"

It must have been two hours since the last visitor had departed, and I was lying on a mat passing away the time smoking cigars, of which I had a good supply, for each visitor had been generous with me. The church bell had some time ago sounded the hour of ten, but, in spite of my repeated requests for a light, I lay in Egyptian darkness. Suddenly I became aware of something moving at the door. Somebody outside was gently inserting a key in the lock, and with a slight click the bolt flew back. I could see against the dim light of a lantern outside in the corridor as a background, the outlines of a man in the half open doorway. The door closed again and I knew somebody had entered. This stealthy manner not only surprised me, but also caused me to feel the least bit alarmed. "Quien vive!" I called out, but in reply only received an alarmed "sh-sh." A match was struck and a lantern lit, that feebly illuminated the apartment. Before me I saw a short, thick-set Filipino, a man whom I had never seen before. Coming up close to me he placed the lantern on the floor and seated himself on a small bench. Then he explained to me the cause of his mysterious visit.

His name was Lazo, and under the civil government he held the position of "Conciejero de la Presidencia." He had entire charge of the building and the servants, a sort of major-domo. But that was neither here nor there; he had come in the name of the Provincial Governor, Don Mariano Acosta, to make me a proposition. He would not alone help me to escape again, but also hide me on certain conditions. The Americans were advancing up the coast and could be expected within a week's time. If I would represent to my countrymen, upon their arrival, that the Governor and all his councilmen were peacefully disposed, and that they extended an honest welcome to the United States Government, he, the Governor, for his part, would allow me to hide until the military had been driven from the town by the advancing forces. Needless to say that I accepted the proposition.

Lazo left the cell again, carefully extinguishing the lantern before doing so, as soldiers still guarded the building. Anxiously I lay there waiting, listening to the occasional challenge of the sentry outside. At last, fully two hours later, a key was cautiously inserted in the lock again, and the door opened. In a loud whisper I heard my name called, whereupon I arose and approached the open doorway. A hand grasped my arm and I was gently drawn outside, where I recognized Lazo by the light of the sentry-box at the entrance. A sentinel was stationed there, but appeared to be dozing, being seated on a bench, his gun between his legs, his back against the wall, and his head sagging down on his chest. We passed the man close by, and I could observe that his sleep was not natural. "Opium," whispered Lazo, pointing to an empty vino glass on the floor. "He will wake up, see the open door, and run away — one soldier less." Evidently my new acquaintance was no fool.

Lazo conducted me up a broad winding staircase into a large, elegant office furnished with massive carved mahogany furniture. A tall mestizo, unusually large for a Filipino, sat at a desk, engaged with his own thoughts and a bottle of vino. As I entered, he greeted me as though I was a long-lost friend, while Lazo introduced him to me as Don Mariano Acosta, Presidente Provincial de Ilocos Sur. The Governor was in a cheerful state of intoxication, although he retained enough of his mental faculties to discuss the question at hand, but he only went over the same ground that Lazo had done. I understood the situation perfectly. I would tell the Americans how good he was, and he would hide me from the military. We both shook hands on the agreement.

The three of us then arose from where we had been seated, and, the Governor leading the way, we went through a long, narrow passage, the door to which seemed to be a part of the wall. Reaching the end after several turns and bends, a second door was opened, and we entered a small room, hardly any larger than the stateroom of a steamer. The furniture consisted of a small iron bedstead, a table, a chair, and two closed bookcases. Evidently the room had been arranged for my reception, for it had been neatly cleaned and everything was in order, candles, matches, writing material, and books. After conversing a few moments longer they retired, telling me to bolt the door from the inside, and never to open unless I heard two taps almost together, and a third after a short interval. That was to be the signal.

To say that my new quarters were comfortable is a mild expression. With writing materials, books, and an abundance of cigars, time would pass rapidly.

I had been alone hardly an hour, when I heard the three taps agreed upon. Slipping back the bolt, I opened the door, and Lazo entered, followed by Bartoleme, the alcaide of the prison, our former jailer.

His greeting was effusive, truly Spanish in that respect, but when he laid a package on the table, which, on being opened, displayed ten sausages and two hundred cigars, I began to "smell a rat," to use a vulgar expression. He also presented me with a beautiful carved cigarholder of carabao horn. Here were peace offerings. What I expected soon followed: Would Señor Alberto write him a letter of recommendation to the American "oficiales," stating how he had always been our friend, and that he desired nothing more than to be a peaceful citizen of the great United States. I could not well refuse him since he had really always been civil and even kind to us, so wrote a short letter, addressed to any American, introducing the bearer, Don Bartolemé, as a man worthy of the consideration of my countrymen for the manner in which he had treated us.

We then conversed on the situation. The town was garrisoned by twenty odd soldiers. Tiño and Villamor were being driven up the coast road, and within a week the Americans would enter Vigan. Alejandrino would not offer any resistance, so my callers expected a peaceful instalment of the American forces, especially if I should be there. Presently they left me, and soon I was dreaming of starry flags and liberty.

Early next morning I heard the signal, and, upon my opening, a boy entered who immediately proceeded to sweep and thoroughly clean out the room, leaving me soap, a basin of water, and towel. Another boy brought in a tray of dishes and began setting the table. Lazo entered, and the two of us sat down to a breakfast such as I had not seen since the wedding-day of Señorita Paredes. While we discussed the victuals, my companion gave me some important instructions. Through a hole in the wall I could observe and hear all that passed in the Governor's office. Within a short space of time the report would be spread that I had again escaped through the treachery of the sentry, who had placed his gun in the rack and disappeared. Should Alejandrino, however, suspect the civil authorities and search the house, I must be prepared. If any attempts were made to open my door, I must drop out of the shell window by means of a rope which was already attached to the sill, and seek shelter in a certain outhouse, from where one of the boys would guide me to safer quarters. All this was very unlikely to happen, but it was well to be prepared for all possible contingencies.

I spent my time reading and smoking until dinner, when a splendid meal with wine, coffee, and cigars was served me. I was evidently worth being taken good care of.

Toward evening I heard voices in the office, and, applying my eye to the peephole, saw a black-robed priest in excited conversation with Acosta. I could not hear all that was said, but such disconnected words as: "Americano — prisonero — escondido" (hidden), etc., reached my ears with an ominous significance. Soon the priest left and I heard no more, but Lazo, who joined me at supper, gave me an account of how Padre Galipay, the self-proclaimed Filipino bishop, had accused the Governor of aiding me to escape. This hotheaded sacerdote was a well-known Insurgent leader, and was often seen on the firing line by our men encouraging the Insurgent soldiers by his presence.

Alejandrino had also been to ask for me, and accused Acosta of being aware of my whereabouts. "I am morally certain he is somewhere in the building," he had told the Governor, "but as I am no longer responsible since I delivered him over to you, I shall not trouble myself to search the rooms. However, Señor Acosta, you are no patriot!"

God bless Joaquin Alejandrino!

Chrisolojo, Castro, and all of the hospital corps had departed during the day with all the sick able to travel, leaving Dr. Martinez, the Spaniard, in charge of the fifty remaining helpless cases, and a few able-bodied nurses to care for them. Don Francisco (he of the saluting drill) had been sent up to Abra as a prisoner by order of General Natividad, being accused of sending secret information to the Americans. Señor Rivera also had accompanied him for having disobeyed General Tiño's orders with regard to American prisoners. It had become known that he had secretly sent Lieutenant Gillmore fifteen pesos, and, as punishment, had been fined five thousand pesos. Refusing to pay this, he was arrested and sent into the mountains, together with Don Francisco. When I asked Lazo how it had leaked out that Rivera had given Gillmore the money, he said that his wife (Lazo's wife) had heard from another woman with whom Tiño was very intimate, that Arnold had confided to the general the part he had taken in the transaction. "Singular," I thought to myself, "how that coincides with the suspicions I formed some months ago, when Chrisolojo told me how Rivera had been arrested."

The long weary days now passed monotonously by, during which time I either wrote down my diary since leaving Bangued, or read a Spanish novel. Acosta had sent me shoes and clothes, but I still wore Alejandrino's uniform.

On the evening of the 25th Lazo came in quite excited. Three American vessels had anchored down in the bay off the main mouth of the Abra River, and were exchanging signals by means of rockets and lanterns. Their searchlights were sweeping the neighboring hills. I felt hopeful on hearing this news, but so many varying experiences had I had of late, that it failed to impress me as it would have done some months before. I slept soundly that night, and did not even dream of the three vessels.

Next morning I was awakened before dawn by a pounding at my door, followed by the signal, opened, and Acosta and Lazo entered hurriedly. "Quick," cried the Governor, "you must run across to the hospital and hide there. The American vessels are making preparations to disembark troops, and Alejandrino has gone down to the beach for a reconnaissance. It is likely that they will return to the town, loot the presidency, and discover you before retreating. Quick, before they return, run across and conceal yourself in the hospital. The doctor there will know what to do."

Downstairs I went into the street and across the plaza to the hospital. I was just in time, for, as I entered the gates I heard a bugle at the other end of the plaza. Alejandrino had proven himself my friend, but there are times when one does not even wish to meet his friends.

Dr. Martinez evidently expected me, for he at once wound a bandage about my head and part of my face, whereupon he conducted me into the old ward. In case the Insurgents entered I was to lie down on a cot among the sick.

As I entered, imagine my surprise at being suddenly embraced by Perez. He had escaped on the march to the river, preparatory to embarking on the rafts, and had now returned to hide in the hospital. Manuel was also there, but he had purposely been left behind to assist Dr. Martinez. Many of the Spanish officers also remained; being friends of Chrisolojo, he had reported them as unfit to travel.

Peeping from the balcony's shell blinds, we saw the soldiers entering the barracks. They had returned from the beach.

For an hour or so we sat conversing, when, suddenly, a loud report startled us all. Again it came, and then: boom — boom — boom, as I had once before heard it in Malolos, but a few miles farther off. Rushing to the balcony, we saw the soldiers flying helter-skelter up the street. An officer on horseback, Alejandrino, undoubtedly, was shouting orders to them, and, as they disappeared from view down an adjacent street leading toward the beach, they had formed into some sort of military order. Twenty-five of them — what did they expect to do?

The firing seemed to be some miles distant, but continued. Suddenly there came a report that shook the building, and a shell hissed over the town, exploding in the jungle between Bantay and Vigan.

The scene that followed beggars description, to use a familiar phrase. Dying men arose from their cots and fell into each other's arms, weeping and sobbing. Spanish officers screamed like maniacs, and an outsider would have thought himself witnessing a scene in a mad-house.

In the midst of the excitement, just as a second explosion seemed to rend the universe to pieces, and again a terrific whirling and screeching overhead brought a shriek from a hundred voices outside, Lazo appeared, and almost forcibly dragged me downstairs into the street and across to the presidency. Here in a group stood all the civil officials, both provincial and municipal, the local president, the governor, the chief justice, the tax collector, and the chief-of-police. As I arrived, a third shell was fired over the town, causing the governor and all his councilmen apparently to leap several feet into the air. The only one who appeared at all composed was a very dark but intelligent-looking young man, who held in his hands a Spanish-English grammar, from which he was repeating the words, "How do you do, gentlemen?" "Ah," he exclaimed, as I appeared, "do I pronounce this correctly?" This gentleman then introduced himself as Señor Ignacio Villamor, Representative of the Province of Ilocos Sur. He was a brother to Colonel Bias Villamor, consequently an uncle to my friend Bernardo.

"Madre de Dios! what shall I do?" exclaimed Acosta to me. "Consider yourself in charge here." I advised him to provide some white flags on long poles, and call out the municipal brass band, all of which he immediately gave orders to have done. Meanwhile, I walked into the middle of the plaza and commenced searching for the cane which I had dropped upon being halted by the sentry at the palace gates. Villamor joined me, and, when I informed him of the object of my search, he likewise began kicking the bushes about.

"Here it is," he exclaimed, holding that precious piece of bamboo up in his hand and passing it to me.

Just then the earth again seemed to split under us, and the limb of a large tree growing within two hundred yards of us was cut neatly off, the shell burying itself six feet in the ground without exploding, fortunately. Here it was afterward dug out.

Hundreds of the inhabitants, men, women, and children now flocked into the plaza, the report that an American was there having spread. Where I was, they thought, they would be safe, for I could certainly not be injured by the shells of my own countrymen.

A discussion was now entered into as to which would be the proper thing: to await the Americans in town or to go down and meet them. I advocated the latter course, otherwise the firing might continue all day, for, elated as I felt at prospective liberty, I admit I should have felt equally delighted had my countrymen ceased throwing those big shells over our heads. I had no doubt that they enjoyed the spectacle at the other end of the arc the flying shells described, but at our end the sensation was not pleasant, to say the least, especially as I had not the same faith in my own immunity from danger as some of the simple natives had.

As we learned later in the day, three persons were killed. One shell burst on the river-bank, a piece of it mortally wounding a woman and a child. Two miles distant another shell exploded in the open rice-fields, killing a poor "taui." But the strangest part of it all is the fact that this woman and man, killed at different points, two miles apart, were brother and sister! All Vigan will tell you this.

A quilez now appeared, and Señor Villamor, Señor Singson (a representative local merchant), and myself seated ourselves inside this vehicle. A white flag fluttered on top, and, the driver whipping up his horses, we took the road toward the beach at a brisk pace.

By this time the bombardment had ceased, but we met men breathlessly running who informed us that the Americans had landed and were advancing upon the town.

Between Vigan and the sea-shore the road passes over two low hills. As we reached the summit of the first of these, Villamor ordered the driver to stop, and watched the top of the other eminence, two miles away. Nothing but the blue sky was visible, however. We waited and watched, anxiously, when, finally, a small black speck made its appearance, then another and another, until quite a column of these tiny figures were observed descending from the brow of the hill. The black mass became bluish, the figures more distinct. In front fluttered something, borne by one of the foremost of the advancing figures, the colors of which, as they became visible to my straining eyes, sent a thrill through my whole being. Never before had those red and white stripes impressed me with a similar sensation.

Our quilez now tore down the hill at a break-neck speed, until we brought to under a tree not two hundred yards from the advancing column. I could now distinguish them as sailors and marines. On foot we walked forward to meet them. I feared my composure would leave me and that I would presently make myself ridiculous. The foremost marine reached out his hand to me as I ran up, and my first impulse, had I given way to it, would have been to throw my arms about his neck and weep on his bosom, but, with a mighty effort, I contained myself, and nearly shook his hand off. An elderly officer, who appeared to be in command, called a halt, and to him I now addressed myself. What I said I have but a faint recollection of, but the officer smiled good-naturedly, and shook hands with me several times.

At length they seemed to understand me, and, taking a cutlass from the nearest marine, I split open the cane and delivered Gillmore's letter. This caused some excitement, for Gillmore's misfortune had evidently made him a famous man. I answered questions innumerable on the spot, and asked as many more, shaking hands with everybody.

These were men of the good ship Oregon; the officer in command was Lieutenant-Commander McCracken. To him I now introduced Villamor and Singson, and the former, as representative of the people, surrendered the town formally. The American officer treated them with the utmost courtesy.

At length, my two native friends and I re-entered the quilez, and, leading the way, returned to Vigan, the inhabitants of which, now headed by the band, flocked out to meet us. When we reached the plaza, the marines, some two hundred, were lined up before the palace. The Governor came out, and I introduced him to Commander McCracken, upon whom he expended just one-half of his entire English vocabulary, "Welcome!" which so impressed the American officer with his knowledge of our language that he at once expressed himself as deeply pleased to meet the Honorable Governor. Acosta understood not a word, so in despair he let fly the other half of his vocabulary, "Good-by!"

All was silent, a hush had fallen over that mighty throng in the plaza. Glancing at the palace, I comprehended what was to follow. A moment later I was rushing wildly up the stairs to the floor above. From the balcony the Stars and Stripes were gliding slowly out and upward toward the flagstaff where a day before the Insurgent banner had fluttered, while down below in the plaza the notes of the American bugles arose.

I arrived just in the nick of time. The flag was half way up, and the next moment I had a hold on the halyard as it dropped from the hands of the sailor who stood on the railing.

Thus I assisted in raising the American colors over Vigan.

Chapter Twenty-Five - In Manila Again

To this day the natives of Vigan speak of Commander McCracken and Colonel Parker, the latter an army officer who accompanied the landing party, as "los buenos," with other flattering adjectives. During their short stay they managed to make themselves very much liked by the people on account of their general courteousness, respect for the rights of the conquered, and the absence of that arrogance rather common to military officials. As I was afterward told by one who had been, and probably still is, a red-hot Insurgent, in sentiment at least, if all American officers were like these two representatives of the army and navy who first governed Vigan, there would now be fewer Insurgents in the hills. My own acquaintance with these two gentlemen, however, amounted unfortunately to but two hours, for, after dinner, to which we had been invited by Acosta, I went down to the landing, to board the Oregon.

Never shall I forget the sensation I experienced, when, on the quilez making a turn around a sand dune, the mighty sea suddenly burst into view, dark blue, calm, apparently slumbering, and there, at least two miles out, that big white battle-ship, which in the morning had hurled those frightful thunderclaps, now innocently glistening in the rays of the sun. What memories were awakened in me! I had seen this proud ship launched in my native city when yet a mere school-boy. Almost within view of the spot where her majestic form had first gradually assumed shape I had spent my childhood's days, but little did I then dream, as I saw her beams and plates skilfully riveted together, that some day she would be the means of saving me from the hands of Filipino Insurgents.

My reception by Captain Wilde and his officers will linger with me as a pleasant memory for many years to come. Considering that I was an utter stranger to them, I had no right to expect it, and, therefore, I doubly appreciate it.

It took me some time fully to realize that I was not dreaming; such kindness and the number of new American faces about me were at first bewildering. The fact that I had actually seen and spoken to Gillmore and his men but nine days previously, made me again the object of a thousand questions, but I, too, was "loaded to the guards" with queries of all descriptions. Dewey, I now learned, had gone home, Otis was still in command, American soldiers had not been slaughtered by thousands, the volunteers had departed, and Ramon Rey had escaped with the two letters — all this was great news to me. Indeed, so stunned was I by all this, that, had they told me that the Salvation Army had come to help fight the Insurgents, I would probably have accepted that with the rest.

During the evening I gave Captain Wilde an explanation of the situation in Abra. Undoubtedly Alejandrino had fallen back with his fifty men to Bangued, thus increasing the garrison there to a force of seventy now under command of General Natividad, Alejandrino being but second in command. Against this force the Spanish prisoners would never rise, of that I felt assured, but a rescue party might save them. Unfortunately the Oregon had not the men to spare for such an expedition, Tiño with several hundred men was fifty miles down the coast. He might reach Abra by means of Tangadan, a pass cutting up into the mountains at Narbacan, twenty miles below Vigan. General Young was driving Tiño up toward this pass. A small force might cut Tiño's retreat off, but it must be done quickly, to do the prisoners any good. Captain Wilde insisted that I should go down to Manila the following morning to explain the situation to General Otis, who, he said, would undoubtedly despatch the required force at once.

The Oregon was accompanied by two smaller vessels, gun-boats, the Callao and Samar. On the latter of these two I embarked the following morning, and soon she was heading for Manila at a ten-knot speed.

At about three o'clock in the morning of November 29th we dropped anchor off Cavite. I did not wake up before daylight, just as the young commander, Ensign Mustin, returned from the Baltimore, the flagship, where he had been to report to Admiral Watson.

"I have orders," he informed me, "to weigh anchor at once and go over to Manila, as the Admiral wishes me to lose no time in presenting you to General Otis."

Half an hour later we were steaming over toward the mouth of the Pasig, and before nine o'clock were moored alongside the quay before the office of the Captain of the Port. Almost immediately the ensign and myself were speeding over the uneven streets of Manila toward the Walled City in a quilez, and at ten o'clock we presented ourselves at the Military Governor's office. We were at once admitted, and for the first time I saw the commander-in-chief of our army in the Philippines, General Elwell S. Otis. Mr. Mustin at once presented Captain Wilde's report, Lieutenant Gillmore's cipher message, and introduced me as the bearer of the latter. To my surprise General Otis knew me at once by name. "You are one of the very first taken," he exclaimed, smilingly, "and we have been on your track for a long time. What is this?" As he said this, he picked up the cipher message. "A letter from Lieutenant Gillmore," explained Mr. Mustin. "Oh!" said the General (his only comment), laying the paper down again without further notice.

The interview lasted about fifteen minutes, but not once during that time was I asked how my late companions had fared or about the state of their health. Not once did the General mention either Gillmore's or anyone else's name connected with the party; in fact he changed the subject by speaking of the necessity of sending provisions and supplies to General Young. At length the ensign stated that both Captain Wilde and Admiral Watson considered it advisable to act at once on the information I had brought, and to employ me as guide.

"Oh, there is no real necessity for that," answered the general; "we can always find native guides."

At last we departed with report and message, the latter still unread by General Otis. I had been told to call again on the day following.

I did "call again" the next day, and also the day after. Meanwhile Admiral Watson had sent notice ashore, through the Captain of the Port, that I might return at once on a vessel leaving for Vigan, the gunboat Wheeling, I believe it was. I told General Otis of this, but all he said was, "Oh, that's a navy vessel; better wait for an army vessel."

At length, on December 3d, General Schwan gave me a letter to General Young, authorizing him to employ me as guide and interpreter. I was told to report each day until an army vessel left for Vigan, but that evening I quietly went over to Cavite and on board the Newark, without notifying the military authorities.

It was then I had an interview with the Admiral, who sent for me, and for some time he plied me with questions regarding the prisoners, as to their health, their treatment, etc. He evidently took a deep interest in their fate.

The same evening I was pleasantly surprised to meet Captain Wilde on board the Newark; he had just come down with the sick Spaniards. The marines had been relieved by two companies from San Fabian, of the Thirty-third Regiment, leaving Colonel Parker in command. The Spaniards had sent to Captain Wilde and his officers a warm letter of thanks for the kindness received at their hands.

Referring to my diary, I see that it was the morning of December 5th that the Newark dropped anchor off Pandan, the harbor of Vigan, where we found the Princeton, Wheeling, and Callao. Lieutenant-Commander Knox, of the Princeton, came aboard, and, as he was to send a boat ashore later on, I accompanied him on board his vessel, after first thanking Captain McCalla of the Newark for his great courtesy shown me on the way up.

While at breakfast Commander Knox imparted to me that there had been no news from Vigan for several days, and it was feared that the Insurgents had cut off communications from the town to the beach. The evening before, an army officer. Colonel Hayes, of the Thirty-first, had gone up unattended, and had not been heard from since.

After breakfast I was put ashore. I hired a horse from a native in the village, and, accompanied by the owner on foot, started up the road toward Vigan. About half way I was met by about half a company of soldiers, headed by an officer who proved to be Colonel Hayes, who had gone up the night before. He also had been seeking General Young, without finding him, the latter not having arrived as yet in Vigan.

The object of this force coming down to the beach was to obtain medical assistance and supplies, as a number of their men had been wounded the day before in an attack by the Insurgents, who had entered the town and fired at them from the houses. Eight Americans had been killed and several wounded, whereas the Insurgents had left over fifty of their dead behind. However, as I was enabled to find out myself later on, a fair percentage of these were non-combatants that our soldiers had killed by firing into the bamboo huts. There were in the town, at the time, about thirty Spaniards, who had escaped from Bangued. As the Insurgents fell, these picked up the Remingtons and fought with our men, and I feel morally certain that to them it made no difference, whether men, women, or children — they simply thirsted to kill FiHpinos, and age or sex was of no importance. God have mercy on us the day we need the assistance of Spanish soldiers in fighting our battles.

I returned to the beach with Colonel Hayes and his detachment. A couple of companies of marines were landed from the Newark, and with these as reinforcements we returned to Vigan. To our surprise General Young had just arrived with two companies of cavalry. I presented myself to him with my letter from General Schwan, and was at once installed as official guide and interpreter.

But a great surprise awaited me. Whom should I meet as guide to General Young but our old friend Ramon Rey. He received me with the effusion of a long-lost father. It seems that for his kindness to us prisoners he had received this appointment at $50 a month. He told me in detail of how he had hidden the two letters in the lining of his clothes, and, feigning desperate illness, had been left behind at San Isidro. He had delivered the two letters to General Lawton himself, but first allowed a newspaper correspondent to copy them. The latter made an attempt to cable them to his paper, the *Chicago Record*, but they fell under the censorship of General Otis, and were suppressed.

Coming up the coast, General Young had driven Tiño and Aguinaldo up before him, the latter switching into the mountains at Tagudin, the former at the pass of Tangadan. Here Tino and Villamor had endeavored to hold the pass, but, after a day's fighting, were driven back to Bangued, General Young sending Colonel Hare and two companies of the Thirty-third to follow them. As I learned later, Villamor had been so seriously wounded here that he had not taken the field again. General Young himself had continued on to Vigan.

Being instructed to do so, I interviewed several of the Spanish prisoners, many of whom I recognized, and learned that the American prisoners had been in Bangued as late as forty-eight hours previous, but that they now numbered twenty-five, having been joined by thirteen others. Arnold had joined them as a prisoner and refused to leave the jail. My clothes had never been found, and two days after my escape the American prisoners had all been closely confined.

Late that night the Insurgents fired upon the town from across the river, and for ten minutes nothing could be heard but the rattle of fire-arms. Next morning I inquired about the casualties, but nobody had been hurt, which surprised me vastly, since the noise had led me to believe it almost a pitched battle.

December 6th, my diary tells me, was the date on which I accompanied Captain Chase with a company of cavalry to make a reconnaissance of La Bocana, and clear the country between of Insurgents who were supposed to be lurking about in bands. Provisions were to be sent up by rafts next day to Colonel Hare, who was presumably at Bangued, but first the pass and river must be cleared of the enemy.

A short distance from town we saw the enemy behind some bushes, and charged him. On we dashed, recklessly, regardless of consequences. "Hurrah for the Stars and Stripes! and down with Aguinaldo!" On we flew like a mighty thunder-cloud one hundred strong. Woe unto the enemy, and had the Insurgent (there was but one) not been already very much dead we would either have taken him prisoner or annihilated him. Poor fellow, a mere boy, he lay there literally riddled by bullets. The soldiers laughed and called him a "goo-goo," whatever that may be, but I failed to see the joke.

Later on we charged the enemy again, and found him to consist of a number of old women and children raking about the mud of a stagnant pool for fish. Our people would have it that they were hiding arms in the mud, and made the poor creatures break up the chain they had formed to drive the fish to one end of the pool. Of course no arms were found, but the day's fishing was spoiled, and I only hope their supper did not depend upon it. Our men had not seen this style of fishing before, consequently didn't understand it nor the natives, and they in their turn did not comprehend us. Nor do I think they ever will.

We reconnoitred all day, but found no real live Insurgents; they were all very much absent. We went as far up the pass as horses could go, but at sunset returned to Vigan, to report to the General that the pass was clear.

It now became necessary to procure rafts, and for this purpose I left town that night for a small village on the main Abra River, to find the raftsmen. As no native could be persuaded to go alone, being afraid to pass the outposts on returning, and as no other American knew where the raftsmen were to be found, this task naturally fell to me. I reached the barrio shortly before midnight and roused the raftsmen, when to my astonishment from each hut rushed one or more Spanish officers. They were resting here for the night, not daring to approach the outposts before morning. I knew most of them, and, drawing me inside one of the huts, one of the officers showed me a small scrap of paper, on which was written:

"**General Young,** Vigan.

"Have left Bangued and am pushing on after the American prisoners, who are but a day's march ahead.

"**Hare.**"

This, I explained to the Spaniard, was an important despatch, and he at once gave it to me to deliver. We returned to Vigan, the Spaniards numbering over twenty, almost all officers.

To approach the outposts was a ticklish affair even for an American, the Newark's marines having a habit of first firing and halting afterward. Before reaching the town we could hear the pop-pop-pop of their rifles almost continuously. It helped to pass away the lonely hours of the night, firing occasionally at shadows, real or fancied, but many a poor native in his bamboo hut suffered for it.

Cautiously we approached the outposts, the Spaniards far in the rear, as I feared they might be taken for Insurgent soldiers in a body. Luckily I was halted first, and ten minutes later the Spaniards were safely housed in the college building. General Young was delighted to receive word from Hare. That he was so hot on the prisoners' trail was gratifying.

My chief ambition now was either to arrest or at least cause the arrest of some Insurgent. As the young officer at Meycauayan had done to me, placing his hand on my shoulder, saying: "I arrest you!" I now burned to do to some

Filipino — the spirit of retaliation was rampant in me. I was to be fully gratified in this respect.

We were informed by a Spaniard that a very fire-eater of an Insurgent, an officer, was hidden in a certain house in town. With five men I was sent to capture him, and my feelings were those of intense delight. Now I shall have my revenge, I thought. We arrived at the house, and while four men were posted so as to prevent any escape, the corporal and I entered, the Spaniard hiding behind an adjacent corner. The man was certainly there, but I couldn't say if he was an Insurgent or not. I soon found that arresting a man was not always exactly what I thought it would be. One old and gray-haired woman fell on her knees and begged us to save her son. Another, a mere girl, clung to the prisoner, and could with great difficulty be separated from him. The two women followed us to the prison, where our man was confined.

Later on I made several more captures of this nature, to satisfy the spite of some lazy cazador who gave the information in order to pay off a former grudge for being made to work for board and lodging. Fortunately Captain Chase released such prisoners immediately, unless there was proof conclusive of guilt.

One day, however, a real bona-fide Insurgent officer was captured while hiding in the home of his family. Some native had given the information and then disappeared, as did all such traitors; they had not, even with the support of armed Americans, the courage to face those whom they denounced. When called upon to act as interpreter between the provost-marshal and this officer, we recognized each other immediately. He was a friend of Bernardo Villamor, and we had met occasionally in the hospital when he had been there to visit his friend. Although taken in civilian clothes, he did not deny being an Insurgent.

There is, or was, a certain class of Filipino officers who attained the rank of lieutenant and sometimes even a captaincy, not from any personal merit, but for the influence their family possessed. They never took to the field and were considered supernumeraries, and upon the approach of the Americans would crawl into holes to hide, objects of contempt to both Americans and Filipinos.

At first I took the above-mentioned officer for one of these; he was a mere boy of eighteen and held the rank of second lieutenant. Villamor had introduced him to me as Antonio Singson, a native of Vigan, and a companion of college days in Manila.

I was now instructed by the provost-marshal to represent to the young man that as he had been taken within our lines in civilian clothes we had every right to treat him as a spy, but if he would reveal the hiding place of any of his associates he might thereby gain his liberty. I noticed a barely perceptible raising of the upper lip as he replied that he knew of none of his comrades in hiding, and if he did he would refuse to tell anyhow. His words were quiet but determined, and I could not but admire the boy's spirit.

About this time it was reported that the Insurgent Captain Reyes, with about one hundred followers, was close by in the mountains, and Singson was sent on parole to inform Reyes that if he would surrender his arms, he and his men might return to their homes unmolested. Singson was gone two days, at the end of which time he returned with the answer from Reyes that he could not surrender without Aguinaldo's permission.

"Tell him," said the American officer, "that Reyes is only a mouthful to us anyhow, and if he wants to join the Insurgents again he can do so. We will find both him and Reyes when we want them."

Before I had time to interpret this, Singson asked me, "Am I still on parole?" "I am instructed to inform you that you are at liberty to go where you please," was all I answered, and he left us.

Several days after this I was visiting a friend, a Señor Reyes (and cousin to the Captain Reyes mentioned above), who gave me an account of the attack on the morning of the 4th, which caused me to open my eyes in amazement. The position of Señor Reyes's house in Vigan enabled him to witness all.

"It was about two in the morning," began Reyes, "when a slight noise outside my window attracted my attention, as of the murmur of voices. I fell asleep again, but was again awakened at about four by voices in the bamboo building behind the hospital, which we use as a theatre. I knew at once what it meant. Shortly before daylight I heard a shot fired, followed by several more, then commenced a general fusillade. The Americans rushed into the middle of the plaza, making use of the monument and stone pillars as breastworks. I saw a company of Filipinos charge up the street past my window toward the plaza. Others had entered the hospital, from where they fired on the Americans. Those that advanced from the street fired several volleys and then retreated. They met others coming up to reinforce them, just under my window. 'Why do you run?' cried the new arrivals. 'We have no more ammunition,' they shouted in return. By this time it was almost broad daylight. At the head of this company marched Captain Ortega, and beside him his brother, Lieutenant Ortega, and Lieutenant Singson. 'Viva! On, my men! on, my valientes!' cried the captain, waving his sword; but barely had he uttered these words, when he fell into his brother's arms. A second volley from the Americans, and the two brothers were lying side by side, dead. Here they were found later by the Americans. The Filipinos were repulsed with heavy loss, but a second time they advanced, being led by their only remaining officer, Antonio Singson, whom I expected to see fall any moment under the murderous fire of the Americans. The Filipinos now evidently had used up all their ammunition, and young Singson ordered a charge with bayonets, but almost every man had been struck and they turned and ran. Antonio followed, but stumbled and fell, and the next moment the Americans, now charging after the fleeing Insurgents, ran over his prostrate body. I thought he had been killed. The Filipinos in the hospital were also driven out, retreating toward the river, the Americans firing at them as they ran."

As this story was told me in confidence, I naturally enough never told of

Singson's true character, whom the American officers considered a mere boy, infatuated by a lieutenant's gilt buttons and shoulder-straps.

I never told the young man what Reyes had confided to me, but my admiration for him increased as I learned to know more of him. We even became intimate friends afterward, and he was to have accompanied me on my return to Manila, but sickness prevented.

A month later, when I once more visited Vigan, Antonio was gone. At first, his brother, with whom I also was on intimate terms, gave evasive answers to my questions about him, until one day when together alone, and I once more expressed my surprise at Antonio's absence, he burst out with some bitterness: "He has joined Tiño again. The American officers could not leave him here in peace, and constantly kept summoning him in order to obtain information of his former comrades. Why is it that you Americans abhor one of your own people who turns traitor, and call a Filipino who joins you against his own, 'mucho bueno'? Antonio would not turn traitor, so to avoid further annoyance he joined his former comrades in arms again."

The last I heard of this young man was a report his brother had received from captured prisoners and which he later confided to me, that he had fallen in a skirmish pierced by a Krag bullet. It was a hero's death! An obscure one, perhaps, but a hero nevertheless.

Again I refer to my diary. On December 7th several hundred Spaniards entered town. They said they had escaped, but let us rather say, they were "unofficially released," since Tiño had ordered them on unguarded. I was talking with several old acquaintances, when who should run up but Pedro and Antonio. "Ah, Alberto! Alberto! mi amigo!" they cried, but Alberto simply turned on his heel and showed his back to them. They seemed to understand and slunk away. I did not even ask what had become of the boy Guillermo, nor do I to this day know.

All these prisoners were shipped down to Manila by steamer, not any too soon, for together with some of our own men they commenced to loot the Chinese stores. I got a "Chino" to point me out one of the culprits, and he was at once arrested.

"Tell the Spanish senior officer this and let him fix the punishment," said Captain Chase, and I did so.

The senior Spanish officer's reply was, "Oh, well, if he has only robbed the Chinos, there's no harm done; let him go; they are not Christians."

"What!" cried the provost-marshal, in a rage, "only Chinos! All right, I'll fix them." They were fixed. Every Spaniard was at once confined in the church until the transports were ready to receive them, and the Spanish comandante was shown but scant courtesy after that.

Several of the liberated Spanish prisoners reported that three of the American prisoners had escaped, met Colonel Hare at Bangued, and gone on with the rescuing party as guides. Instinctively I felt that these three must be O'Brien, Bruce, and Edwards, and this surmise proved quite correct. They had been constant companions, and not the sort to let any opportunity for an escape pass. They could have come down to Vigan with the Spaniards, but instead they had pressed on with the pursuers to help rescue their less fortunate comrades. But I come to their story anon.

It was also my duty to regulate the price at which the market women sold their eggs and cigars to the soldiers, and present their complaints when the latter robbed or cheated them, which was of no infrequent occurrence. Our soldiers are no better than those of other nations in this respect; a great many of them stole, cheated, and even robbed whenever an opportunity presented itself. The officers were ever ready to listen to complaints, but a few days in the guard-house did not strike terror into the hearts of the bullies, and when they came out they were ready to repeat their assaults on helpless natives. Mentally I compared our men to the Tagalog soldiers who garrisoned Bangued, and drew my conclusions in favor of the latter. Never had I seen such scenes before. Some looted the Chinese, others assaulted women, and acts of violence were constantly reported. I am an American, and love my country, but that does not make me blind to such outrages. Later on, however, punishment became more severe and such atrocities fewer, but they never entirely ceased. Natives were afraid to complain for fear of further violence when the offender would be released from confinement. Besides, our officers never would receive the testimony of natives against the soldiers, and this they soon learned. I have heard natives of the upper class complain very bitterly of this.

I was walking about the plaza one morning, watching the women selling their wares. One had placed a table underneath the trees, and was displaying a stock of cigars, cakes, lemonades, fruits, etc. I looked, the old lady seemed so familiar. Yes, I knew her. It was Chrisolojo's mother. I felt a strange sensation in my throat on seeing the venerable lady obliged to earn a precarious living in this manner, she who had been almost as a mother to me. The tears rolled down her wrinkled cheeks as I reached her my hand. We had all called her "Mamma" in the hospital, and I did so now.

"And where is Victorino?" I asked. For some time she could not reply, but at last she sobbed: "God knows — in the mountains, somewhere with Tiño. I fear for my son, so many of our people die before those deadly American bullets." I tried to comfort her. Castro also was "up there," she told me; she had not heard of them since two days before the bombardment. The Señora was up in Bangued, but was likewise ignorant of her husband's whereabouts. In the evening I accompanied the old lady to her home in the outskirts of the town. Their house was small and poor. Here I found Perico, the young nurse, and his father, a brother to Victorino Chrisolojo, both unable to leave the house, as they had no other clothes but of the blue and white striped pattern, the uniform of the Insurgents, and in these garments they did not dare to show themselves.

Only a few days later, upon turning into a side street of Vigan, I ran into both Chrisolojo and Castro, together. For a moment they seemed in doubt as to how I would greet them, but I soon set them at rest on that point. Poor fellows, their clothes were dirty and bespattered with mud, and Castro especially looked sallow and worn. Tiño had told them to return to their families, and I now met them as they arrived. It was a happy moment for me; I could now show them my gratitude, and, needless to say, I did all I could for them. They were not only allowed to go to their homes, but offered employment in our hospital, in the old building where Chrisolojo had formerly been master. I felt almost sad on mounting the old familiar staircase between Chrisolojo and Castro, when I took them up there to present them to Captain Van Dusen, our officer in charge, who received them in the old office where Chrisolojo once had sat with me studying English.

The American officer was very kind to both of my friends, and, as I have already mentioned, offered them employment. This they declined, but Castro volunteered his services in order to attend to several of the wounded Filipinos found in the streets after the fight on the 4th. To this day these two native gentlemen reside in Vigan, but have declined to enter our service officially, and for this I cannot help but respect them. A cousin of Chrisolojo is now health officer to the port of Vigan, but then — he is an "Americanista."

On December 18th a rumor reached us through two Chinese who had been prisoners with Tiño, that Colonel Hare had overtaken the American prisoners in the mountains, and was on the way with them to Aparri in the Province of Cagayan.

The same day I left the Government service, and made preparations to ascend the Abra to Bangued.

Chapter Twenty-Six - Conclusion

ON December 20th, in company with Señor Pedro Chrisolojo, a merchant of Bangued and a cousin to the doctor, I ascended the Abra River on a raft, as I had done previously on September 5th the same year. We started early in the morning and arrived late in the evening, the current now not being half so swift as during the rainy season. A servant had been sent up the day before to prepare my friends' family for our arrival and have a quilez ready to meet us on the river-bank. I had been in Señor Chrisolojo's house but ten minutes when two of the Paredes brothers, Isidro and Mariano, burst in and greeted me with a warmth truly grateful. How much we had to talk about! They knew that I was not drowned, and so did Abasilla; nevertheless the provincial president had not been informed of my disappearance until three days had passed. Captain Hiado had been kept under strict cross-examination for several hours, but they had learned nothing from him. Parties of police had been sent up as far as Dolores to look for me, and my escape telegraphed to all the coast towns. At last they heard that I was once more in the hands of the military authorities in Vigan, but as I had so suddenly disappeared, and the Spaniards from the hospital had reported that a squad of soldiers had come for me in the middle of the night, and, after tying my arms behind me, led me off into the rice-fields, it was naturally supposed that I had been made away with, according to Spanish custom. But the Filipinos as yet have not adopted Spanish methods.

A company of the Thirty-third garrisoned Bangued at this time. Captain Shields, who was in command, had cautioned me against leaving the town alone, as bands of Insurgents infested the mountains. It had been my intention to travel on to Lepanto by horse, and descend to the coast by the pass of Tagudin, but, considering the danger too great, I abandoned this plan.

The day after my arrival, while I was sitting conversing with the Paredes in their home, a young man entered, whom I recognized as Abasilla's former clerk. After greeting me, he turned to Don Isidro and spoke a few words to him in Ilocano, which I did not understand. Isidro nodded his head, and, then, turning to me, the clerk said: "Abasilla has heard of your arrival. He is now hiding outside in the jungle, and dares not enter the town for fear of arrest. He desires very much to see you."

Accompanied by this clerk and Quintin, the youngest of the four Paredes brothers, we rode far out into the neighboring hills, by a winding and well-hidden trail. Had I not had the most perfect trust in my two native companions I might have expected treachery, but that never for a moment entered my mind, although I knew their sympathy lay not with my people. Suddenly our horses galloped into a small clearing and brought up before a bamboo hut. There was a shout from the inside, and Abasilla bounded out and almost dragged me off my horse by main force. His wife was with him, although she could well have remained in Bangued, but she chose to share her husband's hardship. For several minutes the little doctor and I did nothing but slap each other's backs and laugh. We certainly were pleased to meet each other. But soon he explained his troubles. Tiño had given all married men leave to return to their families, and Abasilla had taken advantage of this proclamation, but in Bangued were those who would not hesitate to denounce him as a spy to repay old grudges, for only fools have no enemies, and Abasilla was no fool. He wished, then, to ask my advice as a friend and an American, what course would be the proper one to pursue. I soon settled that question for him. Abasilla returned with us to Bangued, and that very evening I presented him to the garrison officers as my friend and former benefactor. He was not only permitted to return to his old home, but to open up a small apothecary's shop with the old hospital drugs he still possessed. His gratitude to me knew no bounds, simply considerably overestimating the service I had rendered him.

I may here mention that I wrote a letter to Alejandrino, in which I thanked him for the manner in which he had treated me in Vigan. I gave this to a certain party who promised to deliver it, and a month later I met this man again, whose name I feel not to have the right to disclose, and he not only assured me that Alejandrino had received the letter, but gave me a verbal message of thanks from the young colonel. He would have written in reply, but sufficient reasons forbade it. I have good cause to believe the bearer of this message. He furthermore told me that Alejandrino had witnessed the entrance of the Oregon's marines into Vigan from the window of a private house, disguised as a civilian, and an hour later followed his men up to Bangued. It was he who had led the attack on Vigan on the 4th, while Tiño and Villamor fought against Young at Tangadan. On this occasion he had had barely two hundred men, instead of five hundred, as reported, all their ammunition consisting of five rounds, and poor at that.

The scarcity and poor quality of the refilled ammunition is, combined with their inferior marksmanship, undoubtedly the cause of the poor showing the Insurgents always make before our men. That they are cowards or even less courageous than the Americans is proven untrue by the fact that they sometimes stand until half their number are down and all their ammunition gone, knowing that the odds are against them. I am told that often the powder in their cartridges is so weak as to throw the bullet no farther than a few yards beyond the muzzles of their guns. Who, then, can fail to admire their courage in fighting against such odds?

On December 23d I bid my old Bangued friends farewell and descended to Vigan again by raft, as I had come. Together with Ramon Rey I travelled down by the coast road to Dagupan, meeting many old friends again.

Old Pedro Legaspi, presidente of Candon, still held the same position as before, respected and venerated by Americans and natives alike.

Once more I had the pleasure of meeting Colonel Santa Romana, of Namacpacan, or presidente rather, for he was now municipal chief instead of Rosario. I have already mentioned the incident that took place on this occasion, and now I once more assure the reader of its truth.

But what a greeting did our old friend Don Juan Baltazar of Aringay extend to us! Nothing would do but we must remain as his guests for a week, though we finally compromised on two days.

Wherever we went, Ramon Rey and I enjoyed the spontaneous hospitality of the natives, and never could we persuade them to accept pay. Such is the custom of the country.

Shortly after New Year's Day I arrived at Manila, having travelled by rail from Dagupan. Ramon Rey had left me at San Fernando de Pampanga, in order to return to his home in San Isidro, where he now conducts a small store.

As the train stopped at Malolos, strange emotions were awakened within me. Again I saw that living stream of humanity surging, panic-stricken, across the track; the frightened guards urging us on with blows and curses, and the rolling smoke of burning houses on the horizon. A little hut near the railroad crossing I remember as a familiar landmark, and as I see it now I fancy that I again pass it, ragged, hungry, and a prisoner, and almost hear the cries of the refugees!

But what is this? Looking closer as the train begins to pull out from the station and this hut comes into plainer view, I see over the door a large placard, under which a number of big, lazy, blue-shirted soldiers are lounging listlessly. In black, conspicuous letters I now read:

FRISCO RESTAURANT.
Come here for your cool steam beer, only twenty cents a glass.
Frankfurters, hot or cold, only ___ ___ ___

I could see no more. What the price of the frankfurters was I never learned. My vision had burst like a bubble pierced with a needle.

For nearly a month I remained in Manila, living with Señor Ignacio Villamor, who had come down by steamer. Don Ignacio was by profession a teacher in the old Manila University, and now he told me of his plan, together with others to found a college such as Manila had never before seen. The result is the "Liceo de Manila," an institution of which even an American city might be proud.

Somewhere about January 10th the rescued prisoners arrived at Manila from Aparri, numbering twenty-five, and all apparently in fairly good condition, I saw all but Lieutenant Gillmore (who separated from the party upon arriving at Cavite), and now learned all the particulars of the rescue.

A few days after my flight from Bangued the number of American prisoners had been increased by thirteen others. On December 5th Tiño arrived and they were marched off into the mountains. Two days later, from a village called Dunlass, Bruce, Edwards, and O'Brien made a desperate break for liberty and escaped, reaching Bangued safely, where they met Colonel Hare and his men. Instead of continuing their course to Vigan, the trio volunteered their services as guides, and led the soldiers on to Dunlass, where they arrived shortly after the departure of the Insurgents with their prisoners. From there on they followed the trail by means of various clews — a remnant of a pair of old pantaloons, a scrap of paper, marks on trees, rocks, huts, etc. Several times they met the enemy, and fought them. Over steep mountains and through wild gorges the little party pushed on far into Cagayan.

On the morning of the 17th they arrived at the top of a small knoll, and, seeing the figures of men ahead, all lay down and watched. Before them, on the bank of a river, were the prisoners and a number of Tinguianes, all engaged in building rafts, but not one-armed Insurgent could be seen. With a yell the soldiers rushed down on to the party. The Tinguianes vanished like smoke, and a moment later the rescued prisoners were joining their rescuers in loud cheers.

It seems that, finding the prisoners cumbersome, the Insurgents had decided to abandon them, as they had done already with the Spaniards while crossing the Loag valley. Telling them that the Americans were close at hand, and that by remaining where they were they would be rescued within forty-eight hours, the Insurgent officer bid his prisoners "adios," and, together with his men, disappeared. The Tinguianes now came down, but proved friendly, and even assisted them in building rafts on which to travel down the river to the sea-coast.

The day after the meeting between the ex-prisoners and Colonel Hare's men, more rafts were built, and the entire party embarked, floating down the river until Aparri was reached on January 3d. Thence they embarked on the United States gun-boat Princeton, and came down to Manila.

This is the story as related to me by Bruce, Edwards, O'Brien, and their companions, and coincides exactly with what I have been told by soldiers and officers who took part in the rescue.

Lieutenant Gillmore and his men were distributed among the vessels then at Manila. Several went home to the States a few weeks later on the Solace, but the majority are still on duty out on the Asiatic Station.

O'Brien was given a minor position in the Quartermaster's Department in Manila, but has since gone prospecting into the mountains of Cagayan.

Bruce returned to Vigan to establish a store.

Huber, Honeyman, and Bishop, discharged from the army, have since gone to their different homes in the States.

I had the pleasure of meeting Captain Hiado, Lieutenant Bustos, and other companions of the Bangued hospital in Manila. The old captain almost wept as he told me that, with the exception of a few notes, he had lost all my manuscript while fording a river. Every day I had invitations to dinner in the Spanish quarters from all these old friends, until in the middle of January they embarked for their native land on the Spanish transport Leon XIII.

Captain Espina and Comandante Peña I also met later on, in Manila, taken prisoners by our forces, but later released. The former is now, I believe, a member of the native police force of Manila, the latter a civilian.

Toward the latter end of January I returned to Vigan, in order to gather information on certain points regarding my manuscript, which I now commenced to rewrite, from memory and the notes saved by Hiado. I remained here for several months, enjoying the society of Castro, Chrisolojo, and other old friends of the days when the skies were cloudy.

Acosta still continues to be Civil Governor, but in name only, for an American officer soon stepped into that position.

Lucas Paredes fills a similar office in Abra, while Isidro has gone to Manila to study English and practise law.

Bartolemé still rules the Vigan prison as of old, and whenever we meet, he rubs his hands and smiles.

Apparently all is peace and contentment.

But up in the neighboring hills, Tiño, Alejandrino, Reyes, and their faithful followers are still roaming about fighting for the liberty they will never gain. Whenever they come in contact with our forces, a skirmish ensues, partaking more of the nature of a rabbit drive, and about as glorious to our side. The heaps of dead and dying natives are then photographed by our people, and exhibited with such mottoes:

"Can the — d Regiment boys shoot?
 You bet they can
 Count the dead niggers."

This is meant to be humor, but perhaps my sense of humor is defective, for the effect these pictures produce on me is far from funny.

The Government is (1900) strictly military. The municipal presidents are mere puppets, neither more nor less than tools in the hands of our officers. The natives tell me that the taxes are now double what they formerly were, yet a native clerk in the Government employ receives at the most ten American dollars monthly salary. I have myself seen the rates of licenses. A grocery store is taxed fifty pesos monthly, a gambling-house fifty cents (twenty-five cents American). Rents are raised to treble their former standard by our officers, who do not hesitate to pay eighty pesos ($40 gold) for a house for which a native could only afford to pay thirty. Consequently that class which formerly rented comfortable wooden habitations now dwell in bamboo huts. Many of my native friends have been candid enough with me to express their honest opinions, and have not hesitated to declare that they are much disappointed. As one said to me: "Our language and customs are different from yours, and the American officers do not and never will understand us. They say that we cannot rule ourselves, but we were better satisfied during the year of self-government we had, than now. Even if the Tagalogs are in the ascendancy, they are at least of our own race and understand us better than your senators in Washington. How can we be well governed by men who have never even seen a Filipino?"

In the middle of April I departed for my native land, after an absence of almost two years. Bruce was to have accompanied me, but not feeling well enough determined to postpone his leaving until the next steamer. Poor fellow, when the next steamer sailed he was laid under the soil of the country where he had suffered so much. Chrisolojo had diagnosed his case correctly.

I have now no other relic of my experience than Alejandrino's undress uniform coat, which I shall keep as a memento of one of the enemy who treated me as a friend.

As the transport turned her bow north and ploughed through the waters of the China Sea, I leaned over the taffrail and watched the rugged hills of Luzon sinking down on the horizon. A strange sense of loneliness crept over me, for I had just parted, perhaps forever, from those whose friendship had been extended to me under circumstances that proved its quality, where the veneer is thrown off and the man stands forth in his true light.

I had experienced much hardship, even much suffering in that land, but when I compare my experience with that of others in similar situations during our own Civil War, say Andersonville of the South or Rock Island of the North, held by their own race and nationality, then my resentment vanishes, and I am willing to forgive, yes, even a Francisco Donato. Had we been prisoners of the Spanish, or of the French, would we have fared better? No, I think not, nor even as well!

Some of the hardships endured might many a time have been greatly ameliorated, had the men been made to feel in the only officer among them more of the moral influence of a leading mind and of a spirit better befitting the situation in general, and if less efforts had been made in obtaining those personal "rights" and individual "privileges," the claims to which not only had the tendency to embitter them against him, but even frequently caused the most disrespectful bickerings and undisguised ill-feelings, undisguised at times even among those who for reasons of their own felt that loyalty and silence might some day be gold.

Considering the circumstances, the poverty of those who held us, themselves sometimes starving, we ought not to complain. Those who really have come in sufficiently close contact with the Filipinos to know them, and are enabled to judge them without racial or national prejudice, cannot but admit that they are as entitled to be called civilized as other nations, and even more so than some whose representatives we receive at our capital and accord the same honors as those of the most polished nations. Considering the chances they have had, or rather not had, and who their teachers were, the Filipinos have certainly behaved as well, if not better, toward their prisoners, than other nations have done in recent wars.

www.ingramcontent.com/pod-product-compliance
Lightning Source LLC
LaVergne TN
LVHW091253080426
835510LV00007B/244